ACCOUNTABLE

ACCOUNTABLE

Making America as Good as Its Promise

TAVIS SMILEY

with

STEPHANIE ROBINSON

ATRIA BOOKS

New York London Toronto Sydney

ATRIA BOOKS

A Division of Simon & Schuster, Inc.
1230 Avenue of the Americas
New York, NY 10020

First Atria Books hardcover edition February 2009

ATRIA BOOKS and colophon are trademarks of Simon & Schuster, Inc.

For information about special discounts for bulk purchases, please contact Simon & Schuster Special Sales at 1-800-456-6798 or business@simonandschuster.com.

Designed by Joel Avirom and Jason Snyder

Manufactured in the United States of America

10 9 8 7 6 5 4 3 2 1

Library of Congress Cataloging-in-Publication Data

Smiley, Tavis, 1964-
    Accountable : making America as good as its promise / Tavis Smiley. —1st Atria ed.
    p. cm.
    Includes bibliographical references and index.
    1. Government accountability—United States. 2. Political participation—United
States. I. Title.
    JK421.S63 2009
    352.3'50973—dc22
        2008050467

ISBN-13: 978-1-4391-0004-2 (paper over board)

For all who believe in justice for all, service to others,
and a love that liberates

CONTENTS

ACKNOWLEDGMENTS

This book would not have been completed without the tireless work and unconditional support of many people. Their contributions made the book much better than it would have been without them.

We owe a debt of gratitude to the Jamestown Project, with special appreciation to the phenomenal staff, fellows, and board members, including Enola Aird for her insight, advice, and support; Charisse Carney-Nunes, Mark Jefferson, and Professor Ronald Sullivan Jr. for their significant contributions to the book in comments, ideas, and assisting us in articulating our thoughts to make the text more accurate, readable, and coherent.

Our research assistants—Susan Reagan, Jennifer Lane, and Brandi Colander—were top-notch and gave endless hours of indispensable advice.

We thank Candis Hines for her beautiful graphic work on the book.

A special thank-you to Kimberly McFarland, executive assistant to Tavis Smiley, for her organizational and logistical genius, and to Paulette Jones Robinson for her superb editing of this book.

Others lent their specialized expertise to help improve particular chapters, including Nicole Bates, Lawrence Mishel, Damien Jackson, and Carmel Martin.

Finally, we appreciate the efforts of Carolyn Reidy, Judith Curr, and Malaika Adero at Atria Books and Simon & Schuster, for working with us to produce this book and to share with a broad audience the challenges facing our American democracy.

FOREWORD

A nation that is afraid to let its people judge the truth and falsehood in an open market is a nation that is afraid of its people.

—PRESIDENT JOHN F. KENNEDY

Our democracy, as it was envisioned by the founders of the nation, promises citizens a system of checks and balances, including politicians who lead with authenticity. The real test of authenticity in leadership is the willingness of politicians to tell the truth to the American people whether they want to hear it or not.

The 2008 presidential election will undoubtedly go down as one of the defining moments of the 21st century. Inasmuch as the results reflect both an attitudinal and demographic shift in the American electorate, they also represent a long-overdue exercise in active democracy. The inspiring level of engagement among youth, new voters, African Americans, Hispanics, and the electorate in general this time around in presidential politics was almost as significant as its unprecedented outcome.

While this extraordinary event answered a number of questions regarding the changing American electorate, it has also raised as many: How can we keep voters informed and involved in the political process long after the polls have closed? What does it take to keep our democracy active? How do we invest the engagement dividend that we've now realized?

And, as active citizens, how can we be sure that our elected leaders are telling us the truth? Or how do we make sure that those we select to represent us face consequences when they don't tell the truth?

In *ACCOUNTABLE*, the third book in a series, our mission is to equip citizens with the appropriate tools to assess the performance of our elected leaders and us. Accordingly, my coauthor and I present both inspiring and tragic accounts of everyday citizens and arm readers with "Promise Charts" (at the end of the book) designed to compare the actions of our new administration with the initial 10-point agenda outlined in the *Covenant with Black America*, the first book or political primer, published in 2006.

ACCOUNTABLE is the yardstick for measuring whether our politicians, our leaders, and we ourselves have satisfied our respective duties in this democracy. Our purpose is clear and nonpartisan; we pull no punches.

During the run-up to the 2008 presidential election, while I was still the resident political commentator on the *Tom Joyner Morning Show*, I caused quite a stir among the listeners—who are largely African American—by insisting that we hold then-Senator Barack Obama accountable for both his political record and his campaign promises. I wasn't singling him out, but rather applying the same standard to him that we should apply to all. I feel now, as I did then, that it is our responsibility as engaged citizens to expect now-President Obama to live up to the promises that made him an appealing candidate. I want Barack Obama to be a great president. I believe he can be. But only if we help make him a great president by being the kind of active citizens democracy demands.

Certainly, I recognize that this transformative moment in American history is much bigger than me, and even bigger than our iconic new president. I revel in the progressive possibilities that this moment portends. But evaluating accountability, in its truest form, acknowledges neither friends nor enemies, and favors neither faction nor party. True accountability goes hand in hand with good government and representation that an active democracy creates, ensuring all of us—elected leaders, public officials, and private citizens—a role in making America as good as its promise.

We, the people, have a big job ahead to hold our elected officials and ourselves accountable. Therefore, we decided, at the inception of this book, that unlike the titles that precede—*The Covenant* and THE COVENANT *In Action*—we would address readers including and beyond the African American community. *ACCOUNTABLE* is aimed at the total *American* community, in the belief that we need "all hands on deck" in this ambitious and perpetual process, regardless of background, socioeconomic level, or ethnicity. There is certainly strength in numbers, and speaking to this expanded audience is fitting for the considerable size of the mission at hand.

Our mission to make government and ourselves more accountable is not shared by all. Some elected officials, business leaders, and others attempt and often succeed in throwing roadblocks in our path. They sometimes question the timeliness and popularity of our efforts. We believe though that the time is now, that there are legions of fellow citizens who share our concerns. As Martin Luther King, Jr.'s "Letter From Birmingham Jail" reminds us, "Human progress never rolls in on wheels of inevitability; it comes from the tireless efforts of men willing to be coworkers with God, and without this hard work, time itself becomes an ally of the forces of social stagnation. We must use time creatively, in the knowledge that the time is always ripe to do right. Now is the time to make real the promise of democracy and transform our pending national elegy into a creative psalm of brotherhood."

So let us take Dr. King's lead and use our time creatively, arm ourselves with information, go forth and make real the promise of our democracy.

Tavis Smiley
Los Angeles, CA
December 2008

INTRODUCTION

The most important political office is that of the private citizen.
—JUSTICE LOUIS BRANDEIS

In the introduction to the landmark 2006 work, the *Covenant with Black America*, Tavis Smiley tells a poignant story about the legendary African American labor organizer A. Philip Randolph. After dinner at the White House with President Franklin Delano Roosevelt and First Lady Eleanor Roosevelt on September 27, 1940, Randolph was invited to the president's study for cigars, after-dinner drinks, and conversation. There, at Roosevelt's urging, Randolph talked about the dismal conditions for Negro workers and outlined an agenda for government action designed to empower his struggling people.

Roosevelt, after fully acknowledging the validity and merit of Randolph's arguments and the merits of his substantive proposals, challenged the well-known activist with the following words: "Now, go out and make me do it."

While Smiley left the story there and moved on to discuss its powerful implications—namely, Roosevelt's demand that Randolph mobilize the necessary political force so that the president would have no choice but to act—it is time we bring the story full circle by picking up where Smiley left off because the rest, as they say, is history.

On June 18, 1941, at the First Lady's prompting, Randolph, accompanied by NAACP president Walter White, returned to the White House. Presidential historian Doris Kearns Goodwin, in her book *No Ordinary Time*, notes that Roosevelt tried to set a lighthearted tone for the meeting, offering charming stories, but was interrupted by Randolph. "Mr. President, time is running out," the focused organizer said. "What we want to talk about is the problem of jobs for Negroes in defense industries." Randolph, as recorded by the White House Historical Association, continued, "We want something concrete, something tangible, positive and affirmative." He then gave the president an ultimatum: either introduce an executive order to desegregate the defense industry, or 100,000 black workers would march on Washington.

Alarmed by the prospect of a Negro march on the capital, Roosevelt agreed to draft an executive order desegregating the noncombat areas of the defense industry. A relentless Randolph helped draft and edit the order until he was satisfied with its wording. Goodwin notes that Joseph Rauh, a young lawyer assigned to work on the executive order, once quipped, "Who is this guy Randolph? What the hell has he got over the President of the United States?"

Executive Order 8802 was signed into law on June 25, 1941. It declared that "There shall be no discrimination in the employment of workers in defense industries or government because of race, creed, color, or national origin."

Despite his own socialist leanings, Randolph understood the concept of an active democracy. No matter how sensitive or charitable the president was personally, he was a public official who had to be held accountable. As the primary representative of a government "of the people, by the people, for the people," Roosevelt was obliged to account to the masses of citizens and taxpayers over whom he presided. Randolph in turn could be successful in his efforts to affect the actions of the occupant of the highest office in the land only if he first held himself accountable and believed that, as a private citizen, he had the power to do so.

ACCOUNTABLE: Making America as Good as Its Promise celebrates and invites readers to exercise the power of the private citizen. It is the logical successor to two bestsellers: the *Covenant with Black America* (Third World Press, 2006), which sets forth 10 issues critical to our democracy and challenges our public officials to address them, and THE COVENANT *In Action* (Smiley-Books, 2007), which offers a tool kit to help everyday citizens effect change.

The *Covenant* was a groundbreaking effort that drew the focus and energies of the African American and larger community toward critical areas affecting black life—from health to housing, from crime reduction to criminal justice, from education to economic parity. It combined information from six years of symposia and research that empowered African

Americans by explaining how individuals and households could make concrete changes to improve their circumstances. The *Covenant* brought experts and professionals in varied fields together at the annual State of the Black Union and at regional symposia to collaborate on its issues. It galvanized community members across the nation—from pulpits to boardrooms—around the major issues affecting their daily lives.

THE COVENANT *In Action* capitalized on the success and direction of its predecessor by prompting the African American community to act on the goals outlined in *The Covenant*. It encouraged readers to become agents of change in their respective communities and outlined steps they could take to organize, connect, and act to effect change.

The *Covenant* is the "what"; THE COVENANT *In Action* is the "how"; and *ACCOUNTABLE* is the "whether"—the yardstick for measuring whether elected officials and citizens have fulfilled or are satisfying their respective duties in our democracy. Building on these first two installments, *ACCOUNTABLE* serves as a timely report card, one holding public officials accountable for what they have promised to date; too often politicians talk and promise but do not deliver. It also holds the community responsible for its actions . . . or the lack thereof.

ACCOUNTABLE informs citizens how they can help politicians deliver and make democracy active. It tells ordinary people how they can track the performances and promises of their elected leaders, maintaining that these public figures actually represent their interests and ensuring that they, as private citizens, civically engage with government in ways that improve their communities. It is a tool that provides one of the most precious commodities in a democracy: information.

A critical goal of *ACCOUNTABLE* is to identify how citizens together can plant a flag in that land we know as Common Ground. We flesh out that goal by opening each chapter with stories of individual citizens facing the challenges our country is grappling with as a whole. Too often we talk abstractly about health care, the environment, education, and criminal justice. Stories remind us that we are not alone in the world, that we should not consider the problems facing our nation without trying to understand and empathize with the people dealing with these problems.

Another goal of *ACCOUNTABLE:* to help readers answer, "What obligations do we, as citizens, have to—and for—each other?" Author Peter Block defines accountability as the "willingness to care for the whole," one that "flows out of the kind of conversations we have about the new story we want to take our identity from. It means we have conversations of what we can do to create the future."[1] In *ACCOUNTABLE*, we use stories to illustrate the struggles of our neighbors and others, to generate empathy for their difficulties, and to challenge us to *do* something to resolve these difficulties. Equally valuable, these stories—ours and theirs—melt into an active and collective American narrative, reflective of the underpinnings of America's promise.

A final goal is to help readers connect between their individual lives and their political institutions. We commonly speak about government in the abstract. We feel isolated from the larger political process, repeatedly electing the same representatives and expecting a different result. The timely and actionable information in *ACCOUNTABLE* will empower us as citizens to evaluate and have an impact on the politicians and institutions that shape all our lives.

ACCOUNTABLE asks: "How can we create an America as good as its promise?" It strives to set a new standard for those who lead and those who follow by holding our elected officials accountable for what they've promised, and ensuring that they've lived up to the aspirations enshrined in *The Covenant* and acted on in THE COVENANT *In Action.* It also endeavors to hold the entire American community accountable for our own actions within this process.

Each chapter of *ACCOUNTABLE* addresses one or more of the original 10 issue areas outlined in *The Covenant.* Chapter 1 analyzes health care and well-being, presenting a number of reflective cases, both tragic and triumphant, from the field of health. It sketches the development and current status of American health care, highlighting its disparities, its accomplishments, and its potential.

Chapter 2 considers America's system of public education by assessing the impact of standardization efforts, to see if they actually represent an effective method of scholastic accountability. It also considers the racial digital divide, parsing the effects of technological access—or the lack thereof—on individuals and communities.

Chapter 3 explores criminal justice administration, community policing, and civil rights in America. It uncovers the disparities in dispensing justice, argues for more effective and reflective policing policies, and considers the implications of criminal prosecution from a civil rights perspective.

Chapter 4 examines the U.S. economy in light of the current crisis. It analyzes some of the key indicators causing the present crisis and suggests ways to steer our financial ship back on course. It also presents stories that demonstrate how average Americans are struggling to cope financially.

Chapter 5 tackles environmental justice, energy, and infrastructure, describing class- and race-based disparities in the placement of toxic landfills and factories and holding out a vision of livable neighborhoods. It addresses the energy crisis and what our leaders and communities have done to either improve or exacerbate it.

Chapter 6 puts democracy and the electoral process under a microscope, with a particular focus on voter disenfranchisement, gerrymandering, and vote tampering. It proposes key electoral reforms to hold public officials and elected leaders, as well as citizens, accountable for protecting the right to vote—the most fundamental right of our American democratic process.

ACCOUNTABLE concludes—following A. Philip Randolph's lead— by urging Americans to hold their president and other leaders accountable. It reminds that exercising the right to vote is only one part of the democratic equation. We must also ensure that our new president delivers on his promises. Accordingly, *ACCOUNTABLE* includes a series of "Promise Charts" to compare the actions of our highest elected official with *The Covenant*'s 10-point agenda. These charts equip citizens with the tools and information necessary to analyze the performance of our new president and to hold President Obama accountable for his actions. By working with him to ensure his promises are fulfilled, our community is, in fact, holding itself accountable. Together, we all work toward an America as good as its promise.

ACCOUNTABLE also addresses our evolving American identity, encouraging us to resolve deep-seated issues that divide us as a nation. It acknowledges the need for a more representative, collective American story constructed by an aware citizenry that understands the nuances, varying interests, and give-and-take of the democratic process. It promotes a more mature American identity, one that regards our differences as an asset and our disparate interests as more a matter of negotiation than contention.

Many of the stories highlight what happens in a democracy when its citizens fail to hold public officials accountable. One describes a boy whose mother could not afford an $80 dental extraction. Because of barriers to timely health care, the boy developed a toxic abscess that ultimately led to an infection in his brain. Tens of thousands of dollars and a hospital stay later, the boy died from the infection. His death was both preventable and unacceptable in a country as wealthy as America. While his story is heart-wrenching, talking about it, alone, is not enough.

ACCOUNTABLE, consequently, is prescriptive. Each chapter has an "Assessment Checklist" that evaluates whether government and individuals are doing all they can to realize the goals in The Covenant. ACCOUNTABLE equips everyday citizens with tools and enough information to evaluate their public servants. It also allows citizens to evaluate their own efforts in maintaining and improving their life chances.

The notion of accountability is much more than a report card or even some vigilant watchdog process that holds its subject's feet to the intense fires of consequence or induces the reddish blush of ridicule. Accountability, like progress in general, is rooted in the belief that we are significant, a belief that we are worthy and deserving of all the democratic values that condition our national psyche, a belief that encourages an exceptional American consciousness, and that we recite each morning in our public school classrooms. Ensuring that we are doing everything within our power to actualize this belief is the large task at hand.

Cartoons and quotes are interspersed throughout ACCOUNTABLE to inject a lighter, reflective, or inspirational touch. Humor and satire can set or shift the tone; drive home a point; or capture a political moment in a way that policy descriptions never can.

Reaching beyond its predecessors, ACCOUNTABLE focuses on issues facing communities outside the black community, realizing that rescuing our democracy is bigger than any one of us, bigger than any one group, one community, one culture, or one race. It affirms that we must join forces with people of all cultures, hues, ethnicities, income levels, and ideologies to tell a new common American story—to bring about a new American dream, forged from common concerns and brought to life by common action. We can act together or fall apart; either way, the choice is ours. Either way, we will be held accountable for our pain or prosperity by our children, by our times, and, if we are honest, by ourselves.

The prize may be closer than we think. Many things we thought would never happen in our day have happened. King transformed the conscience of a nation. Nelson Mandela was upgraded from a small prison cell to a presidential suite. And in four years, an African American with a unique name went from relative obscurity to become the "leader of the free world." To transform the world, a community, or even a heart, a person must have the fundamental belief he or she holds the power to do so. A. Philip Randolph was known to rally his workers by telling them, "You possess power, great power."

The thought of such power can be frightening. An excerpt from Marianne Williamson's classic poem, "Our Greatest Fear," puts it best:

> It is our light not our darkness that most frightens us
> Our deepest fear is not that we are inadequate
> Our deepest fear is that we are powerful beyond measure.

Perhaps, as they say in horror movies, we should "be afraid, be very afraid." Because if we are, in fact, more powerful than we know and if we fail to account for our own power, and if our communities crumble and our elected officials turn their backs on us, we will have only ourselves to blame.

1
Health Care and Well-Being

Who Holds the Cure?

He who has health, has hope. And he who has hope, has everything.
—ARABIAN PROVERB

In order to change, we must be sick and tired of being sick and tired.
—AUTHOR UNKNOWN

COVENANT ONE
Securing the Right to Health Care and Well-Being

Carol Ann Reyes: Dumped in America

It was a cool Monday evening in late March 2006 in Los Angeles, months away from the sweltering summer when the infamous L.A. smog is at its worst. Traffic was moving swiftly along South San Pedro Street near East 5th Street in the downtown area known as "Skid Row."[2] Known also as the Nickel because of its location along 5th Street, Skid Row is "home" to one of the largest populations of homeless people in the United States. Also known for its tough streets, the Nickel this evening seemed like just another day in the neighborhood, the county's 74,000 homeless seemingly unaware of the headlines of the day.[3]

While they may have been unaffected by the flap over President Bush's wiretapping program or the third-year-almost-to-the-day commemoration of the war in Iraq, L.A.'s homeless were dealing with conflicts that hit closer to home.

One of them was Carol Ann Reyes, a transient Los Angeles resident who spent most of her time not on Skid Row but in a Gardena public park 16 miles south of the city, supporting herself by collecting recyclable bottles and cans. Three days earlier, an ambulance had transported Reyes west across Rosecrans Avenue through Compton to Kaiser Permanente's Bellflower Medical Center for treatment of abdominal pains and injuries resulting from a recent fall. Sixty-three years old, homeless, suffering from dementia and other physical ailments, Reyes remained at the hospital until a decision was made that she had been there long enough.

Though she still had a fever, persistent cough, and perilously high blood pressure, Reyes was discharged by hospital officials without their prescribing medication for her high blood pressure or even taking time to locate the clothes she'd worn upon admission. They simply called a cab, placed her in it donning her hospital gown and slippers, and paid the driver to take her 16 miles north of the hospital to Skid Row, presumably because it is the location of many of the city's homeless shelters.

Hospital officials claim to have called Union Rescue Mission, a well-known shelter on Skid Row, to let them know that Reyes was on her way. Video surveillance footage taken that evening contradicted the directions, showing the taxi driving along San Pedro, making an illegal U-turn, opening the door, and literally dumping her onto the Skid Row streets.

Reyes wandered about in the street and on the sidewalk, lost, without any money, identification, or medical information until a Union Rescue Mission worker noticed her and ushered her to safety and the warmth of a bed. Days later when the news of this story broke, a tearful hospital vice president of communications apologized to her and to the community, vowing that this would never happen again.

But will it? Carol Reyes was not only dumped onto the streets by that taxi; she was dumped by Kaiser Permanente, she was dumped by our failing health care system, and she was dumped by America. And in the year after Reyes' case made headlines, police were investigating 10 different hospitals for allegations of patient dumping on Skid Row, including a paralyzed man found crawling in the streets without a wheelchair and with a broken colostomy bag.[4]

Reyes is just one example of millions of Americans, either uninsured or underinsured, who have been abandoned.

Who should be held accountable for this maltreatment? Who will be accountable the next time?

■ ■ ■

The *Covenant* opens with a chapter, "Securing the Right to Health Care and Well-Being," positioning it as the first and most important covenant.[5] And while the health care crisis in our nation disproportionately affects people of color, to be sure the crisis is an American one—red, white, and blue—pulling at the very fabric of our flag.

There is a proverb that says: "When you are not your natural self, you don't do anything well." This elder wit is trying to tell us that physical weakness prevents accomplishing anything and everything that otherwise might be done. Indeed, when a family member is sick, all other concerns—education, employment, justice, democracy—pale in comparison. Moreover, when a community is sick, that can threaten the economy, the stability, and, depending on the breadth of the problem, the very survival of a nation. And when a nation   is sick, as we have seen with the devastating impact of HIV/AIDS in Africa, it can threaten an entire continent and ultimately humanity.

Few would argue the moral integrity of the aspirational concept of health care as a fundamental human right. It is arguably more important than other so-called fundamental rights—the right to freedom of expression or religious belief. And the right to life, possibly the most important of our fundamental human rights, would certainly be rendered meaningless without a complementary right to health care.

But in America the notion of universal health care and the varied and complicated paths to its achievement have become some of the most vexing and problematic issues of our time. The health care crisis in this country was a pressing political issue throughout the 2008 presidential election. As we inaugurate the second president of the new millennium, it remains the most intractable domestic policy issue, a problem we have been trying to solve since 1914.[6]

A Century of Health Care

In his new book, *Critical: What We Can Do about the Health-Care Crisis*, former Senator Tom Daschle of South Dakota presents a well-researched, exhaustive inventory of America's history of seeking health care reform. The cacophony of today's health care debate does little to remind us that this discussion has been underway in America for 95 years. Daschle explains the early debates during the Progressive Era (1890s–1920s), when reformers sought free medical care and related benefits for workers. All such efforts failed, with opponents decrying national health insurance as socialized medicine. It was the first real national debate on the issue, setting the stage for interest groups—both for and against—to become firmly entrenched in their positions.[7]

During the Great Depression, America had another opportunity to reform the health care system when an advisory committee recommended that President Franklin D. Roosevelt create a system of universal health care as part of his landmark Social Security Act. But Roosevelt decided not to push for a health insurance add-on to Social Security, worried that opposition from the American Medical Association would sink his entire legislative reform effort.[8]

Roosevelt's decision set the stage for the evolution of both the dominance of employer-sponsored health care programs in the United States and the continuing difficulties faced by the millions who remained uninsured, unable to secure protection against the growing cost of illness.[9] Our employment-based system of health care became institutionalized during the World War II era and in the decade following, as the federal government enacted laws that made such plans favorable for the purpose of taxes and labor relations. Today, employer-based health care remains the most prominent form of coverage. This coverage, however, is completely voluntary for employers to provide, and it has shrunk in recent years. In 2000, 65 percent of employees received employment-based coverage; a mere seven years later, just 59 percent were covered, resulting in more than 2 million more people without coverage.

Health care reform remained on the national agenda for most of our presidents in the post-WWII era and beyond—Harry S. Truman, John F. Kennedy, Lyndon B. Johnson, and Richard M. Nixon. Under Johnson, the nation saw the passage of Medicare, "the largest expansion of health care coverage in American history."[10] Medicare guaranteed medical coverage to the disabled and those over age 65, representing a positive first step towards health care reform. Despite this progress, millions of people under 65 remained uninsured, and subsequent attempts to deal with the crisis by Presidents Nixon and Carter, as well as Massachusetts Senator Edward M. Kennedy, failed.

In the 1980s, managed care began to emerge as a beacon of hope. President Nixon signed the HMO Act in 1973, designed to encourage the private sector to create group practices that would be well managed, cost-effective for insurance companies, and more affordable for the insured.[11] The initiative provided the opportunity for a Republican administration to propose an alternative approach that would take the steam out of Senator Kennedy's push for national health insurance. And with the cost of employer-based benefit plans exploding, the "HMO march" began to pick up speed in the 1980s and early '90s. By 1993, 51 percent of all workers received employer-sponsored health insurance provided by some form of managed care plan.[12]

American workers were content by and large with the HMO model as employers began to rely more and more on the concept. Presidents Ronald Reagan and George H. W. Bush largely ignored the health care crisis during the 1980s.[13] Even President Bill Clinton's failed universal health care plan, led by First Lady Hillary Rodham Clinton in 1993, was modeled after HMOs.[14]

As time passed, managed care began to reveal that it might not be the panacea that America had been looking for after all. Some consumers grew frustrated with the way managed care providers impinged on traditional doctor-patient relationships, denied coverage of expensive illnesses such as AIDS and cancer, and refused to pay in some cases for emergency room care.[15] Those fortunate enough to have coverage struggled through the bureaucracy of HMOs, making life-and-death decisions on the basis of cost and benefit. Beyond these frustrations, for individuals such as Carol Ann Reyes, even the broken managed care system was out of reach.

These so-called "management decisions" about a patient's health care have sometimes had grave and even deadly consequences, demonstrating the critical need for serious reform of the health care system for all Americans.

The Hilsabecks: Denied Care Despite Coverage

In 1991, Elizabeth and Steven Hilsabeck were on the verge of achieving the American dream of homeownership in a small town near Austin, Texas. Though the Hilsabecks each earned a good salary, virtually every home in Lakeway, Texas, exceeded their price range until they came across a 2,400-square-foot home priced far below market value. Undaunted by the extreme makeover that their new home would need, the Hilsabecks quickly secured the property and began creating their dream home bit by bit, doing most of the work themselves.[16]

Their dream continued to come true when they learned the following spring that Elizabeth was pregnant, expecting twins. The Hilsabecks flourished as they planned their nursery and finished renovating their home. About six months into her pregnancy, Elizabeth began to have contractions. Staving off the babies for three days, her small-framed body could hold out no longer. She went into labor and gave birth to twins after only 25 weeks of gestation.[17]

The Hilsabecks knew that the prognosis for their new daughter Sarah and son Parker was grim. Each baby weighed only one pound, 13 ounces. But they were grateful for their excellent medical care and Steven's insurance coverage, especially since Elizabeth would have to quit her job to care for her premature twins.

The Hilsabecks were initially satisfied with Prudential's PruCare coverage, which paid hundreds of thousands of dollars worth of their medical costs, leaving them with only a $50 co-payment. Their worries also eased as their daughter Sarah steadily improved. But their son Parker showed no such promise. When the twins were seven months old, the Hilsabecks learned that Parker had cerebral palsy. Without an extensive physical therapy regimen, their doctors advised that Parker might be confined to a wheelchair for life. To make matters worse, only a few days into Parker's treatment, PruCare stopped paying for his care. First, the company said that it would cover only 60 days of therapy over Parker's lifetime, although the actual limit was 60 days per year. The company also made processing mistakes, resulting in erroneous denials. Further tensions mounted when PruCare deemed that Parker's therapy was not covered, claiming it was "habilitative" rather than "rehabilitative" because Parker—who had learned to crawl and was building muscle strength—had never walked before. Finally, the company argued that Parker's medical treatments were not "medically necessary" because there was no guarantee that a child in his condition would ever walk.

Steven tried to find a new job paying more money, but the insurance company for his prospective employer would not cover Parker; Steven was thereby forced to remain in his lower-paying job. The Hilsabecks eventually lost their dream house—and their marriage. But Elizabeth became a crusader for health care reform, and Parker finally learned to walk. Still, this success came at a very high price.

■ ■ ■

Ironically, during the time that the Hilsabecks' story was unfolding, Bill and Hillary Clinton were working on a national level to solve America's health care crisis.[18] For all the bickering that occurred in Washington during the Clinton health care debate, would "Hillarycare" have helped the Hilsabecks? The family had the type of insurance that was being proposed for millions. Perhaps it would have allowed Steven to accept that new job offer without the threat of leaving Parker completely uncovered because of his preexisting condition, but would the new managed care company have made its "management" decisions differently about Parker's care? Would the 1,342-page Health Security Act have redressed Parker's situation at all?

Who is accountable to the Hilsabecks?

The Shaeffers: Health Care Costs
Adding to Family Struggles

Steve and Leslie Shaeffer know something about a managed care company's interpretation of preexisting conditions. More than a decade after the Hilsabecks' ordeal began and Hillary Clinton's H.R. 3600 initiative had ended, the Shaeffers were living the American dream in Murrieta, California—a bedroom community outside of San Diego. Steve was a self-employed tile installer and Leslie was a stay-at-home mom, caring for their four-year-old daughter, Selah. A successful entrepreneur, Steve acquired health care coverage with Blue Cross Blue Shield for his family in 2004, regarding his $498 monthly premium as "the price of peace of mind."[19] Yet when Selah was diagnosed with aggressive fibromatosis—a rare and fast-growing tumor—only a few months later, his peace of mind would be tested.

Blue Cross initially covered Selah's care, including the pre-authorization of much of her treatment. Once her bills exceeded $20,000, however, the company canceled Selah's managed-care coverage, accusing her parents of having left out key background health information when filling out their insurance application. Leslie received a letter from Blue Cross alleging that she and Steve failed to disclose a bump on Selah's chin that would have resulted in a denial of coverage. Leslie countered, saying she took Selah to the doctor after filling out the application, and the doctor told her that the bump on Selah's chin wasn't serious. A few weeks later, doctors discovered the extent of Selah's illness. The four-year-old had surgery for nearly seven hours to remove the tumor, which had spread to her mouth and jaw. Portions of Selah's mouth, jaw, and throat wall were also removed as a precaution.[20]

Blue Cross refused to pay for the operation and threatened to make the Shaeffers repay the $20,000 it had already paid for treatment. Two years later, when the *Los Angeles Times* reported their story, Leslie described her family as being "in big trouble" as the couple faced "more than $60,000 in medical bills and feared the loss of their dream home." They were still struggling to stave off creditors as they tried to figure out how Selah could keep seeing the physician they credit with saving her life.

They thought they had insurance. Who is accountable to the Shaeffers?

■　■　■

Both the Hilsabecks and the Shaeffers had every reason to believe that their managed care insurance providers were looking for any excuse to dodge their children's bills, dumping them much in the same way that Carol Ann Reyes was dumped in the Nickel by the hospital that no longer wanted to help her. Millions of Americans have their own health care horror stories, dealing with the frustrations of managed care, the high cost of private insurance, and the cost-cutting policies of profit-driven hospitals. Their stories, along with those of the Hilsabecks, Shaeffers, and Carol Ann Reyes, have fueled a renewed call for health care reform in the United States.

Disparities in Care

We often speak of the health care crisis in America, but in many ways it is inaccurate to call it a "health care" crisis. After all, this country has the preeminent health care system in the world with its first-rate pharmaceuticals, cutting-edge medical technologies, and unparalleled investment in the health sciences. More precisely, the crisis in America that these stories exemplify is better described as the *lack of access* to the excellent health care that our country undoubtedly provides.

And the crisis is different for different segments of our population. The crisis of Carol Ann Reyes as a poor and uninsured American excluded from the Medicaid system is different in many ways from that of the millions of working-class families who are too well off financially to qualify for state aid but cannot afford to purchase health insurance on their own. Still different are the problems of elderly Americans caught up in an inadequate yet bloated Medicare system.[21]

Then there is the cross-cutting and seemingly insurmountable problem of health disparities in our nation that seems to persist and proliferate no matter how much the overall health of the nation improves. Importantly, though *The Covenant* defined the first covenant broadly as "Securing the Right to Health care and Well-Being," the lens through which this covenant is described was that of health disparities and the impact on the African American community.[22] Indeed, *The State of Black America 2008*, the National Urban League's annual report on the well-being of Black America,[23] devoted a special section in that year's edition to black women's health, opening with a chapter examining the impact of health disparities among African American women.[24]

Health disparities occur when differences "exist in the incidence, prevalence, mortality, and burden of diseases and other adverse health conditions that exist among specific population groups in the United States."[25] With respect to every major disease or public health issue—heart disease, stroke, cancer, diabetes, HIV/AIDS, infant mortality, and addiction—African Americans are among the hardest-hit populations. Disparities also exist in connection with the lack of access to health care. African Americans, as well as other minorities and persons with disabilities, tend to face barriers to receiving health services at disproportionate rates.[26] For example, when *The Covenant* was published in 2006, an estimated 1.8 million African American children had no health insurance, representing 13 percent of black children. More shocking is a statistic for Mexican Americans, revealing that as many as 39 percent of this group in 2006 had no health insurance.[27] And according to *The State of Black America 2008*, 18 percent of all women in the United States have no health insurance, with 2 million of these women (16 percent) being African American.[28]

Deamonte Driver: A Preventable Tragedy

One of those uninsured African American women is Alyce Driver. When her story was told in February 2007, she was a hard-working mom who had held various jobs—in a bakery, as a home-health aide, and as a construction worker—but none of them offered health insurance. She previously had Medicaid coverage for her sons DaShawn and Deamonte, but the family had recently lost its coverage.[29]

Though all states have opted to provide dental benefits to children covered under the State Children's Health Insurance Program (SCHIP),[30] finding a dentist willing to accept these benefits can be a major challenge. Patients have been known to travel up to three hours and to wait many months in search of services. And specialty services, such as surgery as opposed to routine cleanings, are even more difficult to find.[31] In Maryland, where Driver lived, this coverage was offered to her children as an expansion of their Medicaid benefits, but fewer than one in three children in the program received dental care in 2005 because of substantial barriers.[32]

By the fall of 2006, Driver was seeking dental care for both of her sons. Twelve-year-old Deamonte had a toothache. But she was more focused on frantically trying to find a dental surgeon willing to help DaShawn, who needed six teeth extracted. She waited from October 5 to January 16 for a dentist willing to take Medicaid for "emergency" care. However, by the time Deamonte's aching tooth got any attention, Driver learned that the toothache had been caused by an abscess, the bacteria from which had spread to his brain.[33] A few weeks later, he died.

Because Deamonte could not get an $80 extraction, he ended up with a brain infection, a six-week stint in Children's Hospital, two surgeries resulting in $250,000 worth of unpaid medical bills for taxpayers to bear, and—most regrettably—a death certificate.

News of the twelve-year-old boy's death shocked many people, including Robyn Fleming, a former staff member of Goodwill of Greater Washington. She described on the Women's Foundation blog that Driver had been in a vocational program that Fleming had taught, and that she "strived for more for herself and her family. . . . Alyce, along with many other women, came to this program as a last hope. Hope that they will learn something new, hope that they will find support and assistance when they couldn't get it anywhere else, hope for another chance at life!"[34]

But a twelve-year-old is dead because no one could figure out how to fund an $80 visit to a dentist. Fleming wrote, "I feel as if I failed Ms. Driver. But in reality we *all* failed Ms. Driver."[35]

Who is accountable to Deamonte?

A FRAMEWORK FOR ASSESSMENT

The *Covenant* set forth "Securing the Right to Healthcare and Well-Being" as its first and arguably most important covenant. The end of that chapter lays out what individuals, government, and community leaders can do to impact this issue. THE COVENANT *In Action* next provided a toolkit to equip citizens with the instruments to effect change on this and all *The Covenant* issues. *ACCOUNTABLE* now helps any citizen assess whether America has lived up to the aspirations enshrined in *The Covenant* and set forth a measuring tool for future evaluation.

During the 2008 presidential election, the major candidates agreed that the U.S. health care system was in dire need of a makeover. This fact, along with the health care horror stories presented, would lead most people to conclude that we have yet to reach our full potential when it comes to health care. The key questions are what are the potential solutions to this dilemma? Who should take part in crafting them? We must ensure that the entities that are part of the solution—the government, private employers, insurance providers, doctors, hospitals, and citizens themselves—are not unduly burdened by the remedy. Finally, how will the American citizenry know that these solutions are working?

Solutions for Government Reform

With 47 million Americans without health insurance (9 million of whom are children),[36] any governmental solution must be sweeping and comprehensive. The solution must immediately be tailored to assist poor and working-class Americans who do not qualify for Medicaid, are too young to benefit from Medicare, and are either unemployed, entrepreneurs, or employed by businesses that do not offer health coverage. Although most Americans seem to seek a nationwide solution to this crisis, much can be learned from the experiences of state governments that have tackled the issue.

The Commonwealth of Massachusetts attempted such a solution in April 2006 when it adopted the most comprehensive attempt to date by a state to provide near-universal health care coverage. The key components of the Massachusetts plan were to expand eligibility for Medicaid and its State Children's Health Insurance Program (SCHIP). Lawmakers created two new avenues to access the expanded coverage: (1) through Commonwealth Care, a publicly subsidized coverage for adults ages 19 and older with incomes below 300 percent of the federal poverty level; and (2) through Commonwealth Choice: Private, unsubsidized coverage available to any resident who is not offered coverage through his or her employer.[37] Another key element of the plan was it mandated all citizens to carry coverage whether they wanted to or not. Two years after its implementation, the plan is now a victim of its own success: enrollments outpace expectations and state budget officials are struggling with how to pay for the overage.[38]

One of the biggest challenges is the punitive and mandatory provision of the law, requiring Massachusetts citizens to prove on their income tax returns that they carry health insurance or face a penalty for failing to do so. Critics argue that the commonwealth's approach does not guarantee affordability, does nothing to control costs, and thereby excludes broad classes of people, in effect abandoning universal health care. Many who are deemed able to afford the coverage end up spending well over the allegedly capped level of 10 percent of their monthly income on health care.[39]

Massachusetts' challenge with its health care mandate may explain why Barack Obama's plan to move America to "universal" health care did not include such a mandate,[40] opting instead to focus more intensely on cost containment.[41] Upon announcing his plan in May 2007, Obama focused on affordability as its centerpiece, with a specific promise to reduce health care costs for each American family by $2,500. Other key provisions are guaranteed eligibility, notwithstanding preexisting conditions; comprehensive benefits similar to the Federal Employees Health Benefits Program that members of Congress enjoy; subsidies; simplified paperwork; the ability to take your coverage with you to a new job; and a system that would be monitored to ensure high quality and efficiency. Though there is no health care mandate for adults, the plan mandates that children be covered.[42]

The other major Democratic presidential hopeful, Sen. Hillary Rodham Clinton of New York, unveiled her health care plan about the same time. Like the Obama plan, Clinton's "American Health Choices Plan" also recognized affordability and cost-containment as a key strategy in achieving the goal of universal health coverage, but her primary emphasis was "to be the president who accomplishes [the goal of providing quality affordable health care for every American]."[43] For all of the debate during the campaign between Clinton and Obama about health care, the substance of their proposals was strikingly similar. Clinton packaged her plan neatly around three key points: Affordability—America will give tax credits to working families to help them cover their costs; Availability—no discrimination or disqualification for preexisting conditions; and Reliability—if you lose or change jobs, you keep your health care insurance coverage.[44]

The GOP presidential nominee, Sen. John McCain of Arizona, proposed similar health care reform. His plan started with a "Call to Action," envisioning that "we can and must provide access to health care for every American." It focused largely on tax policy, incentives to insurance providers, and tort reform. McCain promised to reform the tax code to give every family a $5,000 tax credit to offset the cost of insurance; to make insurance more portable, following Americans from job to job; and to expand Health Savings Accounts for families. He promised a laundry list of activities, including working with states to develop best practices to facilitate access to health care and lowering health care costs through a variety of mechanisms.[45]

Private organizations and commentators have also offered big ideas about government solutions to the health care crisis in America. In 2008, Project HOPE: The People-to-People Health Foundation published an article, "Building Blocks For Reform: Achieving Universal Coverage With Private And Public Group Health Insurance." "Building Blocks" offered what it called a "pragmatic approach" to universal health care, arguing for a mix of public and private solutions—mandatory employer contributions, an extension of the Medicare system, tax credits, and an expansion of the SCHIP and Medicaid programs.[46]

Overall, the 2008 presidential campaign demonstrated that Americans may finally be ready to resolve the health care crisis in this country. It was a top domestic issue, second only to the related issue of the economy.[47] The major presidential candidates recognized that the federal government needs, at a minimum, a comprehensive plan to address the massive gaps in America's health care system: varied and specific strategies designed to eliminate health disparities and to support poor Americans, working- and middle-class Americans, and the elderly. Now that Barack Obama is president, it remains to be seen whether he can garner the political support to answer this clear call to action by the electorate and whether the electorate will hold him accountable for doing so.

"OUR INSURANCE COMPANY WILL PAY!"

Solutions for Government Enforcement

The government must play a vital role in enforcing any state or federal plan to reform the health care system. Whether the plan relies on private or public entities, or more likely a combination of both, federal and state governments must ensure that fairness imbues the system through oversight and enforcement. By any reasonable measure, Parker Hilsabeck should have been well cared for under his family's policy. But where was the government oversight when Prudential offered his mother ridiculous and often incorrect interpretations of complicated legalistic policy language in an obvious attempt to avoid coverage? And what was the cost to the family of Elizabeth's incessant complaints that were expensive, time consuming, and required an ability to navigate complex systems?

Solutions for Private Employers

The primary solutions for health care reform will be fashioned most likely by the federal government, even though private employers have played a historical, albeit voluntary, role in providing health care to most Americans. As health care costs have skyrocketed, some employers have challenged that role, offering less coverage to fewer employees, resulting in a skyrocketing number of uninsured and underinsured Americans. Consider the story of Gary Rotzler.

Gary Rotzler of Gilbertsville, NY, was one such American caught up in the erosion of employer-based health care. A hardworking, college-educated engineer from working-class roots, he married his high school sweetheart, Betsy, in 1978 and shortly thereafter took a well-paying job with one of Central New York's major manufacturers, from which he thought he'd retire.[48] But in the era of mergers and acquisitions that defined the 1980s, Rotzler's employer was left in the hands of another company that paid a multimillion-dollar departure fee to the former CEO and downsized the company, just like most other manufacturers in that state. Rotzler was fortunate enough to escape the fate that snuffed the dreams of many of his coworkers by landing a new job, where he remained safe for a few more years. But in 1993, his new employer let him go in an era when engineering jobs were nearly impossible to find. He ultimately returned to his original employer, but this time reclassified—as a temporary employee, who did not qualify for health insurance. Rotzler repeatedly requested to be reclassified as permanent so that he could obtain health insurance for his family. His requests fell on deaf ears.[49]

Compounding his situation, his long hours and his quest to work overtime to provide for his wife and now three children distracted him from noticing that Betsy was getting sick. For her part, Betsy delayed seeing a doctor, instead trying a series of home remedies because of their health insurance situation. The family's worst fears were confirmed when Betsy finally confided in Gary, who took her to a local Planned Parenthood clinic, where she learned that she likely had breast cancer. By the time their family was able to arrange treatment at Memorial Sloan-Kettering Cancer Center in New York City, Gary had signed a consent form for treatment, a promise to pay for it, and a few days later, a death certificate. He was forced to declare bankruptcy; his hopes for the American dream and of providing a bright future for his wife and children became a distant ghost of his past.[50]

Rotzler's story illustrates that as insurance becomes more expensive for employers to provide, more employers, even employers of large firms, may stop providing health care. Workers are left with the "choice" of forgoing health insurance at great risk to their families and their overall health care, as in the Rotzlers' situation, or self-insuring, which could expose them to the situation faced by the Shaeffers. But what are employers to do when globalization makes international competition nearly impossible if they must carry the high costs of insuring U.S. workers?

More than six out of 10 employees (63 percent) at most major corporations have employer-sponsored health coverage. But it comes at great cost to corporations that are generally unable to bargain with insurance companies as to cost-containment in an industry that is ancillary at best to the corporations' industry. Meanwhile, the insurance industry has no real incentive to cut its price point for customers who include not only these major corporations, but also the government, smaller corporations, and everyday consumers.

One proposed solution is to look strategically at a major corporation known for cost-containment: Wal-Mart—"a company that understands how low prices can build market share and thus increase profits. Furthermore, it's a company with a culture of cutting costs that has shown no compunction in pushing suppliers to the wall over price. The Wal-Mart motto ought to be, 'Make it cheaper, or we'll find someone who can.'"[51]

Wal-Mart has already applied its "always low prices" strategy to prescription drugs. In 2006, the corporate giant rolled out a program to sell a list of about 300 prescription drugs for only $4. It expanded the program a year later to include additional prescriptions as well as an option for consumers to purchase a 90-day supply of those drugs for only $10. More than 1,000 over-the-counter generic drugs are sold through this program, and higher priced specialty drugs for ailments such as osteoporosis, breast cancer, hormone deficiency, and other women's health problems are sold for only $9. The price point of these prescriptions is no accident. Wal-Mart has apparently studied the weak points of the prescription drug industry, uncovering the point where its customers were being squeezed by their insurance companies with high co-pays and coverage exclusions. It began offering a lower-priced alternative conveniently located in Wal-Mart stores.[52]

The company is starting a similar program to provide medical services, in part through opening walk-in health facilities in its stores in Atlanta, Dallas, and Little Rock. It plans to open 400 clinics by 2010 that will be co-branded with local hospitals. Wal-Mart's competitors include not only Walgreens, CVS, Rite Aid, Costco, and Target, but also insurance companies that are likely already feeling the pressure to reduce co-pays resulting from Wal-Mart's action.[53]

Wal-Mart exemplifies how corporations must work creatively to offer real solutions for consumers. Its "always low prices" as applied to health care are giving citizens more access to health care that they can afford.

Solutions for Insurance Providers

The insurance lobby—which has positioned itself as one of the most powerful groups of lobbyists in Washington, DC—should strive to be part of the solution, rather than part of the problem. In the case of the recent Medicare prescription drug legislation, these lobbyists even influenced the law that prevented the federal government from negotiating with drug companies on cost.[54]

In an era where the people are desperately seeking change on issues including health care and the economy, insurance companies must see the writing on the wall. Citizens will no longer support conditions that have health care costs on track to approach 25 percent of the gross domestic product in less than 20 years.[55] Large corporations in a global economy cannot sustain the former situation, and this new era will certainly bring forth Wal-Mart-style competition with insurance companies that will ultimately impact their bottom line.

In June 2008, America's Health Insurance Plans (AHIP) Center for Policy and Research released a technical memo detailing AHIP's proposals to improve the affordability of health care.[56] (AHIP is the national association representing nearly 1,300 member companies providing health insurance coverage to more than 200 million Americans.) This positive step indicates that insurance lobbyists understand the times and that they will clearly benefit from being included in the national conversation on solutions. In fact, the substance of their affordability proposals contains ideas such as health information technology reform that parallel those set forth in President Obama's proposal. What is needed, however, is trust building and a fully integrated conversation among consumer advocates, AHIP, and governmental actors.

Solutions for Doctors, Hospitals, and Pharmaceutical Companies

Community leaders and health professionals will be crucial to making health care reform real and creating immediate change. They have access to the communities at need and know firsthand which problems are most pressing. They can fashion solutions that address real problems practically and effectively.

For example, a group of African American cardiologists realized in the 1970s that while heart diseases affected the black community disproportionately to the rest of the nation, there was little awareness of this higher risk, let alone ways to prevent their onset. Black communities were not receiving the attention or energies of the American Heart Association and other health organizations. These 17 doctors held themselves accountable as a community and created the Association of Black Cardiologists to raise awareness about heart disease and stroke in the black community. Not only did they provide health education for citizens, they also realized that forming the next generation of leaders was crucial to continuing their mission. Equally precarious: that there were too few African Americans in the medical profession, and specifically in cardiology.

The group did not wait for extensive support and funding. Instead, it launched initiatives for community education, beginning by using churches as centers for blood pressure screening. These community programs were soon supplemented by a fellowship program designed to motivate and prepare new African American cardiologists. Today, the group hosts symposiums, runs continuing education programs for physicians, and remains committed to its mission to educate the African American community about the dangers of heart disease.[57]

Another effective yet simple solution: In response to rising prescription drug costs facing senior citizens, the Cristo Rey Community Center in East Lansing, MI, created a Prescription Assistance Program to help seniors navigate the programs available to receive prescription drug assistance. Many prescription drug companies have programs providing free or reduced-cost medication to those with demonstrated financial need. These programs, however, present a maze of paperwork as an obstacle to receiving assistance. Cristo Rey works as an advocate to help its clients receive the assistance to which they are entitled. The program has helped people like Anthony and Joan, a couple in their late 60s. They could not afford their monthly medications, which cost more than three thousand dollars; much of this huge expense is not covered by Medicaid. The couple's only source of income is Social Security benefits, which total little more than $1,000 per month—barely enough to cover maintenance and living expenses. The Prescription Assistance Program provides Anthony and Joan with an advocate to help them fill out their application to the pharmaceutical companies, to provide the required documentation, and to follow up every three months so that they don't run out of medicine.[58]

Solutions for Individuals

Achieving health care goals should not begin with arguments about Medicaid extensions and universal insurance coverage. Each and every one of us must be held accountable for our own health and well-being. We must understand that eating healthy and exercising is more than a cliché of the latest health care marketing campaign. Taking action to be responsible for the nutrients and toxins that we introduce to our bodies and deciding to stay physically active are actually expressions of civic participation and engagement. Similarly, partnering with our doctors for prevention is a much more active and democratic strategy than hiring a doctor after the fact to correct health problems that could have been prevented.

Roosevelt Johnson is a well-respected psychologist in Silver Spring, MD. In March 2008, Dr. Johnson was healthy, happily married, the father of three successful adult children, and a deacon at his church in Washington, DC. He led a healthful and fulfilling life. For years Johnson maintained a partnership with his personal physician. As an African American male over age 50 and with two older brothers who had survived prostate cancer, Johnson knew that he could not "sit in the back seat" where his health was concerned; nor did he want the "passenger's seat." When he reached his late forties, he educated himself extensively about prostate cancer and decided to "drive his own car." He learned of the dangers of prostate cancer and the latest developments in testing and prevention. He took that information to his doctor, who told him additional PSA testing was unnecessary. Johnson didn't let this stop him; he decided that with his risk factors, he would reject the standard medical advice to just complete an annual PSA screening. He opted instead to be screened quarterly, knowing this might require him to pay for the tests out of his own pocket. He reasoned that if he had cancerous cells too early to detect from a PSA screening, waiting another 365 days for his next one could have deadly results. Johnson even convinced his doctors that his tests should be covered by insurance because of his high risk factors.

Johnson's resolve paid off in 2007. His March screening revealed a slight elevation in his PSA blood level, as compared with his previous results. Though the elevation appeared trivial and remained within the acceptable medical range, true to form, Johnson insisted that his doctor probe further to uncover the source of the slight elevation. Days later, after a biopsy that he had insisted be performed, he and his wife sat before that same doctor, who delivered the results: early-stage prostate adenocarcinoma—a highly aggressive form of cancer. The good news: the probability that it would be neutralized and contained. Because he educated himself on his risk factors and demanded early testing, Johnson discovered the cancer at an early stage, worked with his doctor to address his surgical options, and was able to avoid chemotherapy and radiation.

Johnson used his illness as a way to continue his lifelong vocation— teaching and ministering to his community. He took his son with him to his procedures and doctor's appointments, so that his son would realize the risk his family history would eventually pose to him. Johnson later testified in church about his experience; the response was immediate. He recalled, "men started coming out of the woodwork," discussing the shame they felt at their diagnosis, the fear that kept them from getting screened. His decision to educate and hold himself accountable has had a ripple effect— "breaking the silence" about prostate cancer in his community and leading others to do the same.

ACCOUNTABLE ASSESSMENT CHECKLIST

The most powerful tool we have as citizens to effect change is our vote. We should not allow our elected officials to make promises in their campaigns without fulfilling their obligations once in office. Use this list to hold our new president accountable on health care.

Campaign Promises 2008: Health Care

BARACK OBAMA AS PROMISED . . .

* Will make a new national health care plan available to all Americans with guaranteed eligibility; comprehensive benefits; affordable premiums, co-pays, and deductibles; simplified paperwork; easy enrollment; increased portability; and choice.

* Will provide tax relief for small business.

* Will create a Small Business Health Tax Credit to assist small businesses in providing employee health care.

* Will mandate health coverage for children.

* Will help patients by improving disease management programs and increasing transparency in health costs.

* Will lower costs by increasing competition in the insurance and drug markets.

Use this checklist to evaluate whether the entities that can make a difference are doing all that they can to help America realize the goal of the first Covenant: "Securing the Right to Health care and Well-Being." Reexamine this checklist every six months to assess progress.

OUR PRESIDENT

☐ Have you made implementation of a health care plan a priority within the first 100 days of your administration?

☐ Have you exercised good judgment, reached out to a broad number of constituencies who will be affected by health care reform, and engaged in transparent dealings that will strengthen the chances that implementation of reform will succeed?

☐ Have you retained the ability to oversee the new reforms, ensuring that neither private nor public entities behave unfairly or unethically?

☐ Have you provided for unbiased entities to evaluate the success of the new reforms at regular intervals to determine if benchmarks have been met?

OUR U.S. CONGRESSMEN AND CONGRESSWOMEN

☐ Have you made health care reform a priority issue?

☐ Are you using monitoring and enforcement mechanisms to ensure that insurance companies, doctors, hospitals, pharmaceutical companies, and all entities in the health care system act in good faith and do not violate federal or ethical standards?

☐ Have you voted to expand health care coverage for children?

☐ Are you working to make health insurance more affordable for all Americans?

OUR GOVERNOR AND STATE LEGISLATORS

☐ Have you shown leadership on health care reform even where the federal government may be lacking?

☐ Do you have a plan to fill in gaps in health care coverage created by a federal plan?

☐ Can you implement that plan if necessary?

☐ Do you have an enforcement mechanism to ensure that insurance companies, doctors, hospitals, pharmaceutical companies, and all entities in the health care system always act in good faith and do not violate state, federal, or ethical standards?

OUR COMMUNITY LEADERS
AND FAITH-BASED ORGANIZATIONS

☐ Do you have a plan or an initiative to monitor the political progress of health care reform promises made by our governmental leaders and to advocate when necessary?

☐ Do you have a plan or an initiative to educate your members about the progress of health care reform and about the availability of health care options in our community?

☐ Have you educated your members about health, nutrition, screenings, and risk factors for degenerative diseases such as diabetes, cancer, hypertension, and heart disease?

☐ Do you implement programs to improve the health of your community members, such as disease screenings, blood pressure checks, or fitness initiatives?

YOU AND I

☐ Do I eat a healthy diet?

☐ Do I exercise regularly?

☐ Do I know where the health facilities in my community are and what services they offer?

☐ Do I have a primary physician whom I see at least once a year?

☐ Do I see myself as the best advocate for my own health?

☐ Do I understand the importance of cancer, HIV/AIDS, and other health screenings, and undergo the appropriate tests at the recommended intervals as determined with my doctor?

☐ Do I talk to my family, neighbors, children, friends, and community members about important health issues—insurance coverage, access to services, and making health care affordable for all Americans?

☐ Do I talk to my family, neighbors, children, friends, and community members about maintaining a healthy lifestyle, such as the value of eating a healthy diet, exercising regularly, and seeing a physician at least once a year?

2
Education

Success in Our Schools

Education is the kindling of a flame,
not the filling of a vessel.
—SOCRATES

A child miseducated is a child lost.
—PRESIDENT JOHN F. KENNEDY

COVENANT TWO
Establishing a System of Public Education in Which All Children Achieve at High Levels and Reach Their Full Potential

COVENANT TEN
Closing the Racial Digital Divide

Jolita Berry: Attacked and Abandoned in Her Own Classroom

Jolita Berry was a teacher until the morning of April 4, 2008. On that Friday—a date that Berry will never forget—she was viciously assaulted by one of her students.[59]

Her assault occurred during art class; she taught art at Reginald F. Lewis High School. What provoked the incident? Why would a student repeatedly strike her teacher? Berry says she asked the student to sit down. The student refused. More than refusing to follow her teacher's instructions, the student confronted Berry, saying that she was "gonna bang" her. Berry told the student to "Back up, you're in my space. If you hit me, I'm gonna defend myself." Students in the classroom urged their fellow student to "hit her," Berry recalls, and without any further warning, the female student did precisely that; she repeatedly struck Berry until she was pulled off of her teacher.[60]

You might be tempted, with good reason, to believe that this incident was not as bad as it seems or that perhaps the teacher was exaggerating, or that the incident has been overblown. You might believe that, except that the entire assault was captured on video—not by a school-provided security camera, as one might expect, but by another student in the classroom with a cell phone. A student recorded the entire incident and, adding insult to injury, the video was posted to MySpace and can still be seen on YouTube.[61]

The video is difficult and disturbing to watch: Berry, on her back and on the floor, trying to defend herself; the student flailing away at her, inflicting injuries both to her shoulder and to one of her eyes. Perhaps the most difficult part of all: watching her students cheering and encouraging her assailant to continue to assault her. All of this, it bears repeating, in a public school classroom.

What many considered even more outrageous than the assault itself was the reaction of the principal, who—rather than immediately removing the student from the situation—suggested that Berry had provoked the attack by asking the student to step back and saying that she would defend herself.[62]

Who is accountable to Jolita Berry, and thousands of teachers like her, who are struggling to teach under the most trying circumstances and who are blamed for why our schools are failing? Who is accountable for supporting our teachers? Furthermore, when did we expect and accept having security cameras, metal detectors, and other prison-like surveillance measures in our public schools?

■   ■   ■

"Establishing a System of Public Education in Which All Children Achieve at High Levels and Reach Their Full Potential," the second of the 10 covenants presented in *The Covenant,* focuses on the declining state of our nation's public school system. Our public schools are in an almost unbelievable state of disrepair. Most vulnerable to the shortcomings of our system of public education are African American, Hispanic American, and poor American children of all ethnic backgrounds. Our schools are failing these children on a scale that ought to have citizens taking to the streets in protest and bombarding our means of communication with messages of outrage. That we, the wealthiest and most powerful nation on earth, would expose any of our children to the level of dysfunctionality and harm that is typical of too many of our public schools is, in a word, shameful. That we have learned to live with this state of affairs is damning.

The problem with our schools is not a local one, although we have learned to think of it that way. Neither is it merely a problem for "other people's children," as Lisa Delpit famously put it,[63] or for "inner city" children—one of the many unfortunate euphemisms we use to avoid the problems of race and education that still plague our nation. Providing the best public education possible is a covenant that we must keep with all children. And our public school system is failing all our children. It is also failing our nation.

Our public school system is failing our nation because education is not solely about securing, for all our children, the opportunity to fully cultivate their individual potential and to live the kind of productive and complete personal and professional lives that education often brings. Education is, of course, about securing for our children their individual right to life, liberty, and the pursuit of happiness. But it is about something more: a means for securing better life chances and outcomes for all citizens should be the bare minimum of what we hope to achieve through our public schools.

The Key to Democracy: An Educated Citizenry

Education has always been about more than our individual lives; it is also about the present and future health of our democratic experiment. It is impossible to overestimate the importance of an educated citizenry to a promising and promise-keeping democracy such as we imagine our republican form of democracy to be. Government in the hands of the people will require that the people be educated people if they are to keep democracy's promise that the people—and only the people—are sovereign. Education should be about not only preparing our young people for lives of individual fulfillment; education should also prepare our young people for the benefits and burdens that are part of the challenges and responsibilities of citizenship in a democratic society. Turning our backs on our students is turning our backs on our country's future. Poorly educated, disengaged citizens will not be able to preserve what is best about our democracy, and they certainly will not be positioned to agitate to make our democratic project better than they found it.

"Above all things I hope the education of the common people will be attended to, convinced that on their good sense we may rely with the most security for the preservation of a due degree of liberty," wrote Thomas Jefferson to James Madison in 1787.[64] More than two centuries later, Jefferson's words still resonate.

Given the importance of education to our individual lives and to the overall health of our country, how did we allow our system of public education to fall into such a state of emergency?

Leaving No Child Behind?

Notwithstanding 100 years of school reform, the urgency to reform our schools is not a new phenomenon; America's schools used to be the envy of the world. Beginning with the U.S. Department of Education's 1983 report, *A Nation at Risk,* we began to see and to understand that America was no longer leading the world in educational measures.[65] How we came to lose our preeminence in education is the subject of countless articles and books. That substantial reform of our public educational system is immediately necessary, however, is not in dispute. The poor state of our public schools is one issue on which Americans of every stripe agree, as is the desire to find a solution to the problems that ail our schools. Where reformers traditionally disagreed was how best to solve any given problem—at least until the signing into law of the No Child Left Behind (NCLB) Act on January 8, 2002. The passage of that legislation signaled, at least initially, a collective desire by politicians on both sides of the aisle to address our crumbling public school system.

No Child Left Behind was by any measure an extraordinary moment of agreement as to how best to redress the myriad of problems facing our public schools; it was a welcomed step toward turning our schools back toward excellence. At the heart of NCLB is a focus on outcomes-based assessments, known now as standards-based education.

The emphasis of this approach to reform is relatively simple: by setting high expectations and establishing measurable goals, individual student outcomes will be improved. In theory, No Child Left Behind represents a crucial first step in reforming our schools; to improve, we must hold our students, teachers, schools, and society accountable. Moreover, the law's provisions requiring accountability for the progress of minority, limited-English-proficiency, and special needs students have forced schools to focus on those pupils previously swept under the rug. These provisions represent a dramatic improvement in how our schools and school systems do business. However, the failure of NCLB lies not in the goals themselves, but in the measures and methods chosen to achieve them.

How do we measure outcomes and achieve goals under standards-based reform efforts? Testing; more specifically, standardized testing. NCLB requires states to develop standardized testing to be administered to students at different grade levels, if (and here is the rub) schools are to continue receiving federal funding. Schools, however, are far too often left without the funding and professional support necessary to improve teacher performance, curriculum, classroom size, and other factors essential to improving student performance. Instead, struggling schools too often focus on teaching to a test and meeting an overall quota; they should be focused on educating students who then will succeed in developing skills crucial to future schooling and careers; this will lead to success on test day. Meeting quotas has become the goal more than teaching children. When this occurs, we fail to prepare them for fulfilling and responsible lives as adult citizens in our democracy. Students like Indira Fernandez are failed when we focus on educational ends at the expense of educational means.[66]

Indira Fernandez: Failed by Passing

Indira Fernandez graduated from the High School of Arts and Technology in New York City in 2007. She graduated despite having "missed dozens of class sessions and failed to turn in numerous homework assignments." Fernandez would not have graduated, however, if the decision had been left to her math teacher, Austin Lampros, who gave her the grade that his records indicated that she earned: a failing one.[67]

Lampros was overruled by Fernandez's principal, Anne Geiger, who permitted Fernandez to retake the final exam after two days of personal tutoring by other math teachers—a benefit not afforded to her classmates. Even though she received a 66 on her final, her grade for the course was still a failing one. Again, Geiger intervened, awarding her a passing grade and allowing her to graduate.[68]

There is a lot to this story about teachers' unions and administrative oversight. There is a lot here about retaining committed young teachers like Austin Lampros (he resigned over this episode). This story even raises questions about the rise in New York City's graduation rates. But the real questions this story raises have to do with Fernandez.

Although she may not yet be aware of it, Fernandez is the real loser here. Receiving a diploma without the skill sets that diplomas are supposed to signify is the worst kind of dishonesty we can display toward our young people when it comes to education. And although Fernandez may not agree, she should not have graduated if she did not meet the standards necessary for graduation. But Fernandez is not a special case. We routinely promote children to the next grade level, even when we know that they are a year or two or several years behind in terms of the skills they should have acquired to move on.

This is part of the problem that standards-based education is supposed to address, but what really happens to students who do not meet the standards, especially when entire school buildings are filled with students who are several grades behind? How do standards-based outcomes help students who we already know are several grades behind?

Beyond Testing: Ensuring High Standards for Each Child

Focusing on outcomes and performance is a necessary part of improving our public schools, but it is not sufficient. Testing is not a cure-all. Even if all our students were at or above grade level, the work of education would not be complete. Being an educated, whole, critical, and compassionate human being cannot be assessed by a test. Nor should we try to assess the wholeness of being that real education seeks to facilitate with a test. Our fixation with tests and outcomes obscures the circumstances that contribute to poor test scores.

There are other flaws with focusing too much on testing. Our emphasis on testing and outcomes almost assumes that our students come to school orderly, motivated, and well-behaved. Social networks are presumed in place that encourage educational success. Yet somehow either the teachers are not competent enough to teach, or the students, though focused on learning, are just not able to learn enough to deliver on test day. We have to stop posing solutions that have little connection to the real problems being faced by our public schools. We have to break out of the circular reasoning of outcome-focused solutions: the children perform poorly because they fail to do well on the tests, and because the children fail to do well on the tests, the children perform poorly. Instead, we need to ask the most unwieldy and most difficult question: Why?

Why are our public schools doing such a poor job of educating our children? The answer is not a terribly complicated one: too many of our schools do not have a culture of learning. As renowned educator Lorraine Monroe has remarked, "What is distressing is that we already know what good schools look like. We already know what to do to provide quality education. It is just that we have chosen which children to do it for."[69] And this is all our fault and all our responsibility. Would better teachers help? Of course they would. But we have to be careful not to assume that all or even most of our teachers are incompetent, simply because they are the easiest targets. Would better parents help? Of course, a stable family life is, arguably, the most crucial factor in a child's development. But blaming parents who themselves may not have obtained a solid education or who may find themselves with work requirements that do not easily allow them to guide their children through school will not solve the problem. Would a culture geared toward the virtues of learning help, instead of the vices of material acquisition at all costs? Well . . . we can dream, can't we? Would more testing help? Only if a culture to help our children excel on tests is in place. Testing should come last in the process, not first. Preparation comes first.

Having high standards must also mean having high standards for the kind of preparation we give students before requiring them to exhibit high standards on a test. And where the proper means for preparation are unavailable, where there are no rigorous standards or expectations for bringing our children up to level and beyond, testing is little more than a sham. What does a 10th grade student who reads at a 6th grade level think about being given a test administered at a level beyond what she knows is her capacity? How do you penalize this student's current teacher and principal when she has been passed along four grades beyond her current abilities by previous teachers and principals? And what is gained by penalizing schools—schools that we already know have students who are several grade levels behind in reading and math—when their students fail to pass a test we already know they aren't qualified to take?

We have to teach our students first. We have to demand excellence from them by demonstrating excellence in what we are willing to provide for them. We must not accept excuses for some children failing and others doing well. Before we hold our children accountable, we have to be sure that we have done everything we can as adults to *make* them succeed.

Tests are important tools for holding students and teachers accountable. Our children deserve tests that accurately measure their abilities. This means demanding innovation from educational and political leaders to move away from the easy standardized tests and explore more holistic, performance-based assessments. In the hands of good teachers, tests demonstrate student progress, highlighting areas of proficiency and weakness, allowing teachers to tailor instruction to student needs. When the test becomes the main event, as is the case in far too many American schools, students suffer.

Until we face the problems our schools face and start providing answers to questions we are afraid to ask; until we stop using our schools as dumping grounds for problems that schools are hardly designed to address, we will never be able to provide the kind of education all our students deserve and desire. Our children need for us to face the difficult questions honestly. Otherwise, we will have more students making headlines, like the following Milwaukee teenager.

Julia D'Amato and Her Struggling Student

When Julia D'Amato, principal of Reagan College Preparatory High School in Milwaukee, WI, was punched twice by a fifteen-year-old female student in her office, knocked unconscious, and hospitalized for a fractured back resulting from the assault, we did not know even half of the story.[70] What set off the teenager on the day she was sent to Principal D'Amato's office? Something quite small. Something routine. In the cafeteria, some fellow students accidentally spilled fruit on her pants. This incident probably resulted in some laughing and teasing by her classmates. She lashed out at them, cursing all the way to the principal's office. When she arrived there, she would not calm down, even though her principal repeatedly requested that she do so. Next, the teenager struck her principal—another "out of control" student doing what "those" kinds of students do. Who can imagine actually striking an adult of any kind, much less an authority figure?

Normally, the story ends there.

We shake our heads in disbelief while declaring, often aloud, what kind of children are these and move on. Children hitting principals should strike us as foreign and utterly unacceptable. So, being typical, again, we move on. Maybe we did this when reading the story of Jolita Berry. And why wouldn't we? The news reported on Berry only, and the focus, rightly so, was on one vivid and visual example of the kind of challenges too many teachers face daily. What, you wonder, would provoke a child to strike a teacher while other children laughed and looked on?

We don't know much about the student who assaulted Berry, but— thanks to the work of a journalist who was willing to ask tougher questions—we do know a lot about the child who assaulted Julia D'Amato.[71]

At five, she and her three brothers witnessed a gang murder. Their mother, in a desperate attempt to shield her children from the violence of their surroundings, moved the family from Chicago to Milwaukee. After only a few days there and after being bounced from shelter to shelter for disruptive behavior, the mother—unable to secure a place to live—called officials to take custody of her children. By the time authorities arrived, the mother decided against turning over custody of her children. Noticing that the children were disheveled and that the mother's behavior was erratic, officials placed the mother in a mental health facility and her children in the temporary custody of the state.[72]

But that custody was not temporary; state custody was permanent. The little girl's family would never be together again. Her mother disappeared, rumored to have returned to Chicago, where drug addiction, prostitution, and mental health problems ensued.[73]

The girl was separated from her brothers and entered into the foster care system. A pattern soon emerged: the child would get along well initially in her new environment, only to soon display violent behavior that would lead to being placed in another home. At the age of eight, she would bang her head against the wall, hurting herself; she even tried to commit suicide. In time, the girl would violently lash out at others—other children and other adults. From the time she was separated from her mother, the girl was moved to more than 30 different placements in the foster care system.[74]

The usual services were provided for this troubled child: therapy, social and psychological interventions of all kinds, and medication in the form of anti-depressants. In therapy sessions with her siblings—she was able to see her siblings through group therapy sessions—a caseworker reported that she felt the most unwanted of all her siblings. What might be hardest to believe is that throughout all the trauma she has experienced, the girl remained a good student. In the eighth grade she was reported to have earned a 4.0 grade point average and received an honor for helping disabled children learn Spanish.[75]

She entered high school as an excellent student. But from the beginning, she was a difficult fit for the academically rigorous and highly structured Ronald Reagan High School. Plans were created to help her manage her anger, but, in the end, she could not control it.[76] This is the girl who, unable to control her rage, struck and injured her principal.

And this girl, whose name we do not know because she is a minor, is not alone.

There are many girls and boys like her attending public schools every day. In Milwaukee Public Schools, the system in which this girl is still a student, 20 percent of the student body received special education assistance during the 2007 school year.[77] Many of our children attend school carrying the kind of burdens this girl is still carrying, coping with traumas that often prove too much for them. Who is accountable for these children who do not have parents to guide and focus them through life? What are we to do with students like this when they negatively impact the learning of other students? Should we segregate them? This teenager was an exceptional student despite all she had been through. What do we do to those students who spilled fruit on her and provoked her outburst? What do we do for her principal?

The easy answer might be that she is an extreme case, but the reality is that she is not. For our most vulnerable children—children living in poverty, children who are the children of parents and sometimes grandparents who do not have a quality education or quality jobs—school is always being attended under heavy burdens: poverty, violence, joblessness, difficult home lives, and indifference to education. These are the burdens weighing on too many of our children who must navigate them even before they set foot in a classroom.

We do ourselves a disservice by thinking that merely introducing standardized measures for excellence can address many of the problems our students face in school. This is not an argument against standards. We need school and community-driven standards of excellence. But standardization is not the answer. Testing for outcomes, though important, is hardly a panacea for all that ails our schools. Before we provide answers to what ails our schools, we have to have the courage to be honest about the context in which many of our struggling schools operate. We make teachers an easy target when we expect them to impart knowledge to students when many of our teachers spend more of their school day attempting to perform the duties parents, social workers, and psychologists are having a difficult time performing. We make parents easy targets when we refuse to address the kind of social conditions that have always pushed education to the back burner of their lives—parents who are coping as best they can in their day-to-day lives, lives that don't immediately connect education with life outcomes. Parents who are unable or unwilling to risk the pain that deferred dreams often bring should not be blamed when we do not have the kind of social nets in place that allow even the poorest among us to live with some modicum of integrity and pride, required conditions for dreaming. And we make students easy targets when we don't ask ourselves what are the kind of school experiences they are really having; what kinds of burdens are our disadvantaged (and advantaged) children daily bearing?

Are our most vulnerable children thus incapable of learning? Should they be exempt from the challenges of excellence? No. For our least advantaged children, education is their last best chance for living fulfilling and meaningful lives. In other words, students who have less need to be pushed harder—stroking them alone is not the answer, though love is an essential ingredient to teaching a child. They will need to work harder to achieve their dreams. Requiring excellence without a willingness to fully support the work of excellence, however, is the worst kind of cynicism.

Who is accountable for a child's future when a child is without a supportive home, able or committed parents, or has parents whose work keeps them from being able to check homework and attend PTA meetings? Who is accountable for the other burdens—poor health care, inadequate housing—borne by that child each day, making learning even more difficult? What is a child to do when we adults, who should be responsible for educating our children, refuse to even look at the problem through a child's eyes? What are we willing to do and how far are we willing to go to provide the right kind of education for the most vulnerable among us?

■ ■ ■

The girl whose name we do not know would have been in a much better position if she had a loving, stable, and supportive home life. Nothing is more important to a child's development than her parent or parents. But even a loving, stable, and supportive home life does not always prove to be enough to protect one's children from the tragedies that exist in our school system. Just ask Mai Abdul Rahman.[78]

Mai Abdul Rahman: A Parent's Struggle in Today's Schools

Mai Abdul Rahman is an active parent. She is a former teacher and is involved in the PTA. She earned her bachelor's degree in political science from Drake University and is pursuing her Ph.D. in urban school reform from Howard University. Rahman is so active, in fact, that she ran, albeit unsuccessfully, for a seat on the District of Columbia's School Board in 2007. She is known in the District as a public figure who cares about the quality of education not only for her children, but also for all children attending school in the District. You might think that such an active parent could protect her own child from disruptive behavior that is usually found in our failing schools. But Rahman was unable to protect her son from violence at Woodrow Wilson Senior High School.

In March 2008, Rahman wrote to DC Schools Chancellor Michelle Rhee (she sent copies to Mayor Adrian Fenty and deputy mayor for education Victor Reinoso, among others), describing the incident in which her son was assaulted. "He walked unaccompanied into the gym and found himself surrounded by five 9th grade students," she wrote. "For several minutes, they proceeded to punch him in the face until 12th graders broke it up."[79] (Doctors reported that Rahman's son was fortunate not to have suffered a fractured skull or diminished vision as a result of his attack.) She continued, "On the same day, a 9th grade student was also 'jumped,' a term used to describe the violent assault of one group that belongs to a gang as they hit and maim their lonely victim. All these violent crimes occurred a day after Wilson security had discovered a gun that was found through the metal detector scanner in a student's bag." Her e-mail further stated, "This school year, Wilson has had a rash of violent student assaults and countless number of robberies. I am sure you are aware that our students are often victims of the same crime two or three times. . . . So far in the last three weeks both the Hawk security guards and DC police have confirmed to me that they have made four arrests of students in the school facilities for a combination of assaults and other criminal activities." Rahman's e-mail also stated that the assailants, students who roam the hallways, "lack the proper tools to maintain class interest and focus, so they are rarely in class to the delight of most teachers who are tired of the discipline issues" and that assailants at Wilson often "capture their attacks by video and circulate them with little fear of being caught."[80]

Wilson has long been considered one of the top-performing high schools in the District of Columbia. Its distinguished alumni include billionaire Warren Buffett, broadcaster Derrick McGinty, famed boxing writer Bert Sugar, and the current mayor of the city, Adrian Fenty. Wilson is not your stereotypical inner-city school where we, regrettably, accept environments that are not conducive to learning. But, like many of our public schools, Wilson is subject to the same kind of atmosphere and behavior that is a major contributor to what is wrong with our schools. We can continue to tell ourselves convenient truths, but the simple fact is that at any given public school in our country, at all levels of schooling, there does not exist the kind of environment necessary for learning—and we are all accountable.

In response to Mai Abdul Rahman's complaints and persistence, the students who assaulted her son were arrested and expelled. (What are we to do about the assailants?) Also in response to Rahman's complaints, Chancellor Rhee restricted students to eating their lunch in their classrooms while a long-term solution was sought. Much like the locking down of a prison, the Chancellor was compelled to take this drastic step to restore order at Wilson High School.

School Mismanagement

Neither Chancellor Rhee nor Mayor Fenty is to blame for what happened at the high school. They inherited a system in complete disarray: students behind in grade level, financial mismanagement, and deteriorating, even hazardous, school buildings. Those are just a few of the problems plaguing District schools. Thirty-three percent of poor fourth graders across the nation lack basic math skills; in the District that rate nearly doubles, to 62 percent of its poor students.[81] Moreover, three-fourths of all the elementary students in the District are classified as poor enough to qualify for free or reduced-cost lunches.[82] The results of the 2006–2007 DC Comprehensive Assessment revealed that 62 percent of elementary students were not proficient in reading and nearly 70 percent of elementary students were not proficient in math. Among secondary school students, 65 percent of students are not proficient in reading, and 67 percent are not proficient in math.[83]

The physical school buildings in the District tell an equally tragic tale. It takes on average 379 days for principals to have repair requests identified as dangerous conditions or urgently need to be completed. Of the 146 schools in the District, 113 had requests for a leaking roof to be repaired in 2007, and 127 of the same schools have requests pending for electrical work.[84] Most unsettling among the physical plant problems is the condition of the school cafeterias. A round of inspections in 2007 revealed that 85 percent of the cafeterias had violations, including "peeling paint and plaster near food, inadequate hand-washing facilities, and insufficient hot water"; more than one-third of school cafeterias showed evidence of rodent or roach infestations within three years leading up to 2007.[85] Ariel Smith, an after-school volunteer at one of the District's schools, was initially disheartened by the "mice scurrying around the cafeteria and kindergarten classroom," but later discovered: "These kids are so used to it [the mice], it doesn't faze them anymore. First it upsets you, then you get used to it, then you work around it."

As for mismanagement, two stories will suffice. The District paid $25 million for a computer system designed to track and manage personnel within the school system, but it had to be discarded because there was no accurate list of employees from which to build the database.[86] The school system does not even have an accurate list of the students in the system, even though it pays a consultant $900,000 a year to keep count.[87]

The misery goes on and on. But how can we expect our children to learn in these kinds of physical conditions? How can children possibly believe we care about them when we allow them to attend schools in such disrepair? What kind of outcomes can we honestly expect when we can allow children to accustom themselves to learning in the midst of vermin? All this in the school system of the capital of the most powerful nation in the world?

Who is accountable for this?

A FRAMEWORK FOR ASSESSMENT

The *Covenant* set forth "Establishing a System of Public Education in Which All Children Achieve at High Levels and Reach Their Full Potential" as its second covenant. The end of the education chapter imagines what individuals, government, and community leaders can do to impact this issue. THE COVENANT *In Action* next provided a toolkit to equip citizens with the instruments to effect change on this and all of *The Covenant* issues. *ACCOUNTABLE* will help citizens assess whether we have lived up to the aspirations put forward in *The Covenant* and give them a measuring tool for future evaluation.

During the 2008 presidential election, the major candidates agreed that the U.S. public education system needs reform. The tragic stories just presented further attest to the sad state of affairs. The key questions still to consider are: what are the potential solutions to this dilemma? How can we hold our leaders accountable to the promises and solutions that convince citizens that they deserve our vote? And how will citizens know that these solutions are working?

Solutions for Government

Both President Obama and Senator McCain acknowledge the myriad of problems plaguing our public school system. While McCain and Obama have publicly supported NCLB, both have questioned the efficacy of all aspects of this historic legislation.

McCain's plan for turning our public schools around focuses on choice. He maintains that parents should not be forced to keep their children in under-performing schools, believing that "all federal financial support must be predicated on providing parents with the ability to move their children, and the dollars associated with them, from failing schools." McCain also believes that we should have a competition model for attracting and maintaining the best teachers. Finally, the former GOP nominee is against nationally imposed standards, preferring to leave the question of standards to state and local officials and boards.[88]

Obama's plan begins with his concern about the underfunding of the NCLB, which has led to being unable to provide high-quality teachers, among other concerns. His plan focuses more on repairing and developing institutional supports that assist parents in the education of their children, such as expanding Early Head Start and Head Start programs. Obama would place a sustained emphasis on recruiting and retaining the best teachers. And his plan looks beyond secondary education to college education and proposes ideas for reducing its rising costs.[89]

To succeed, both plans will require enough flexibility to address the problems besetting our public schools. We must be suspicious of any solutions that feel too much like a magic bullet. Reforming our system of public schools cannot be reduced to one school of thought, nor can it be reduced to political platforms. We have to be vigilant enough to force our elected officials into keeping all our options open.

Solutions for Private Employers

The Washington2Washington Project was launched by Microsoft in 2000 with the goal of linking two classrooms (one from the State of Washington and the other from Washington, DC) through using innovative and cutting-edge technology. The two schools were SEED Public Charter School in Washington, DC—the nation's first urban, public boarding school—and Sequoia Junior High School in Kent, Washington.[90]

Bringing two schools from different coasts with different student populations together to learn from and with one another was and is an innovative educational opportunity. By using cutting-edge technology—Microsoft spent hundreds of thousands of dollars to facilitate this program—to advance educational opportunities, Microsoft is setting the pace for and only scratching the surface of the kind of classroom experiences we should come to expect in our future. Support from the private sector is essential to providing the kind of education that will prepare our students for the 21st century.

Solutions for Community Leaders

In 1982, Robert Parish Moses became frustrated that his daughter's school did not offer algebra to eighth graders. He made a simple request of her teacher: would his child be allowed to sit apart in math class and do more advanced work in mathematics. The teacher's response was equally simple: why not come to class and teach his daughter Maisha and several advanced classmates more sophisticated math, math that would put them on course to take college preparatory mathematics.

Moses accepted, and the Algebra Project was born. This is the same Bob Moses who organized in the South during the 1960s; the same Bob Moses who worked with the Student Nonviolent Coordinating Committee, and the same Bob Moses who collaborated with Fannie Lou Hamer to establish the Mississippi Freedom Democratic Party to fight for the voting and civil rights of African Americans in the South.

For Moses, the Algebra Project is an extension of the work of the civil rights movement. Where the movement's work was to secure the fundamental right to vote, the Algebra Project's work is to secure the "right of every child to a quality public school education."[91] Moses' innovative and original approaches to teaching mathematics by linking the importance of math to everyday experiences has been replicated in more than 200 middle schools. The real challenge, however, cuts deeper for both Bob Moses and the Algebra Project: "This work is really a much larger deal; this issue of really changing the culture of the community around the education of its children [is the work the Algebra Project is doing]."[92] It is also the kind of work more of us will have to engage in to turn our schools around.

■ ■ ■

Today more than ever, education does not stop at the school door. The Internet has revolutionized how we access information, transforming employment opportunities and the culture at large. Too often minority and low-income communities have fallen behind, creating a digital divide that perpetuates the challenges already facing such groups. But change is coming: A program has successfully begun to bridge this gap in Philadelphia; it allows neighborhoods to access the Internet as a group, thus reducing the cost of connection to less than $15 a month.

This program has literally changed the worlds of Taah, Maya, and Theodora Cox, three generations of women living in Philadelphia. Theodora, at 64, enrolled in the One Economy Program, an eight-week computer training course that would allow her to purchase a computer for $120 and obtain broadband access for $10 a month. Overcoming her fear of intimidating technology, she successfully completed the program. She goes online to research kidney treatments that have helped her daughter Maya cope with the kidney disease that struck her as a teenager, just as she gave birth to her own daughter, Taah. Today, Theodora sells candles online, and Taah, an elementary school student, is the technology whiz of her class.

Solutions for Principals, Teachers, and Schools

In response to the rigid standards imposed by NCLB, some schools have instituted an equally rigid program, focused on winning the test scores "game," doing whatever it takes to get the requisite percentages that deem a school successful. Other schools have decided to focus on student achievement and improving the experiences of all children in their district. While resisting the urge to simply play the numbers game, these schools have achieved lasting gains, demonstrated by the students whose lives have been changed.

In Kennett Square, PA, school officials didn't need testing to confirm what they already knew: one-third of their student population was Hispanics who had recently immigrated and were struggling to succeed. Kennett Square school superintendent Rudolph Karkosak resisted the NCLB mentality that all students are the same and will learn the same way. Instead, he knows what years of experience have taught him, that different students respond to different techniques, and "local school districts can manage the flexibility needed to address changes in a community." Rather than hide the struggling students in his district, Karkosak started a series of programs aimed at every level of education, from kindergarten to high school, to address the needs of his English-language learners. The district extended the kindergarten school day, providing extra literacy classes for struggling students. In middle school and high school, programs were started to keep students invested and energized about school through mentoring and tutoring programs in partnership with local community organizations. These initiatives were so successful that the school began steering these students not just toward graduation, but to college. In 2006, 28 Hispanic students entered college, earning $320,000 in scholarships.[93]

In the meantime, test scores improved. All the district's elementary schools met their yearly progress targets in 2007, and the middle and high schools continued to show impressive gains. Kennett Square demonstrates that if you focus on educating and motivating students, the numbers will follow.

Uncommon Schools

Finding strategies for education reform has required innovation in how we organize and develop schools. From this realization has sprung a public school choice movement—advocating choices for students and parents within public education in the form of charter, magnet, and alternative model schools. One such program, Uncommon Schools, reminds us of what is possible in education. Begun with one charter school in Newark, NJ, in 1997, Uncommon Schools now provide a model of how school culture and high expectations can radically improve student achievement.[94] The Uncommon Schools require extraordinary commitments from students and teachers: school is in session 11 months a year; students are often at school for 10 hours a day. Parents and students must pledge to work hard and do everything in their power to put school first. Why do students commit to such a demanding schedule? Because it works. At the Uncommon Schools, students, known as "scholars," know that their effort will eventually pay off. Last year, 100 percent of North Star Academy (one of Uncommon Schools' Newark sites) graduating seniors enrolled in college. And the program has found no shortage of students willing to sacrifice; the schools' waiting lists often exceed 2,000 students.[95] Not surprisingly, despite largely low-income and traditionally disadvantaged student populations, Uncommon Schools consistently outperform state averages on NCLB assessments, demonstrating that good teaching and student engagement will lead to improved test results.

ACCOUNTABLE ASSESSMENT CHECKLIST

The most powerful tool we have as citizens to effect change is our vote. We should not allow our elected officials to make promises in their campaigns without fulfilling their obligations once in office. Use this list to hold our new president accountable on education.

Campaign Promises 2008: Education

BARACK OBAMA AS PROMISED . . .

- Will invest 10 billion dollars in a "Zero to Five" plan to provide critical support to young children and their parents to get children ready for kindergarten.

- Will reform No Child Left Behind by providing the necessary funding for the law and improve assessments to track student progress and improve student learning in an individualized manner.

- Will improve No Child Left Behind's accountability system so that we are supporting and not punishing schools in need of improvement.

- Will address the dropout crisis by drafting legislation to provide school districts with funding to invest in intervention strategies in middle school.

- Will expand high-quality, after-school activities by doubling federal funding and thus serving one million more children.

- Will recruit new teachers by creating Teacher Service Scholarships that will cover four years of undergraduate or two years of graduate teacher education.

- Will reward teachers by promoting new and innovative ways to increase teacher pay that are developed with teachers, not imposed on them.

Use this checklist to evaluate whether the entities that can make a difference are doing all that they can to help America realize the goal of the second Covenant: "Establishing a System of Public Education in Which All Children Achieve at High Levels and Reach Their Full Potential." This chapter also promotes the 10th Covenant: "Closing the Racial Digital Divide." Reexamine this checklist every six months to assess progress.

OUR PRESIDENT

☐ Have you made implementation of your education plan a priority within the first 100 days of the new administration?

☐ Have you worked to expand the measures by which schools and school districts are evaluated, examining not just testing data, but also special education programs, graduation and dropout rates, attendance rates, and other measures of student achievement?

☐ Have you improved the funding of educational programs to make No Child Left Behind possible?

☐ Are you investing in our schools to help all groups of children learn and be held to high standards?

☐ Have you provided for unbiased entities to evaluate the success of the new reforms at regular intervals to determine if benchmarks are being met?

☐ Did you assemble a team of experts on education to help make informed decisions about education policy?

☐ Have you provided support to early childhood education?

☐ Are you addressing the digital divide by improving access to the Internet and improving technology in our schools and communities?

OUR U.S. CONGRESSMEN AND CONGRESSWOMEN

☐ Is education reform a priority issue for you?

☐ Have you made early education a priority by expanding and supporting preschool programs?

☐ Do you support the inclusion of social studies, music, and art in the curriculum?

☐ Is funding early education, teacher training, and higher education programs a priority?

☐ Will you introduce or support initiatives to institute merit-based teacher pay?

☐ Do you support the development of charter schools, locally and nationally?

☐ Will you support funding for programs to bring more computers into homes and schools?

OUR GOVERNOR AND STATE LEGISLATORS

☐ Are you showing leadership in education reform, even where the federal government may be lacking?

☐ Do you have a plan to fill in gaps in education coverage where the federal government is remiss?

☐ Do you support reforms that help all students, especially those traditionally disadvantaged, to achieve and meet high standards?

☐ Do you have a testing program that holds our state to high standards in comparison with the rest of the nation?

☐ Have you worked to equalize funding through the school districts in our state?

☐ Have you tried to bring affordable, high-speed Internet access to your constituents?

OUR LOCAL LEADERS

☐ Do you have a plan to attract, hire, and retain strong teachers?

☐ Have you worked with parent and teacher groups to understand the education issues facing our community?

☐ Have you organized programs to help educate parents about ways to support and assist with their children's learning?

☐ Will you help your constituents become comfortable with new technology by increasing funding for such programs in schools and community centers?

OUR COMMUNITY LEADERS AND
FAITH-BASED ORGANIZATIONS

☐ Do you have a plan or an initiative to monitor the political progress of education reform promises made by our governmental leaders and to advocate when necessary?

☐ Do you educate members about the progress of education reform and the availability of education options in this community?

☐ Do you help students achieve by organizing after-school or summer programs that provide enrichment and remediation for children?

☐ Have you helped people in our community participate in our local schools, through fund-raising, volunteering, and voting on educational issues?

☐ Do you work to educate parents on helping their children succeed?

☐ Do you help promote literacy in our community?

☐ Do you offer programs to help parents interact positively with teachers and school administrators?

☐ Do you offer additional programs to expose students to different opportunities, such as racial and ethnic history, college tours, vocational training, life lessons, character education, and problem-solving skills?

YOU AND I

☐ Do I read more than I watch television?

☐ Do I read to my children?

☐ Do I have Internet access at home?

☐ Is my child at the appropriate reading and math levels for her or his age?

☐ Do I watch too much television at home? Do I allow my child to watch too much television or spend too much unsupervised time on the Internet?

☐ Do I monitor the music I allow my children to listen to and limit the amount of time they spend playing video games?

☐ Am I on a first-name basis with the principal of my child's school and his or her teachers?

☐ Do I regularly attend Parent-Teacher Association meetings?

☐ Do I know the children with whom my children are friends?

☐ Do I know the names of the parents of my children's friends and talk regularly with them about our children?

☐ Do I talk to my family, neighbors, children, friends, and community members about important education issues?

☐ Do I talk to my family, neighbors, children, friends, and community members about the value of education?

☐ Have I volunteered at a school in my community, whether through a career day, school event, or fund-raising activity?

☐ Am I aware of the different educational options for my child at every level of schooling?

☐ Do I attend parent-teacher conferences each semester and always discuss my child's progress with him or her?

☐ Can I advocate for my child if he or she needs extra services, such as tutoring, enrichment, or special education services?

☐ Do I know the skills and materials my child is responsible for this year and educate myself about those topics so that I can help support my child?

☐ Do I check my child's homework every night?

☐ If I am not a parent, do I support children in my family or community by providing advice, positive reinforcement, and a strong role model?

☐ Do I insist that teachers and administrators establish classroom environments that promote excellence for every child?

3

Unequal Justice

Balancing the Scales

Injustice anywhere is a threat to justice everywhere. We are caught
in an inescapable network of mutuality, tied in a single garment
of destiny. Whatever affects one directly, affects all indirectly.

—MARTIN LUTHER KING, JR.

Bad laws are the worst sort of tyranny.

—EDMUND BURKE

COVENANT THREE
Correcting the System of Unequal Justice

COVENANT FOUR
Fostering Accountable Community-Centered Policing

Affording Justice

A young mother of four is in trouble. Her children are between two and seven years old, and she is an addict.[96] As with most addicts, she engages in behavior that she would otherwise find objectionable: She lies. She cheats. She steals to feed her habit. While stealing is independently bad, this woman stole from a charity, one that provided medical resources to needy people. She solicited prescriptions for Percocet and Vicodin, filled the prescriptions using the names of the charity's employees, and kept the drugs for herself.[97] The young woman admitted, "I knew what I was doing, I knew it was wrong, and I couldn't stop."[98] Percocet and Vicodin, both opiates, are listed as Schedule II narcotics under federal law. This means that each stolen pill carried up to a one-year prison term.[99]

This young mother hid her addiction from the public well. She managed to adopt a child during the period that she was receiving and ingesting illegal drugs; her usage should have disqualified her from becoming an adoptive parent.[100] Most states will remove children from homes where a parent is a drug abuser,[101] but this woman escaped the government's intervention. Neither the prosecutor's office nor Family and Children's Services had any idea that she was an addict. Sometimes taking more than 20 pills per day, she hid her addiction from family and friends for three years.[102]

Here, the record grows cold. We do not know the ways in which her addiction manifested itself in her home and within her marriage. How were her children impacted? Were there periods of neglect? We have no answer to these questions; but we do know that drug addiction tends not to be one's own private hell. Family, friends, and loved ones usually suffer as well.

Eventually, her family intervened. She stopped using; her life was back on track. No public shame. No criminal record. Her family remained intact. But she was still not quite out of hell. One year later, a former employee of the charity, who had discovered the woman's theft, alerted the Drug Enforcement Administration (DEA). Now the government knew; an investigation by the DEA and the U.S. Attorney's office ensued. Her crimes could have landed her a 20-year prison sentence. She was in trouble. She knew what to do and had the resources to do it: hire a powerful and respected lawyer. She did. He quickly negotiated a settlement that avoided any criminal record whatsoever. Instead, she paid a fine for the drugs she stole and entered a pretrial diversion program. (A diversion program, as the name implies, "diverts" potential felons and misdemeanants from the criminal justice system by providing a period where the defendant agrees not to break the law and to follow any additional obligations that the court imposes.) Typically, the drug-addicted defendant is required to attend counseling programs or a drug treatment center. Once the defendant successfully completes the diversion program, the prosecutor will dismiss the case, which is how the young woman's story unfolded. She was now completely out of hell. She could put the issue behind her—as a matter of law.

This woman's story differs from the stories that many others could tell. Although blacks comprise 12 percent of the country's population and only 13 percent of drug users, they make up a breathtaking 57 percent of state inmates convicted of drug crimes. By comparison, whites constitute 70 percent of the population and 68 percent of drug users, but represent only 23 percent of drug offenders in prison.[103] Justice plainly is not equal. Unlike the hundreds of thousands of African Americans and Hispanics languishing away in prison, this woman who stole Percocet and Vicodin spent no time behind bars. Her marriage, job, and relationship with her children were preserved. So, what accounts for the difference in treatment between this woman and the millions of black and brown citizens in jail?

Disclosing her identity partly answers the question: her name is Cindy McCain. She married the 2008 Republican presidential nominee, Sen. John McCain, in 1979.[104] From 1989 to 1992, she was addicted to Vicodin and Percocet. At the time, she was the founder of a not-for-profit group, the American Voluntary Medical Team (AVMT), which funded trips by doctors to Third World countries desperately in need of medical expertise. McCain persuaded some of the volunteer doctors to write prescriptions that she filled in the name of AVMT staff members.

Who should be held accountable for this story? Who should be accountable to the millions of Americans—first offenders, even—who sit behind bars while others have their cases dismissed, or who benefit from diversionary programs?

■　■　■

Three years ago in *The Covenant*, "Correcting the System of Unequal Justice" and "Fostering Accountable Community-Centered Policing" examined the promise—and pitfalls—of the American criminal justice system. The promise of our democracy is still clear, a strong symbol of which is the U.S. Supreme Court, a remarkable edifice in Washington, DC. Above the massive stone figures on the face of the high court we find these words, emerging almost organically, out of the very marble from which the figures are carved: EQUAL JUSTICE UNDER LAW. These four words represent the best of what America aspires to be: a country where neither race nor creed nor station in life becomes the measure of the quality or quantity of justice one receives.[105]

Such is the theory of equal justice under law in the United States. The pitfalls presented in *The Covenant* remain at least as pressing today. The reality for black and brown and poor people is unfortunately different. Minority populations are over-policed, over-prosecuted, and over-sentenced, resulting in these populations sitting in jails and prisons at rates highly disproportionate to their population. Cindy McCain's story is instructive. She experienced the criminal justice system in a way different than most. How do we make sense of the way in which she was treated?

Many read the Cindy McCain story and decry the disparate treatment, concluding that she should have been treated like everybody else: prosecuted to the fullest extent of the law. Such a conclusion misses an important lesson that the Cindy McCain story teaches. Rather than demanding that McCain be treated like the millions of poor and minority defendants across the country, we should demand that those defendants be treated like Cindy McCain. In other words, we should raise the standards of representation in the criminal justice system to ensure fairness and equality. This does not mean that the system should treat everyone equally badly; we should push the poor to the top, rather than pull the rich to the bottom. The law handled Cindy McCain properly, recognizing that drug abuse is a sickness—a treatable disease; it provided an avenue to compel treatment without destroying a family by processing her through the criminal justice system. Courts, prosecutors, and law enforcement alike should aspire to treat the many like the few, not the few like the many.

Millions have suffered because a loved one has been convicted for drug possession. The spillover effects can be disastrous: Children lose their fathers; wives, their husbands; families are torn apart because of the over-prosecution of what it is—an illness that deserves medical assistance. Locking up addicts without concern for treatment is both fiscally irresponsible and penologically ill-conceived.

Yet this is precisely what we have been doing since the United States began its "war on drugs" in the 1980s. The impact of drug-related incarceration on families has been devastating. Many authorities suggest that the massive increase in incarceration has not led to a corresponding decrease in crime rate.[106] To the contrary, the war on drugs has resulted in the prosecution of low-level, nonviolent drug possessors.[107] The resulting disruption to families and destabilization of neighborhoods has led to a pervasive cynicism about government generally and law enforcement particularly.

Cindy McCain's story is a perfect illustration of why the war on drugs, like so many others, is wrongheaded. Her hurt was no more significant than that of the nameless, faceless millions separated from their families. Her life was no more important than the lives of working and poor women of all races who found themselves trapped in a cycle of addiction. They deserved the legal treatment she received—and they are entitled to it. Equal protection under the law requires that we accord everyone's life equal dignity and respect. Our collective failure to do so renders those four words—equal justice under law—hollow, a meaningless engraving on that stately Supreme Court building.

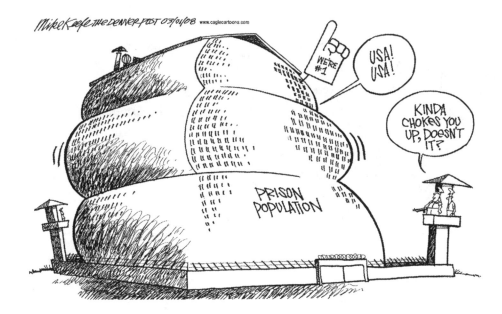

Frances Johnson: A Community Pillar Struck Down

Frances Johnson is a 68-year-old grandmother who suffers from cancer and diabetes.[108] A pillar of her District of Columbia community, she works with and mentors at-risk children. Several years ago, Johnson became an activist after neighborhood children witnessed a drug raid on their building. She converted her walk-in closet into a dollhouse and classroom. Children regularly visited her apartment, did homework, and engaged in dramatic play. The kids pretended to be doctors, lawyers, and even presidents. This safe haven is but one example of Johnson's altruism. She remains a fixture in her community—never a part of the problem, always a part of the solution.

Johnson is also poor, like far too many citizens in our nation's capital. She requires public housing to have a roof over her head. To be poor, fighting cancer, suffering from diabetes, and relying on public assistance might lead even the best of us to lose faith in the democratic possibilities of volunteerism. But not Frances Johnson. Her volunteer public service work continued unabated; that is, until her nephew was arrested for a minor marijuana possession charge. Her nephew lived with her and helped care for her. Two weeks after his arrest, the police raided Johnson's apartment, based on a warrant arising out of the nephew's arrest. During the raid, the police found a cuff link box with a small amount of marijuana in it. Although the criminal case that resulted from the cuff link box was dropped against her nephew, Johnson's ordeal was just beginning.

Pursuant to the federal government's "one strike and you're out" policy, the District of Columbia Housing Authority initiated proceedings to evict Johnson from her public housing complex. President Clinton announced his own "single strike" federal policy, whose purview included 3,400 public housing complexes in 1996.[109] "[T]oday [mark]s a clear signal to drug dealers and to gangs. If you break the law, you no longer have a home in public housing. One strike, and you're out." Some lauded the policy, arguing that it would reduce drug usage. But critics were many. "This really is a program where you don't even get up to the plate," Mark Kappelhoff of the ACLU told CNN. "You're thrown out without . . . having a conviction or even an arrest."[110] Because of Johnson's long history of service in the

District, several members of the DC Council wrote letters of support for her, urging the Housing Authority to reconsider its decision to evict her. The Housing Authority did back down, but Johnson's landlord, NDC Realty, has filed two eviction lawsuits against her. Johnson says she has trouble sleeping these days, not because of her chemotherapy sessions, but because she doesn't know whether she will have a place to live.

Think about it: a senior citizen, a pillar of the community, who may be thrown out on the streets, not for anything she was accused of doing, but because her nephew allegedly had a small quantity of marijuana in her apartment. There is no claim and no evidence whatsoever that Johnson had any knowledge of marijuana being in the house. Nevertheless, she faces eviction and an uncertain future. More immediately, her nephew was forced to move out. He assisted his 68-year-old aunt as she navigated the complicated terrain of cancer treatment and medication. No more. At least not at the level that he once helped his aunt.

An innocent senior is punished for the conduct of her nephew. Who should be accountable if Frances Johnson cannot keep up with her cancer treatment regimen? Who should be held accountable if she becomes homeless? Who will be held accountable if she is unable to secure public assistance for her future housing needs, owing to her nephew's prior conviction? And what is to become of her nephew? Should we even care?

Disparate Disenfranchisement

The collateral consequences to criminal convictions are many and often have devastating effects on both the individual and his or her family. Felony disenfranchisement laws represent one of the most significant civil rights challenges of our era. The Sentencing Project estimates that 5.3 million Americans cannot vote due to state laws that prohibit people with felony records from voting.[111] As with all aspects of the criminal justice system, black men draw the short straw. An estimated 13 percent of black men are disenfranchised because of a felony record.[112] Following is a state-by-state breakdown of the impact of felony disenfranchisement laws on citizens and how those laws impact blacks particularly, as tabulated by the Sentencing Project.[113]

DISENFRANCHISED FELONS BY STATE[114]

State	Total Felons	Voting Age Population	Disenfranchisement Rate
Alabama	250,046	3,392,779	7.37%
Alaska	11,132	459,529	2.42%
Arizona	176,103	4,051,499	4.34%
Arkansas	57,691	2,043,701	2.82%
California	283,124	26,064,483	1.09%
Colorado	28,636	3,397,937	0.84%
Connecticut	22,854	2,647,997	0.86%
Delaware	46,677	618,649	7.54%
District of Columbia	730	454,981	0.16%
Florida	1,179,687	13,094,945	9.01%
Georgia	283,607	6,387,956	4.44%
Hawaii	6,530	960,466	0.68%
Idaho	17,416	994,305	1.75%
Illinois	45,825	9,422,938	0.49%
Indiana	26,245	4,591,742	0.57%
Iowa	121,418	2,250,634	5.39%
Kansas	27,863	2,028,426	1.37%
Kentucky	186,348	3,123,645	5.97%
Louisiana	98,190	3,318,779	2.96%
Maine	–	1,018,982	0.00%
Maryland	111,521	4,130,817	2.70%
Massachusetts	10,140	4,946,304	0.20%
Michigan	49,788	7,541,065	0.66%
Minnesota	38,784	3,810,605	1.02%
Mississippi	146,155	2,120,013	6.89%
Missouri	93,752	4,297,142	2.18%
Montana	4,145	701,847	0.59%
Nebraska	61,996	1,298,451	4.77%
Nevada	43,594	1,659,757	2.63%
New Hampshire	2,587	981,456	0.26%
New Jersey	127,178	6,506,779	1.95%
New Mexico	18,080	1,372,580	1.32%
New York	122,018	14,657,367	0.83%

North Carolina	73,113	6,319,805	1.16%
North Dakota	1,466	487,010	0.30%
Ohio	45,487	8,620,509	0.53%
Oklahoma	49,541	2,633,289	1.88%
Oregon	14,228	2,710,424	0.52%
Pennsylvania	41,626	9,534,761	0.44%
Rhode Island	20,793	832,115	2.50%
South Carolina	48,523	3,123,648	1.55%
South Dakota	3,271	568,883	0.58%
Tennessee	94,258	4,447,269	2.12%
Texas	522,887	15,878,347	3.29%
Utah	5,970	1,608,540	0.37%
Vermont	–	481,661	0.00%
Virginia	377,847	5,587,563	6.76%
Washington	167,316	4,634,864	3.61%
West Virginia	10,800	1,419,453	0.76%
Wisconsin	62,342	4,139,405	1.51%
Wyoming	20,198	380,169	5.31%
U.S. Total	5,259,350	217,766,271	2.42%

These numbers are remarkable because they are so starkly inconsistent with notions of fair and equal democratic participation. That more than 13 percent of black men compared to only two percent of whites are disenfranchised must be understood as a civil rights issue, which has to be addressed and remedied. In 1963, the U.S. Supreme Court coined the phrase, "one person, one vote,"[115] which captures a core constitutional value: namely, that every citizen has a vote, and the vote of every citizen counts. Indeed, voting is regarded as the most significant expression of our democratic tradition, a central pillar upon which our democracy rests. Yet states are disenfranchising millions of fellow citizens who have paid their debt to society. They have no vote and have become politically voiceless. This is anathema to values essential to our democracy.[116]

Another major consequence of being a convicted felon is ineligibility for government benefits. The inability to receive federal student loans, Section 8 housing (as we see in Frances Johnson's story), and, in some cases, medical benefits erects roadblocks to full integration into the community.[117] The Legal Action Network recently completed a comprehensive two-year study, "After Prison: Roadblocks to Reentry: A Report on State Legal Barriers Facing People with Criminal Records."[118] The study found that "people with criminal records seeking reentry face a daunting array of counterproductive, debilitating, and unreasonable roadblocks in almost every important aspect of life."[119] The network has outlined the enormous legal barriers that ex-felons face:

- Most states allow employers to deny jobs to people who were arrested but never convicted of a crime.

- Most states allow employers to deny jobs to anyone with a criminal record, regardless of how long ago or the individual's work history and personal circumstances.

- Most states ban some or all people with drug felony convictions from being eligible for federally funded public assistance and food stamps.

- Many public housing authorities deny eligibility for federally assisted housing based on an arrest that never led to a conviction.

- Most states make criminal history information accessible to the general public through the Internet, making it extremely easy for employers and others to discriminate against people on the basis of old or minor convictions, for example, to deny employment or housing.

- All but two states restrict the right to vote in some way for people with criminal convictions.[120]

Considering these barriers, ex-felons find it increasingly difficult to find and maintain employment. In fact, 37 states have laws that permit employers to consider arrests that never led to a conviction.[121]

Ryan Matthews: Guilty Until Proven Innocent

Shortly after his 17th birthday, Ryan Matthews was arrested and charged with murder in 1999. Witnesses to the murder described the assailant as "short," no taller than 5'9". Even though Matthews is at least six feet tall, and even though none of the three witnesses could identify Matthews, the New Orleans district attorney prosecuted the case. The allegation was that a masked man shot and killed the owner of a convenience store.

As is often the case, Matthews was unable to hire an attorney and, therefore, was assigned an attorney paid for by the state. His court-appointed attorney was both inexperienced and unprepared. After only three days of trial—in a capital murder prosecution—the testimony was finished and the judge ordered closing arguments. Deliberating for several hours, the jury first reported that it could not reach a verdict. The judge responded by ordering the jury to continue deliberating until such time as it reached a unanimous judgment. The jury returned a guilty verdict, and Matthews was sentenced to death.

A few years later, Matthews' appellate lawyer recognized that the trial lawyer was ill-equipped to deal with the DNA evidence. The new lawyer had the DNA on the assailant's mask tested and compared with Matthews' DNA. It turned out that the murderer's DNA did not match Matthews' DNA. Matthews was not the assailant; better yet, the DNA affirmatively matched the DNA of someone already in prison for a murder that occurred two months after the one for which Matthews was convicted and which was committed only a couple of blocks away from the convenience store murder. Faced with irrefutable DNA evidence that proved Matthews' innocence, the state dismissed his case.[122]

Who should be held accountable to Matthews and his family for the years he spent behind bars? Who should be held accountable for making an innocent man believe that he was going to be put to death?

Death Penalty: Irreversible (In)Justice

In the United States, the death penalty "is a sad and ugly badge of shame."[123] These words are from Judge George Bundy Smith in an opinion in which he was simply fed up with unjust and unequal application of the death penalty. Death is the most final, most severe, and the only irreversible penalty in our criminal justice arsenal. Given these realities about the death penalty, politicians should take the utmost care to ensure that any judgment imposing the death penalty is applied fairly and impartially. The Fourteenth Amendment to the U.S. Constitution, in part, reads, "nor shall any State deprive any person of life, liberty, or property without due process of law; nor deny any person within its jurisdiction the equal protection of the law."

For decades, the application of the death penalty has violated "the equal protection of the law." One of the clearest examples of this is the famous Supreme Court case *McCleskey v. Kemp*, 481 U.S. 279 (1987). Part of the record of that case revealed that "taking into account 230 nonracial variables . . . prosecutors sought the death penalty in 70 percent of the cases involving black defendants and white victims; 32 percent of the cases involving white defendants and white victims; 15 percent of the cases involving black defendants and black victims; and 19 percent of the cases involving white defendants and black victims." Notwithstanding this startling correlation between race and the death sentence, the Supreme Court upheld the application of the death penalty in that case and has upheld it in others. This is unacceptable in a democracy. Even if one is a proponent of the death penalty, that most final of all criminal sentences should not be based, even slightly, on race.

Community-Centered Policing

The U.S. Department of Justice, Office of Community Oriented Policing Services (COPS) defines community policing as follows:

> Community policing focuses on crime and social disorder through the delivery of police services that includes aspects of traditional law enforcement, as well as prevention, problem-solving, community engagement, and partnerships. The community policing model balances

reactive responses to calls for service with proactive problem-solving centered on the causes of crime and disorder. Community policing requires police and citizens to join together as partners in the course of both identifying and effectively addressing these issues.[124]

Community policing represents the most significant reform in policing in the last 100 years. It positions law enforcement as partners within a community as opposed to occupiers of a community. Under this partnership model, police and the community work together to solve what they understand to be common problems. The important point here is that community problems are conjointly the problems of the residents *and* the police. The police are part of the community; this is how it must be for community policing to be effective. The police and community work together to find creative solutions to solving crime in the community.

The *Covenant* lists several programs and initiatives from around the country that work to make community-based policing a reality in the fourth Covenant, "Fostering Accountable Community-Centered Policing." The *Covenant* catalogs how police are being held accountable to the community. This information is readily available. Policymakers know what works—and what doesn't; they know which policies are likely to maintain good working relationships between the police and the community and which ones are likely to generate animosity, mistrust, and tension between the police and community. What is missing is the political will to implement programmatic change that both protect public safety and respect the civil liberties of community residents. The *Covenant* introduced the Ella Baker Center's Bay Area PoliceWatch to the wider community, for example.

This program endeavored to "police the police" by documenting police abuses and educating the community about its civil rights. Programs such as PoliceWatch are necessary only when law enforcement is viewed as occupiers—a force that regularly abuses the civil rights and liberties of the community's residents. A model of community policing, on the other hand, does not position the police as oppositional; they work with the community to ensure just results. They are not in the community only to lock people up; they are there "to protect and serve."

One simple policy change jurisdictions can implement to facilitate community policing is residency requirements. Police officers who have a stake in the community they serve behave differently than those who are outsiders and have no interest in seeing the community not only survive, but thrive.

On the street police officers are, for the most part, discretionary actors in the criminal justice system. They decide whether to arrest and whom to arrest. They even make the initial charging decision (which the prosecutor usually rubber-stamps). Police officers who know the community and the residents are better equipped to exercise their discretion responsibly. For instance, police officers familiar with the community can better decide whether to empty a bottle of beer and take "Tommy" home, knowing that Tommy's mom will deal with him swiftly and severely, or to arrest Tommy, charge him with a misdemeanor, and saddle him with a record that will impact his life chances. Community policing, properly conceived, can lead to a productive, nonconfrontational relationship between the community and the police. This, in turn, will lead to communities whose civil rights are respected and where civil rights violations become the exception and not the rule.

A FRAMEWORK FOR ASSESSMENT

The *Covenant* set forth "Correcting the System of Unequal Justice" and "Fostering Accountable Community-Centered Policing" as covenants committed to examining and providing solutions for the failures of democracy and frequent injustices generally faced in America. These problems are especially acute for communities of color. At the end of these two chapters, we imagined what individuals, government, and community leaders can do to influence their related issues. THE COVENANT *In Action* next provides a toolkit to equip citizens with the instruments to effect change on these and all of *The Covenant* issues. *ACCOUNTABLE* now will help citizens assess whether we have lived up to the aspirations put forward in *The Covenant* and give them a measuring tool for future evaluation.

During the 2008 presidential election, candidates weighed in on our criminal justice system, but only barely. Crime and crime policy seemed to be an area that both candidates stayed away from. Remarkably, neither McCain nor Obama listed "Criminal Justice," "Crime," "Crime Policy," or any variant thereof on his official presidential website. To be sure, each addressed crime policy, but one had to really dig through their respective websites to find their policy proposals. Both candidates vowed to be "tough" on crime, with Obama promising to be both "tough" and "smart" on crime. What exactly that means, we do not know. What is clear is that the problem of crime in America has not gotten better, even as we continue to incarcerate more and more of our citizens. The challenge for the next president will be to treat the causes of criminality in America. Criminalizing more and more people, stamping people with criminal records that they wear as a permanent scar, isn't helping.

Solutions for Government

The United States has more than 2 million people in jail. This represents more people in jail and a higher percentage of imprisoned citizens than any other country in the world, even more than Iran, Iraq, or any country in the so-called axis of evil. To the extent that deterrence is a primary goal of the criminal justice system, the level and extent of incarceration in America appear not to be doing the trick.

The key to establishing sound criminal justice policy is, at once, remarkably simple and prohibitively difficult. It is simple because programs exist that work, programs with demonstrably proven results. It is difficult because effective policing usually is not politically popular. "Lock 'em up and throw away the key" seems to make for better political theater. Harsh incarceration is quick and satisfies the public's sense of just retribution, whereas programs designed to prevent crime take longer to yield results and are susceptible to claims of being soft on crime.

The lion's share of criminal justice policy, of course, is a state affair. The federal government, however, can create incentives for states to fund programs that work. Getting more law enforcement officers on the streets, for example, is low-hanging fruit. Study after study proves that one of the most effective strategies for fighting crime is having more police dispatched in communities. Three programs in particular can be funded by the federal government. First, the COPS program, which put 100,000 additional officers on the street, can be re-funded. Empirical studies show that increased police presence under the COPS era actually reduced both crime and arrests. At present, the COPS program has been defunded.

Second, President Obama should propose funding for the LEAD program, which provides federal funds for police officers who wish to pursue advanced degrees and learn about the most recent advances in criminology. Finally, policymakers should bring back the PoliceCorps program, which was proposed but never implemented during the Clinton administration. PoliceCorps is designed to be similar to AmeriCorps, but for police. Government would subsidize education costs for young people who want to engage in public service by joining the ranks of law enforcement and agreeing to serve for a predesignated time in an underserved community.

Solutions for Community Organizations

Communities should take an active role in the state of policing in their community. As demonstrated in this chapter, criminal justice has civil rights implications, from voting to jobs to housing. The collateral consequences of contacts with the criminal justice system can so debilitate individuals and the communities in which they live that community organizations must work to avoid these negative outcomes.

Several community organizations have partnered with institutional actors to have a formal say in community policing and prosecution. By way of example, Community Court Initiatives are popping up all over the country. In these programs, "quality of life" crimes are prosecuted in community courts, consisting of community residents, merchants, and institutional actors, such as social workers. Quality-of-life crimes include shoplifting, petty gambling, minor drug violations, and similar misdemeanors. Rather than subjecting the accused to the traditional criminal process, Community

Court Initiatives are responsible for adjudicating the guilt or innocence of the accused and, if guilt is determined, fashioning an appropriate remedy as punishment. Usually, punishments include community service and fines, rather than jail and probation. The idea is that communities best know their own residents and know what type of "punishment" will best protect the community and serve the interest of justice. That is to say, community members are in the best position to determine whether one of their own is incorrigible or amenable to a second chance. Community Court Initiatives also recognize that first offenders who enter jail for minor offenses often come out much more disposed to criminal behavior than before. Jail, then, must be a last option, not a first.

ACCOUNTABLE ASSESSMENT CHECKLIST

The most powerful tool we have as citizens to effect change is our vote. We should not allow our elected officials to make promises during their campaigns without fulfilling their obligations once in office. Use this list to hold our new president accountable on correcting our unequal system of justice.

Campaign Promises 2008: Unequal Justice

BARACK OBAMA AS PROMISED . . .

- Will ban racial profiling by federal law enforcement agencies and provide federal incentives to state and local police departments to prohibit the practice.

- Will reduce crime recidivism by providing ex-offender support such as job training, and substance-abuse and mental health services.

- Will eliminate sentencing disparities between crack and powder-based cocaine.

- Will use drug courts to give first-time, nonviolent offenders a chance to serve their sentence, where appropriate, in the type of drug rehabilitation programs that have proven to work better than a prison term in changing bad behavior.

- Supports capital punishment for only the worst crimes.

Use this checklist to evaluate whether the entities that can make a difference are doing all that they can to help America realize the goal of the third and fourth Covenants, "Correcting the System of Unequal Justice" and "Fostering Accountable Community-Centered Policing." Reexamine this checklist every six months to assess progress.

OUR PRESIDENT

- ☐ Have you made implementation of a plan to eliminate racial profiling a priority?

- ☐ Have you exercised good judgment in decision making regarding the scope of capital punishment?

- ☐ Have you sought to examine and reform racial disparities in sentencing laws?

- ☐ Have you provided federal support to state and local entities in creating innovative solutions to reduce crime?

- ☐ Have you provided for unbiased entities to regularly evaluate the success of the new reforms to determine if benchmarks are being met?

- ☐ Have you created programs to prevent recidivism in the federal criminal justice system?

OUR U.S. CONGRESSMEN AND CONGRESSWOMEN

- ☐ Have you supported or introduced legislation designed to reduce racial disparities in the criminal justice system, such as racial profiling and sentencing disparities?

- ☐ Have you examined the problems facing our state or district so that you can advocate for practical solutions regarding criminal justice?

☐ Have you introduced legislation that reduces sentencing disparities along racial and ethnic lines?

OUR GOVERNOR AND STATE LEGISLATORS

☐ Have you created programs to prevent recidivism in the state criminal justice system?

☐ Do you have a plan to address the specific problems of crime and justice facing our state?

☐ Have you investigated and implemented new technologies to allow public safety personnel to be more effective in fighting and preventing crime?

☐ Do you support state and local law enforcement in mandating high standards for officer conduct and fair treatment for all people?

☐ Do you mandate that local and state officials meet with community members to discuss issues and challenges of the criminal justice system facing local communities and the state as a whole?

OUR COMMUNITY LEADERS
AND FAITH-BASED ORGANIZATIONS

☐ Have you researched the criminal justice issues facing your community?

☐ Do you have a plan or an initiative to educate your members on both preventing crime and ensuring a system of equal justice?

☐ Have you educated your members on the dangers and consequences of a criminal conviction?

☐ Has your organization created a plan to help prevent crime in your community?

☐ Have you organized meetings with local and state law enforcement officials to discuss problems and work together to craft solutions to issues of criminal justice?

YOU AND I

☐ Do I educate myself about the events occurring in my community regarding crime?

☐ Do I talk to my friends, family, children, and neighbors about these issues and events?

☐ Do I know how the criminal justice system in my community, state, and nation functions?

☐ Have I ever visited a courthouse or jail in my community?

☐ Do I talk to my children about how to deal with an encounter with any law enforcement official?

☐ Do I know where and how to report police misconduct if it should occur?

☐ Do I attend community meetings about issues related to crime and criminal justice?

☐ Do I know how to find out what the law is in my community?

☐ Do I know if my community has free legal services available to residents?

☐ Have I taught my children about doing the right thing and obeying the law?

4

The Economy

Securing the Means Necessary for Pursuing Happiness

We have always known that heedless self-interest was bad morals; we now know that it is bad economics.

—PRESIDENT FRANKLIN D. ROOSEVELT

Don't let your mouth write no check that your [behind] can't cash.

—BO DIDDLEY

COVENANT EIGHT
Accessing Good Jobs, Wealth, and Economic Prosperity

COVENANT SEVEN
Strengthening Our Rural Roots

Cynthia Porter: Hard-working, Dedicated, and Struggling to Survive

Sometimes when Cynthia Porter cannot find or pay anyone to drive her to work—she does not earn enough money to buy a car—she walks several miles in the dark of night, sometimes well past midnight, to get to work because, as she says, "I'd rather walk and be a little late than call in. I'd rather make the effort. I couldn't just sit here. I don't want to miss a day; otherwise I might be fired." There is no public transportation in Marion, Alabama, to take her to and from work for her 11:00 p.m. overnight shift.[125]

What kind of job does Cynthia have that requires her to work the graveyard shift and to walk there so late at night out of fear of losing her job? Is it a job that pays an exceptional wage? A job with the kind of benefits package that would motivate any of us to do the same because the benefits far outweigh the risks?

Porter is a certified nursing assistant employed by a nursing home. She earns $750 a month. She pays $150 rent for a small shack with plywood floors, a sunken toilet, and a broken heater, which her landlord refuses to fix. This is home to Porter and her two children.[126] Her responsibilities include helping elderly residents with the toilet, changing bedpans, and repositioning patients every couple of hours to prevent them from developing bedsores. When she is not directly assisting patients, she cleans wheelchairs and dining rooms, mops floors and scrubs refrigerators, clears out closets and drawers. At the end of her shift, she is responsible for getting her elderly patients ready for their morning meal.[127]

One might assume Porter is unhappy with her job or that she is desperately seeking another one that pays more and provides benefits; a job that makes it easy for her to afford Clorox or shampoo; or that pays her enough to purchase a washing machine and dryer to avoid scrubbing the family's clothes in her bathtub on hands and knees before she hangs them on a line to dry.[128]

But Porter does not feel that way at all. "I like helping people. . . . I like talking to them and shampooing their hair. I like old people. If they are down, I can really make them feel better. The patients say, 'Nobody loves me or comes to see me.' Sometimes I help the residents play dominoes. Sometimes their hands shake, but I hold them. It's a lot of fun for them. I tell them 'I love you,' and give them a hug. I like being a CNA; I'm doing what I want to be doing."[129]

This is a snapshot of rural poverty in our country—low-paying jobs, substandard housing, poor or nonexistent public services. It is not just rural America, however, that suffers from the inability to earn a life-enhancing wage.

This story, based on an article published in *The Nation* a few years ago, is not an isolated incident. Our country is filled with Cynthia Porters: decent, hard-working, engaged, and compassionate citizens who work hard all day, or in her case, all night, and who still live below the poverty line. "Give me your tired, your poor, your huddled masses yearning to breathe free" are words engraved on the pedestal of the Statue of Liberty, and these words have inspired generations of immigrants to come to our shores, become citizens, and put our promise of a decent, meaningful, and dignified life for all willing to work hard enough to achieve it to the test.

Our country's promises are not being fulfilled for Cynthia Porter and for those just like her.

Are we comfortable with allowing more than 30 million Americans to be among what we describe as the "working poor"?[130] When did it become *American* to allow fellow citizens to work honestly and hard and yet have no security or stability? How can we tell ourselves we are the greatest, most powerful nation on the earth, while allowing one in four of our workers to languish in low-paying jobs that barely allow them to eke out a living?

Who is accountable for making sure the tens of millions of Cynthia Porters in America earn a livable, secure, and decent sustaining wage for their hard work?

■   ■   ■

In *The Covenant,* we focused on our economic disposition—steadying our attention on the challenges facing the most vulnerable among us. What we found was not beyond repair, but enough to justify serious concern with our current condition and its debilitating impact on the less fortunate. The adage, "the rich get richer, and the poor get poorer," has never been more appropriate in our country's history than today. Or, as the famous blues singer Billie Holiday crooned, "Them that's got shall have, them that's not shall lose . . ." Three years after the publication of *The Covenant,* "them that's not" are still losing.

Teetering Toward Disaster

The year 2000 seems a lifetime ago. Employment was up, the federal budget was balanced, and the economy appeared strong. The year marked the third consecutive one in which there was a federal budget surplus. "It was," to borrow from Charles Dickens, "the best of times."

Eight years later, we are experiencing the latter of Dickens' profound coupling of phrases, "the worst of times." And it is anybody's guess how long it will take to recover from what billionaire Warren Buffett describes as "an economic Pearl Harbor."[131] How did we get to this point? Were there warning signs? Could this financial meltdown—the worst since the Great Depression—have been avoided? Who could have imagined, except for the eclectic and often prescient George Soros, that this crisis could have happened?[132]

The housing crisis is at the eye of this financial storm. The past few years saw an unprecedented rise in homeownership. With interest rates low, loans were made available for citizens to achieve the quintessential pillar of the American dream: a home of their own. Many lenders, in search of reward without risk, approved easy loans with adjustable mortgage rates.

Imagine, for example, you purchased a home with a mortgage of $1,500 a month, a bit of a stretch on your budget. Now imagine there is a condition in your mortgage contract stipulating, under certain conditions, your mortgage could balloon to $2,000 or $2,500 a month. It is doubtful you could continue to pay for your new home. To further complicate matters—and to avoid risk—lenders bundled mortgages together into tradable securities to be sold on Wall Street. With the housing market growing unabated, these securities became attractive to investors worldwide. They were sold many times over, as is the nature of securities, and the risk of individual homeowners becoming unable to pay their mortgages was passed down the line. The assumption, of course, was that the housing market would continue to expand. It is the nature of bubbles, however, to burst. The housing bubble did: balloon payments kicked in, mortgages could not be paid, and foreclosures began.

The negative rippling spread all over the world, soaking up investors holding these mortgage-backed securities with their value uncertain. Consequently, banks, hedge funds, and investors no longer know how much the burst bubble has drained from their overall portfolios.

Think of it another way: Bank A routinely lends to Bank B but is no longer certain Bank B can repay its loans because Bank A does not know how much of Bank B's assets are exposed to the housing market, and neither does Bank B. No one, therefore, trusts anyone to repay loans, which then freeze and, on a larger scale, we eventually find ourselves in the middle of a worldwide economic crisis. Gone are the days when the flow of capital was largely regulated or contained within national boundaries. Like the Internet, world markets are all connected. And when the largest economy on the face of the earth catches a cold—more like pneumonia in the current case—the rest of the global economy is on life support.

Despite the fact many in the media have blamed this entire crisis on people who could not afford homes they purchased—a cynical attempt to scapegoat ordinary citizens as today's "welfare queens"—the root of the problem lies with lenders. Financial institutions, searching for profits without risk, put easy capital on the street and passed the risks along to the next investor. Consumers, however, must be held accountable for their role in this crisis as well. For too long, we have been living on credit and not on what we could actually afford. But the true culprits in the housing crisis occupy bank corridors and Wall Street, where a ravenous desire for financial reward without end inflated the housing bubble.

Affixing blame is the least of our problems; when the smoke clears, we need to remember how we got here and be vigilant in implementing measures to prevent repeating this catastrophe. For the most part, banks are not lending, and when banks don't lend, payrolls are not met, growth stalls, and, in the worst case, depression—worldwide depression—sets in.

We are, by all indications, facing the greatest financial crisis since the Great Depression. This presents additional challenges to the long-term structural problems facing working families, minorities in particular. We should not lose sight of the need to manage an economy that will provide all Americans with an opportunity to earn a livable wage. After all, as Americans, this is what we are promised.

As in *The Covenant*, we highlight long-term indicators of economic health, such as jobs that pay a livable wage, the relationship between homeownership and wealth building, or long-term shifts in our modes of productivity, such as the evaporating manufacturing and industrial sectors of our economy. These areas reflect economic performance over time and are factors we must revisit to provide opportunity for all.

Although the outlook for our economy is bleak, this is not the worst moment in our country's economic history. The most difficult was the Long Depression between 1873 and 1896, where difficulties persisted for more than 23 years. It was once inconceivable for us to imagine living through such a moment, given the relative economic stability we've enjoyed as a country since the Great Depression of 1929. Other moments of economic difficulty have been overcome, beginning with the Panic of 1797; the 19th and 20th centuries were checkered by three depressions and numerous economic panics and recessions.

The point? We have been here before and, in all likelihood, we will visit economic hardship again. There are no all-encompassing, final solutions for our economy.

While we place our current moment in context, we do not suggest the economy is a force of nature whose laws must be uncovered and obeyed, much like the laws of gravity, to prevent an economic fall. This kind of ideology—economics as a force of nature outside of the direction of human agency except for trying to uncover its laws—is a lot of what has gotten us into our present state.[133] There is no one correct way to guide an economy, especially given many countries are as productive as the United States but offer higher incomes and significantly less inequality for those least well off.

We will never have all the necessary information to predict economic outcomes. The economy is, and always will be, subject to panics, moods, and collapses despite our persistent study of it. Still, unlike the laws of gravity, it is responsive to decisions we make and can be shaped by the leadership and policies of our institutions. For example, we are in a financial squeeze on working families that extends more than three decades, where their productivity has not generated commensurate improvements in their living standards. This has not been by accident. Policies have been implemented by legislators and the corporate world who wish to see the economy primarily benefit the "haves." As impersonal as the economy may seem, human beings are always the ones making decisions and setting policies that have a direct bearing on our economic condition, for better or for worse. This logic guided many of the safety nets and regulations that were instituted under the New Deal and reinforced by the Great Society: markets are fickle but necessary, and we need to provide a net to protect citizens from indecent standards of living when the economy turns for the worse.

Jerry Roy and Larry Mathews: Losing Retirement Security and a Way of Life

When Jerry Roy first went to work at General Motors (GM) in Flint, MI, in 1977, he was convinced his future would be secure. "When I got there," he recalls, it was "like I'd died and went to heaven." His feelings were not uncommon, given generations of Americans before him had earned their living and their retirement packages with GM and other major domestic manufacturers. He was the fourth generation of Roys to work for GM or its one-time subsidiary, Delco. His great-grandfather John went to work for

GM, relocating to Michigan from Missouri during the Great Depression. His grandfather Edward worked at Delco during World War II. His father, Gerald, worked at both GM and Delco and remembers the days when the plants never closed: there were three shifts covering 24 hours.[134]

Many employees, like Jerry Roy, continued the honorable work of their parents and grandparents, assuming U.S. manufacturing would continue to provide for homeownership, medical benefits, safe pensions, and overall stability. After all, for the better part of a century, it had served as the foundation for blue-collar families to send their children to college where they, in turn, could gain the talents necessary to join the ranks of white-collar workers in the upper middle class.

Those days are regrettably long gone at both GM and Delco, as they are for many once-powerful manufacturing giants. Since 1998, 3 million manufacturing jobs have been lost; in 2003 Bethlehem Steel folded, costing thousands of jobs and pensions. A year later, Levi Strauss closed the doors at its last of more than 60 factories.[135]

Less than 50 years ago, 53 percent of our economy was accounted for by manufacturing. By 1988, only 39 percent of the economy was attributable to manufacturing. By 2004, that number had dwindled to 9 percent.[136]

Despite 28 years of service and his family's proud industrial legacy, Jerry Roy may lose his retirement fund and is facing, like so many others, a severe cut in pay or the actual loss of his job.

Remember Ross Perot's famous line about that "giant sucking sound"? It was, he claimed, the sound of manufacturing jobs lost to the then-proposed North American Free Trade Agreement (NAFTA). This quip was met with laughter at the funny little man from Dallas; no one is laughing anymore. His insights into the effects of NAFTA were spot on. Moreover, it is not just the jobs lost because of increasingly intense competition from low-wage nations. Conventional economic wisdom tells us that imports push downward on the wages of those who remain in manufacturing, and when people lose jobs in the "traded sectors," they compete with other workers, thereby lowering wages in "nontraded sectors." Fourteen years after the institution of NAFTA, many of us are feeling these effects; and the future suggests, without a change of course, we will continue to lose the jobs that allowed many citizens to achieve the American dream—citizens like Larry Mathews.

Like Jerry Roy, Mathews comes from a family of autoworkers, but he isn't encouraging his son to follow in his family's footsteps. As he puts it, "Given what we've lost here in the past decade, I really didn't want to see him come to work at GM or Delphi . . . the security just isn't there." Still, he considers the painful possibility of having to call his son back home from college in Michigan if proposed pay cuts go through at Delphi.

"I bet those executives (at Delphi) don't have to make those calls."[137]

They don't. And more and more Americans are faced with not having the income to put their children through school. Who is accountable to Jerry Roy, Larry Mathews, and the millions like them?

What will become of those families, communities, cities, and even states that have depended on heavy industry for employment? Local economies, in particular, are jeopardized when industries fold or pack up and leave for other countries with lower wages, nonexistent labor laws, or lower costs overall. CEOs, boards of directors, and shareholders are the winners in this game at the cost of cities such as Detroit, Pittsburgh, Dayton, and Flint.

We say people will have to be retrained and seek new industries to find jobs that promote stability and possibility. But little or no funding exists for such training. Even highly skilled jobs—engineers and computer scientists—are under pressure from the global economy.[138]

How will we manage to get through the stormy winds of this 21st-century economy? Where will we turn for answers? Where will we find the resources necessary to weather this storm and plant the seeds for a brighter economic future? Without secure jobs, we could face a drastic shift in what we now understand to be the American way of life, one largely reflected by the quest for homeownership. Our homes are commonly our most valuable asset. Sadly, Americans of all backgrounds are losing their homes at record rates. People of color—Hispanic and African American in particular—are taking the biggest hits during this housing meltdown.

The Foreclosure Crisis: Losing Our Most Precious Assets

The recently released *Foreclosed: State of the Dream 2008* is a timely and powerful indictment of the disparities that still exist between white Americans and black and brown Americans with respect to the current housing meltdown. The total direct loss from subprime loans over the past eight years is conservatively estimated to be between $356 billion and $462 billion. Not accounting for the spillover effects from lowered property values, lender losses, and taxes, black and brown Americans could lose between an estimated $164 billion and $213 billion from loans taken during the same period.[139]

This study contends the reason for this disparity is plain. The recent subprime meltdown as it relates to people of color has been "racially predatory," and "persistent racial and economic inequalities that continue to manifest broadly in U.S. society are at the root of this crisis and need to be addressed for any policy solutions to be truly successful."

Federal data bear this out, indicating that people of color are more than three times as likely to have subprime loans. High-cost loans account for 55 percent of loans to blacks, but only 17 percent of loans to whites. If subprime loans had been distributed equitably, losses for white Americans would be 44.5 percent higher, and losses for people of color would lower by 24 percent.[140]

Homeownership is the most valuable asset most Americans possess and, as with all assets, it can be leveraged to provide the means to weather a financial storm or finance a child's education. According to the authors of *Foreclosed*, "while approximately 29 percent of people of color fall below the poverty line, 79 percent of black people can be considered asset poor, compared to 40 percent of their white counterparts. Being 'asset poor' means that an individual or family, without the flow of income, cannot maintain their current economic lifestyle for three months."[141]

Homeownership is like comfort food, promulgating a sense of stability and security. The promise of stability is what motivated Lillian Mitchell to move her family into what was then a white neighborhood in Atlanta in 1968. That same promise is what her husband, now widowed, is trying to hold on to today.

The Mitchells: Duped into Near Foreclosure

George Mitchell recalls his move to Atlanta's Westwood neighborhood 40 years ago as a tranquil move, surprisingly not filled with violence by his new, white neighbors.[142] There were no "come over and get acquainted" invitations either.[143] Not too long after the Mitchells moved in, their white neighbors moved out, which was of no consequence to the Mitchells: They had their dream—a home of their own.

Soon, many others, like the Mitchells, would find their dreams in Westwood and other areas of Atlanta, a city long considered a haven for black Americans. Today, Westwood is feeling the brunt of the subprime meltdown. Eighteen thousand homes faced foreclosure during the first quarter of 2008 in Atlanta, representing a 40 percent increase over the first quarter of 2007. The Mitchells are struggling to keep themselves off of this list.

George Mitchell, like so many Americans, found himself the victim of aggressive, predatory mortgage loans, which have placed his home and the home of his children and grandchildren in jeopardy. Less than 10 percent of all subprime loans were passed on to first-time homebuyers, according to the Center for Responsible Lending.[144] Over half of the subprime loans on the books have been used to refinance existing home loans; the Center for Responsible Lending reports that the foreclosure totals at the end of this meltdown will outstrip minority gains in homeownership by more than a million families.[145] These losses are not ones black and brown Americans can withstand.

In 1967, when the Mitchells purchased their home, homeownership counted for 67 percent of black wealth and 40 percent of white wealth. But the wealth disparity between blacks and whites has ballooned since the late sixties; not counting homes, black wealth is but 1 percent of that for whites.[146]

Mitchell fell victim to the predatory lending patterns that have threatened the homes of millions of families. After years of almost no lending history against their mortgage—an exception was made to pay the final two years of a daughter's college tuition—the Mitchells found themselves with an avalanche of loans at rates and terms beyond their home's value. Even a cursory look at his finances—a senior citizen in his seventies on a fixed income—would have indicated his inability to make mortgage payments once the rates ballooned.

Mitchell initially kept these problems from his children, but after falling two months behind on his mortgage and unable to pay his gas, water, electricity, and phone bills, he told his children about the mistake he was lured into making. Luckily for him, his children are assisting him with his bills so that they won't lose their family home.

Millions of Americans unfortunately do not have family members who can help save their homes. The impact of this massive loss of homes and wealth is far reaching. Communities with boarded-up homes and unkempt lawns attract crime, squatters, and vagrants, simultaneously dragging down property values of homes in the neighborhood and in adjacent neighborhoods. The impact on children may be the most far-reaching of all; studies show that children in families who lose their homes are frequently scarred in ways socially, emotionally, and educationally that we are only beginning to track.[147]

Who is accountable for guiding us to a place where no American adult works without the possibility for advancement; where there are jobs that point the way toward better tomorrows; where there are secured, decent retirement incomes; and where—in the worst of times—we provide social safety nets that preserve our dignity until we can get back on our feet?

A FRAMEWORK FOR ASSESSMENT

The *Covenant* set forth "Accessing Good Jobs, Wealth, and Economic Prosperity" and "Strengthening Our Rural Roots" as two covenants linked by their intention to speak to economic challenges facing all vulnerable Americans. Each chapter ends with what we imagine individuals, all levels of government, and community leaders can do to impact their related issues.

Solutions for Government

During the 2008 election season, Democratic presidential nominee Obama felt the struggling American economy was the most pressing issue facing Americans. The loss of jobs to globalization, the need for innovation in American industry, the rising costs of health care, and the need for tax relief as an economic stimulus were just a few of the items he was weighing on his to-do list.

Obama pledged to make permanent tax cuts, but only for middle- and working-class Americans, while repealing tax cuts for upper-income brackets. He sought fiscal discipline by adding a requirement that all new federal spending be paid for by additional revenue or cuts in other programs. He promised at least $10 billion in direct assistance to Americans hit hardest by the foreclosure crisis; he also promised to support a 90-day foreclosure moratorium for homeowners acting in good faith. In response to the fall 2008 economic crisis, Obama supported the $700 billion Wall Street bailout package proposed by the Bush administration. He advocated reform of Wall Street, the nation's financial center, including requirements that firms provide more disclosure of activities and increased oversight of investment banks. If victorious, Obama promised he would promote a $50 billion emergency stimulus package to jump-start the economy, with funds specifically targeted to improving infrastructure, schools, and aid to local governments.

Solutions at the State and Local Levels

Local and state officials can encourage entrepreneurship and support local businesses. The New York State Small Business Development Center, a partnership of public and private entities, has created more than 50 resource centers statewide to provide counseling and training to small business owners, especially to women, veterans, people with special needs, and minorities. The center also focuses on projects that advance job development, investment, and economic growth to help small businesses boost the state's economy.[148]

The Small Business Development Center has nurtured a variety of businesses. It assisted Jorge Rodriguez in opening a Mexican restaurant in Brooklyn; it provided credit counseling and acted as a liaison with federal and state agencies to resolve outstanding tax issues that had prevented the restaurant from opening.

The program also helped Elaine Wilshire launch Elan-Sa International, a handbag manufacturer. After being laid off in 1997, Wilshire began taking classes in fashion design. Despite a visual disability, she found a niche in crafting unique purses and accessories for friends. With the help of a Business Center advisor, Wilshire developed a business plan, created a marketing strategy, and obtained a start-up grant.

Rodriguez and Wilshire are among the 275,000 New Yorkers helped by the Center since 1984, obtaining $3.4 billion in assistance and creating or saving 127,000 jobs. The Small Business Development Center provides a model of how private and public entities can collaborate to promote local business and, in doing so, strengthen local economies.

Solutions for Business and Community Leaders

Kalamazoo was once a leading manufacturing city in western Michigan. In the past decade, however, the city lost thousands of jobs to fleeing industries and globalizing businesses.[149] The beginning of a turnaround occurred in 2007, when Kaiser Aluminum Corporation chose Kalamazoo as the home for a new $80 million office-and-research center employing 150. Kaiser chose Kalamazoo from at least three other finalists in part because of The Kalamazoo Promise, an initiative that will strengthen the city's workforce. A group of anonymous philanthropists have pledged to donate at least partial college tuition to all seniors who graduate from the city's public schools. Kaiser leadership established the program to distinguish Kalamazoo as a city committed to increasing the educational level of its residents.

More signs that the city's turnaround is on track: The program, and the businesses it has attracted. Despite large companies like Pfizer cutting thousands of local jobs as recently as 2006, in 2007 and 2008, Kalamazoo's graduation rates increased 21 percent, and families are relocating to the city, increasing school enrollment by 12 percent. Other companies have followed Kaiser, including MPI Research, a pharmaceutical company; Fabri-Kal, a local plastic product producer; and others, bringing hundreds more jobs to the area. This progress has spilled over into the real estate market as home sales have increased. Most of all, The Promise has imbued Kalamazoo with a sense of optimism, something it had been missing for too long. Other cities are noticing the city's success as corporations, foundations, and private donors have pursued similar programs in El Dorado, TX; Peoria, IL; and Denver, CO.

Solutions for Individuals

Individuals dealing with an economic downturn need to take advantage of local programs that provide information and assistance with credit and homeowner issues. Sydney Porter dealt with possible foreclosure of her Sacramento home by attending a local workshop about dealing with foreclosures and mortgage default.[150] The retired Californian has a five-page call log of all the different parties she has called for information and assistance, including her lender, mortgage company, and real estate broker. Porter took advantage of an advisor provided by the local housing agency to help keep people in their homes and keep future pressure off city social service agencies. The pair agreed to contact Porter's lender to try to request a modified loan. Until the decision is received, Porter is preparing for all possible outcomes, learning about alternatives to salvage the equity she already has in her home and to regain control of her financial situation. Despite her struggles, Porter provides a positive example of a proactive approach to financial troubles by arming herself with information, taking advantage of local resources, and persistently defending her rights.

ACCOUNTABLE ASSESSMENT
CHECKLIST

The most powerful tool we have as citizens to effect change is our vote. We should not allow our elected officials to make promises during their campaigns without fulfilling their obligations once in office. Use this list to hold our new president accountable on the economy.

Campaign Promises 2008: The Economy

BARACK OBAMA AS PROMISED . . .

▪ Will support a $50 billion emergency economic stimulus plan to create 1 million jobs for rebuilding infrastructure and schools and helping local governments avoid budget cuts.

▪ Will provide $10 billion in relief to state and local governments hardest hit by the housing crisis to ensure continuity of vital services.

▪ Will introduce new legislation that would give families the option of withdrawing as much as 15 percent of their retirement savings—up to a maximum of $10,000—without facing a tax penalty this year or next.

▪ Will increase regulations, oversight, and disclosure requirements for financial institutions.

▪ Will cut taxes for middle-class Americans.

▪ Will invest in next-generation technologies in manufacturing and industry to create 5 million new "green" jobs for Americans.

▪ Will raise the minimum wage to a "living wage" for American workers.

▪ Will create a rating system and a credit card bill of rights to attack predatory credit card practices.

Use this checklist to evaluate whether the entities that can make a difference are doing all they can to help America realize the goal of the seventh and eighth Covenants: "Strengthening Our Rural Roots" and "Accessing Good Jobs, Wealth, and Economic Prosperity." Reexamine this checklist every six months to assess progress.

OUR PRESIDENT

☐ Have you made the implementation of your economic plan a priority within the first 100 days of the new administration?

☐ Have you addressed pressing financial issues, both for individuals and for financial institutions?

☐ Are you implementing your planned tax reform as promised during your campaign?

☐ Have you implemented new regulations to increase accountability and transparency in the financial sector?

☐ Have you assembled a team of experts on economics to help you make informed decisions about economic policy?

OUR U.S. CONGRESSMEN AND CONGRESSWOMEN

☐ Have you made economic reform a priority issue?

☐ Have you used your vote to promote sound fiscal policy?

☐ Have you considered the interests of your constituents in making economic decisions?

☐ Are you addressing long-term and short-term problems facing the nation?

OUR GOVERNOR AND STATE LEGISLATORS

☐ Have you shown leadership on economic reform even where the federal government may be found wanting?

☐ Do you have a plan to fill in gaps in economic reform that the federal government may have overlooked?

☐ Are you addressing those communities most affected by recent economic crises?

- ☐ Are you working to attract and retain strong and stable businesses in our community?

- ☐ Have you worked with labor and other local groups to understand the economic issues facing our community?

- ☐ Have you worked with local leaders to develop programs to help educate citizens about ways to support and assist with improving the economic situation?

OUR COMMUNITY LEADERS
AND FAITH-BASED ORGANIZATIONS

- ☐ Do you have a plan or an initiative to monitor the political progress of economic reform policies and promises made by our governmental leaders and to advocate when necessary?

- ☐ Do you have a plan or an initiative to educate members about the progress of economic reform and on the availability of education options in our community?

- ☐ Do you help people in our community participate in our local economic reform, through awareness raising, volunteering, and voting on economic issues?

- ☐ Do you educate members about how to manage their personal resources?

- ☐ Have you worked to promote financial literacy in our community?

- ☐ Do you offer additional programs to expose members to different economic opportunities, such as investment clubs, vocational training, and job opportunities?

- ☐ Do you help people in our community understand basic economics?

YOU AND I

- ☐ Do I read the business section of my newspaper?

- ☐ Do I prepare a monthly budget and stick to it?

- ☐ Do I monitor my credit rating at least once every six months?

- ☐ Do I work toward eliminating debt?

- ☐ Do I pay my bills in a timely and consistent fashion?

☐ Do I have a savings account and dedicate __ percent of my earnings to it monthly?

☐ Do I talk to my family, neighbors, children, friends, and community members about important economic issues?

☐ Do I talk to my family, neighbors, friends, children, and community members about the value of understanding the economy and how it affects us?

5

The Environment, Energy, and Our Aging Infrastructure

Protecting Ourselves and Our Planet

Treat the earth well: it was not given to you by your parents, it was loaned to you by your children.

—ANCIENT NATIVE AMERICAN PROVERB

We simply must balance our demand for energy with our rapidly shrinking resources. By acting now, we can control our future instead of letting the future control us.

—PRESIDENT JIMMY CARTER

COVENANT NINE
Assuring Environmental Justice for All

COVENANT FIVE
Ensuring Broad Access to Affordable Neighborhoods That Connect to Opportunity

Sheila Holt-Orsted: The Verdict Is Cancer

Sheila Holt-Orsted of Dickson, TN, started treatment for breast cancer in November 2007. Her story, though unfortunate, would not be as compelling had it not been for her family's long history of speaking out against the toxins that flowed from the Dickson Landfill onto their land. Dickson is located about 35 miles west of Nashville and is home to an area landfill that has allegedly been leaking toxins into the family's well water for four generations. Holt-Orsted's breast cancer was the final verdict on the township's failure to address the family's extensive list of complaints about health issues. "I think people should stand up and take back their communities," says Holt-Orsted. The list of charges was so staggering that it landed the family in the national media spotlight, including CNN, the *Washington Post*, and *People* magazine. The family members who remain on the property now use city water; in the meantime, the family has several lawsuits pending. The United Church of Christ described the case as "a poster child of environmental racism."[151]

Dennis Schmidt: A Man's New Island

Communities like Dickson have been fighting for years against environmental racism—the placement of facilities such as hazardous waste treatment plants and oil refineries in minority and low-income communities. Many of these same facilities are also responsible for the inordinate use of fossil fuels and the release of carbon dioxide into the atmosphere that is now causing a warming trend on earth.

Two years before Holt-Orsted's diagnosis, Dennis Schmidt enjoyed the achievement of a lifetime: he discovered an island. For a man devoted to exploring the arctic terrain of Greenland, his discovery was the realization of a dream come true. His discovery had a downside, though; the island was made possible by global warming. It almost certainly would have been discovered several years ago if it had not been completely covered by glacial ice. With the melting of the icecaps, the geography of Greenland is rapidly changing, certain evidence of the effects of climate change on our planet. Schmidt has tentatively—and appropriately—named the island Uunartoq Qeqertoq, Inuit for "the warming island."[152]

Polluting our earth, our environment—whether through dumping toxic materials into our water supply in low-income and minority communities or releasing toxins into the atmosphere, thereby overheating our planet—has long been a priority concern of Professor Robert Bullard. The director of Clark Atlanta University's Environmental Justice Resource Center, Bullard pioneered the environmental justice movement, which was born out of a confluence of the social justice and environmental movements.[153] The movement was born more than two decades ago from Bullard's groundbreaking research, which proved that members of communities of color were more likely than others to live near hazardous waste sites, putting them at higher risk for sickness or death. His extensive knowledge and exceptional scholarship inform the introductory essay he authored in *The Covenant*.

Bullard describes the toxic landscape this way: "We're seeing elevated asthma rates, we're seeing higher-than-average cancer rates, we're seeing lots of diabetes and kidney failure."[154]

Not surprisingly, this phenomenon could be attributed to factors such as residential segregation, housing discrimination, economic injustice, and lack of awareness of the pertinent issues. Bullard has authored two authoritative texts on this issue and has collaborated notably with the Environmental Protection Agency (EPA) among other agencies to ensure that the federal government properly assessed environmental justice issues in all its environmental decision making. Bullard and the opponents of environmental racism whom he inspired helped Holt-Orsted get the media attention and legal assistance that strong-armed the town into finally addressing her family's concerns.

Bullard's victories extend all across America, with a particular emphasis on the South. In some cases he has helped affected citizens collect millions of dollars in compensatory damages; in others, he has helped them fight an intractable system of entrenched and often deadly racism.

Along with the troubling impact of environmental racism, some believe a major problem is our society's whitewashed view of the environmental movement in the first place. "We suffer the most in this pollution-based economy," offered environmental activist Van Jones in a March 2008 PBS interview with Tavis Smiley. As head of the Oakland, CA-based Ella Baker Center for Human Rights and author of the *New York Times* bestseller *The Green Collar Economy*, Jones stresses the need for environmental inequalities to be framed in a way relevant to communities of color. "If you're going to have a green and clean economy, green the ghetto first,"[155] Jones continued, borrowing a quote from South Bronx (NY) activist Majora Carter. Jones cites the impact of global warming and Hurricane Katrina on people of color while emphasizing the need for urban dwellers to use solar panels, weatherize their homes, and grow and demand affordable, organic produce.

"The environmental movement is no longer just for the hybrid crowd or the people who care about polar bears," Jones adds. "It's about putting the tools, technology, and training in our young people's hands to go out there and fix America."

■   ■   ■

"Ensuring Broad Access to Affordable Neighborhoods That Connect to Opportunity" formed the foundation of the fifth Covenant, urging us to strategize around the issue of livable neighborhoods. This covenant asks if you have considered joining a self-help housing project such as Habitat for Humanity and building your family or another family a home. It asks if you have considered finding multiple ways to get home or to work or to school—walk, bike, ride public transit, or carpool—or organizing neighborhood groups to advocate for expanded and better public transit services and safe pedestrian walkways.[156] These principles are exemplified in "smart growth" efforts sweeping our country.[157] Smart growth must also be considered through an environmental justice lens that demands that communities of color speak for themselves and are included in urban planning strategies that will surely impact them.[158]

In this chapter, we examine both of these covenants in the context of the energy, environmental, and infrastructure crises facing this country. These energy and environmental challenges are monumental, and the consequences from our hesitation to address them have already had dire impacts on all Americans, particularly on those already suffering from injustices. This chapter recognizes the interrelatedness of the energy, environmental, and infrastructure issues confronting our nation and asks how we citizens can hold ourselves and our government accountable for dealing with them. While broader in scope than the original construct of environmental justice and hazardous waste, this chapter retains *The Covenant*'s "justice" lens by broadly examining environmental issues as complex questions that run a grave risk of burdening those who can least afford to bear them.

Small Business Energy, Economic Stressors

C. Buren Williford established Southern Piping Company (SPC) in 1965. According to the SPC website, "The only assets at that time were his two strong hands, an unequalled drive for excellence, and a good head for business."[159] Williford hung out his shingle on a small building in Wilson, NC, with only one employee. But he was full of hopes and dreams for the future.

Over the next four decades, SPC grew to be one of the largest and most respected names in the plumbing and mechanical contracting industry in North Carolina. As the company grew, Williford was able to provide a solid, rewarding life for his wife, Peggy, and his children, and he instilled his drive for excellence in his children, who now own and operate SPC.

Buren's son, Tim, is the company vice president. He attended a small liberal arts college in Virginia and later Mercer University School of Law. After five years of practice, Tim joined the family business, quickly becoming a leader in his community. He combined his legal and business skills to become a Wilson County Commissioner and is active in the Plumbing-Heating-Cooling Contractors Association, which represents over 4,000.

Through the association Tim Williford forged relationships with many other contractors, all small business owners—entrepreneurs who comprise the engine of economic growth. But he has seen a disturbing trend through his association work. Fuel costs are stressing small businesses. In testimony before the U.S. House Committee on Small Business in April 2008, Williford discussed the impact of rising gas prices on America's small businesses. He testified that one firm in his association saw its fuel costs rise to $70,000 in 2006, up from $47,000 in 2005. If current trends continue, he explained, that company will spend as much as $88,000 in 2008. Another member company had its fuel costs triple, and Williford noted that "this is all happening at a time when the downward price pressure of the market won't allow us to raise our prices!"[160]

At SPC the problem is even more acute. In 2007, the company spent nearly $1 million for oil and gas products. For 2008, the company estimates that number to rise by as much as a half million dollars. And the options for cutting costs are limited, Williford reports. The company has had to resort to reducing employee benefits. "For example, we recently shelved plans to implement a wellness program for our employees. We have also postponed additional spending on our safety program. We view these initiatives as crucial to our efforts to keeping a safe, healthy, and productive workforce. However, increased fuel prices are forcing us to make a very difficult choice."[161]

America's Addiction

As we mentioned earlier, issue number one during the 2008 election campaign was the economy. And aside from the mammoth near-collapse of the American financial system, the biggest economic issue was the country's energy costs. Fuel costs rose to astronomical heights during 2008, stressing food distribution networks, small businesses, and daily life for ordinary families. If small businesses truly drive American economic health and job creation, then rising fuel costs have created a multicar train wreck, figuratively speaking.

America's addiction to foreign oil threatens our economic and national security. In 1970, the United States imported 24 percent of its oil. In 2008, we import as much as 70 percent. At current oil prices, we will send $700 billion to foreign nations in 2008 and an astronomical $7 *trillion* over the next decade. The "good" news is that the problem has become so acute that solving our energy crisis is now seen as a mainstream priority that all Americans want resolved. The challenge remains in charting our path to energy independence.

America typically needs energy for two purposes—transportation and electricity generation—with transportation producing the fastest-growing demand by far. Fuel (highly refined oil) is the most common source of energy used for transportation; alternative forms of energy do exist in this country, including both natural gas and biofuels.[162] Some people argue that an easy way to reduce our reliance on foreign oil is to drive automobiles that use natural gas as a fuel source. The technology exists today; about 150,000 cars on the road use natural gas.[163] Many experts find gas to be an attractive resource because it is cleaner, cheaper, and more domestically abundant than oil.[164] Natural gas offers a temporary alternative, but it is not a limitless resource. Nor are natural gas power plants as clean as their proponents contend, still emitting dangerous toxins in communities that are likely to be of color or economically disadvantaged.[165] While natural gas may end up helping America reduce its oil consumption, experts, environmentalists, politicians, and communities will have to work together as this resource is expanded. And exploring other alternative sources of energy—biofuels, wind, solar, and geothermal technologies—must continue.

Biofuels are derived from recently dead biological material, such as photosynthetic plants, and common agricultural food staples like corn. Biofuels are a promising technology because of their potential to produce energy without releasing a net increase of carbon dioxide into the atmosphere. Fossil fuels, to the contrary, are derived from the fossilized remains of dead plants and animals that took hundreds of millions of years to create; they produce so much carbon dioxide that they return it back into the atmosphere. Carbon dioxide is a greenhouse gas and contributes to global warming. Biofuels are promising because most cars on the roads in the United States today can run on a blend of biofuel, thus reducing our oil consumption. Critics note, however, that biofuels can interfere with food production, local economies, and even the global food crisis by inflating the demand for certain crops.[166]

Much of the promise in the area of alternative energy exists in the electrical generation sector. Wind and solar power have received tremendous attention and hold vast potential. For example, experts call the United States "the Saudi Arabia of wind power," with the Great Plains states demonstrating the greatest wind energy potential of anyplace in the world.[167] Similarly, solar is a clean source of energy that produces no emissions during generation and, with new technology, is as available and renewable as the daily sunrise.[168] These concepts—deriving energy from the wind and the sun—are easy for most people to grasp, and the technologies for each are progressing daily.

Geothermal—another form of alternative energy—generally refers to underground heat, as it is energy generated in the earth's core. Water and heat generate energy in hydrothermal power plants. The United States has been at the forefront of geothermal electricity as compared to other countries, with California and Nevada leading the way.

While alternative forms of energy hold tremendous promise, they also have environmental, economic, and political consequences that may impede them from being implemented on a larger scale until the technology becomes more feasible to meet our national energy demands. Promoting building and appliance efficiency, smart growth, vehicle efficiency, and industrial efficiency all deserve our attention. By demanding and insisting on more energy-efficient appliances and vehicles and by requiring that the same is done on an industrial level, we are doing our part in promoting a more energy-efficient nation.

Katrina and Consequences

Our overreliance on fossil fuels such as oil is contributing heavily to global warming—a phenomenon that most of us agree now is real. On June 22, 2006, the National Research Council of the National Academies of science, engineering, and medicine published a major book, concluding "with a high level of confidence that the last few decades of the 20th century were warmer than any comparable period in the last 400 years."[169] Moreover, that global warming is "very likely" *man-made*—the result of greenhouse gas emissions—is generally accepted by the world scientific community, as is evidenced by a United Nations report issued in March 2007 by the world's top climate scientists.[170] The scientists concluded that man-made greenhouse gas emissions are to blame for fewer cold days, hotter nights, killer heat waves, floods and heavy rains, devastating droughts, and an increase in hurricane and tropical storm strength, particularly in the Atlantic Ocean.[171]

In the days following Hurricane Katrina, mainstream news media and others made much of this potential global warming–hurricane connection. While a consensus exists on the ineptitude of the federal, state, and local responses to this disaster, there is no such consensus around the causation. Scientists have speculated that everything from "atmospheric fluctuations to the periodic warming of the Pacific Ocean known as El Niño might be responsible."[172]

Resolving this debate may not matter because scientific research has determined "hurricane wind speeds have increased about 50 percent in the past 50 years."[173] Post-Katrina science has confirmed that while it is premature to determine whether global warming has actually made recent hurricanes, typhoons, and cyclones worse, it is likely that greenhouse warming will cause hurricanes in the coming century to be more intense on average and have higher rainfall rates than present-day hurricanes.[174]

■ ■ ■

The debate over global warming and hurricanes was meaningless to Jimmy Ellzey as he stood studying the wreckage of the Tivoli Hotel in Biloxi, MS, the Tuesday after Hurricane Katrina hit. "That's J.D.," he said, as he eyed a pair of bare feet sticking out of a square hole in a concrete slab, "and that's Sue," as he looked toward a pale white knee, barely visible under the slab.[175]

Jimmy Ellzey had been the manager of the Tivoli, a residential hotel that had been a landmark on the Mississippi coast, known for its parties and fights, its marriages and divorces, and even for its giant hot tub. In 1969, the Tivoli had even survived Hurricane Camille, a Category 5 monstrosity that remains the strongest storm to have ever entered the United States mainland on record.[176] During Katrina, however, one of the government-sanctioned casino barges broke free from its moorings, flattening the hotel, killing eight people inside, including J.D. and Sue, and converting the hotel's dicey daily lore into a patchwork of stories about what used to be.[177]

Ellzey saw another victim: a man who had beat him at poker the night before. He didn't know the man's name but reflected on the $10 score from the card game. It seemed hard to believe that in the hours since, Ellzey and his girlfriend Rhonda had narrowly escaped death by jumping into the surging water as the cinder blocks gave way behind them. Had they waited any longer, they would have fared no better than J.D., Sue, and the unknown man whose luck apparently ran out after that poker game.[178]

■ ■ ■

Hurricane Katrina highlights so many problems on different levels in our society. In addition to the obvious issues of preparedness, homeland security, and equity (in every sense of the word), Katrina profiles for us a natural disaster that science confirms will occur either on our homeland or elsewhere again and again.

That our government was unprepared when Katrina hit is a matter of fact. Exacerbating that fact is that we were also warned. In the months following Hurricane Katrina, we learned that the White House received warnings of the storm's likely impact 48 hours before it hit.[179] These warnings were detailed, including predictions of massive flooding, breached levees, and major loss of life.[180] State and local government leaders exhibited similar ineptitude. A bipartisan committee investigating the preparation and response to Katrina found that despite adequate warning 56 hours before landfall, the governor of Louisiana and the mayor of New Orleans delayed ordering mandatory evacuation in New Orleans until only 19 hours before landfall. The investigators concluded that the failure of complete evacuations led to preventable deaths, great suffering, and further delays in relief.[181] The investigators' other findings were widespread and systemic: massive communications failures; command and control was impaired at all levels; failure to implement the National Response Plan; the lack of military coordination; the lack of preparedness of the Department of Homeland Security and the state of Louisiana for a catastrophic event; the collapse of local law enforcement and public communications leading to civil unrest; difficulties in coordinating medical care and evacuations; and capacity constraints on charitable organizations.[182]

The 2008 hurricane season gave federal, state, and local governments as well as nongovernmental organizations a chance to implement some of the "lessons learned" from Katrina. In the days leading up to a storm that was predicted to be more devastating than Katrina, nearly 2 million Gulf Coast residents were evacuated by plane, bus, and train. Images of residents on rooftops and of sickness in the Superdome hovered as distant memories of our nation's past.[183] Local and state officials were so prepared that they even housed residents' pets so that people would feel more assured about evacuating.[184] The Red Cross was also better prepared, having spent $80 million since Katrina to upgrade its communications systems as well as to stockpile cots and other supplies in disaster-prone regions.[185]

In the end, however, the Gulf Coast was spared a hit reminiscent of Katrina—an unexpected mercy because, notwithstanding the Red Cross's tripled capacity to feed relief victims and provide volunteers, a nonpartisan report released by the Government Accountability Office found that a "large-scale disaster would 'overwhelm' the Red Cross and other nonprofit organizations that have federal responsibilities for assisting the government in feeding and sheltering victims of natural disasters."[186] Essentially, it seems that while so many people in the United States are appropriately focusing on preventing and preparing for the *potentiality* of a terrorist attack, at least as many or more should also be focusing on preparedness for the *eventuality* of a natural disaster. Policymakers must act *now* to prepare for and prevent the consequences of inevitable climate change—food shortages, disease, and unplanned human migration.[187]

The National Hurricane Center of the National Oceanic and Atmospheric Administration is charged with tracking the meteorological statis-

COMMUTER KNIEVEL

tics, damage, and casualties of hurricanes and cyclones.[188] As Americans become more familiar with sweeping hurricanes domestically, others beyond our shores are experiencing similarly devastating natural disasters. In Bangladesh, a November 2007 cyclone killed in excess of 1,700 people and destroyed thousands of homes.[189] In the aftermath, Bangladesh farmers hinted to reporters that the cyclones are symptomatic of the larger problem of climate change, citing their observations of water problems, reduced productivity, diminishing trees, and pollution. What makes Bangladesh unique is the scale of such devastation, given the size of the country, with its population of 150 million and a landmass roughly the size of Wisconsin, a state that is home to only 5.5 million people.[190]

The United Nations Office for the Coordination of Humanitarian Affairs assists following natural disasters by dispatching missions for aid. Fourteen such missions were sent around the world in 2007, a record nine in Latin America alone. This new need for assistance, primarily in response to hurricanes, was identified as "possibly a glimpse of the shape of things to come, given the reality of climate change."[191]

Recently Haiti has been reminded of its vulnerability to hurricanes. What is interesting is not the increased devastation that recent hurricanes appear to guarantee, but the manner in which such events are being reported. In an op-ed article published in the *Los Angeles Times*, the writer argued, "[Haiti's] governments, both the dictatorships and the democracies, have done almost nothing to stop deforestation or to protect Haitians from the next big storm."[192] The tone has shifted from attributing infinite power to the hands of "Mother Nature" to calling the government to action by implementing preventive mechanisms to curb the intensity of natural disasters in response to a changing climate. Such a change in tone is indicative of the media's embrace of environmental realities and challenges that inherently impact our world.

Mercedes Gorden: Total Collapse

The Haitian example is illustrative of the challenges that severe climate change can place on a nation's aging infrastructure. Four successive storms in 2008 have knocked out bridges and roads and caused a spike in food prices, devastating life in the hemisphere's poorest country.[193] A newly refurbished hospital that had been devastated in 2004 by Hurricane Jean was again wiped out in 2008 by Hanna.[194]

Haiti is a long way from Minnesota; the tiny island was the furthest thing from Mercedes Gorden's mind as she drove home from work August 1, 2007. She had just returned from Las Vegas for a friend's wedding and was no doubt thinking about her own fiancé, Jake Rudh. She was also super excited to be celebrating her new promotion at the Best Buy corporate headquarters and was generally thinking about all the good things in her life.[195]

As she drove onto the Interstate 35W bridge, Gorden recalled an uneasy feeling she had been having since bridge construction had begun. Once she reached the midpoint, in bumper-to-bumper traffic, Gorden felt the concrete below her buckle and saw pavement in front of her ripple. "It started coming at me like a wave in the ocean," she recalled. "I could feel it first."[196] Then, her car fell 60 feet, landing accordion style. Gorden later remembered, "It just felt like a war zone. . . . It was absolutely chaotic. It was catastrophic. It was absolutely unbelievable."[197] She took stock of her condition after her car struck the pavement. She was all right except that her legs were pinned underneath her dashboard. Good Samaritans who had rushed to the scene stayed with her until rescue workers could take over.

Firefighters used the Jaws of Life to free Gorden from the wreckage. "When I saw it, I was absolutely shocked," she said of her lower leg, twisted nearly at a right angle. "It was gruesome. It was pretty sick looking." More than a year after the bridge crushed her legs, Gorden still has to rely on the kindness of others to make it through the daily challenges of life. She continues intensive physical therapy and has suffered with arthritis and challenges to her vocal cords. There have also been public perception challenges with the 35W Bridge Victims Fund,[198] established so that Gorden and the other victims would be eligible for $10,000 in lost wages. No victims received payment from that fund until well over a year after the accident.[199] Many people erroneously believe that the fund is paying for the victims' expenses, but many like Gorden are suffering economic hardship. She and her fiancé are recording their ever-changing personal stories on a web log at CaringBridge.org.[200]

■ ■ ■

Our aging infrastructure and the environment must be analyzed together because our infrastructure is no longer sustainable—a direct result of our poor energy policy. We depend on infrastructure to provide safe drinking water, commutes, travel, and affordable housing. We have always understood that routine maintenance is required for our highways, bridges, and buildings; what we are only recently beginning to learn is that *updating* these systems with more energy-efficient technologies and fuels is critical to establishing an infrastructure that will be able to handle our growing population and needs.

Congress has recognized the need to update infrastructure but has been unsuccessful in passing meaningful legislation to get it done. Senate Bill 1926, the National Infrastructure Bank Act of 2007, was intended to establish funding for qualified infrastructure projects. It would designate qualified transit, public housing, water, highway, bridge, and road infrastructure projects for loans. As of June 2008, the Senate was still holding hearings on this initiative.

Meanwhile, the House of Representatives has been working on two pieces of infrastructure legislation. The first, H.R. 1495, the Water Resources Development Act of 2007, would provide for conservation and development of water and related activities, while authorizing improvements to rivers and harbors by the U.S. Secretary of the Army. The second, H.R. 1587, the National Levee Safety Program Act of 2007, would enhance the safety of levees under the direction of the Secretary of the Army. While pending legislation reflects our growing concerns, we need more immediate action considering that the costs rise daily to operate our aging infrastructure.

■　■　■

Bridges were not built to last forever. They age, and they will need to be re-paired or replaced, irrespective of the cost. Falling bridges make headlines; so do sharply rising energy costs because of an outdated power grid. Often overlooked, however, are the additional infrastructure updates required for steam pipes and water mains. The depth and breadth of our infrastructure needs are immense and will require collaboration at all levels.

Infrastructure frailties show up in other areas caused by poor main-tenance as well as old age; some is merely ill-equipped to adequately support present and future generations. We have witnessed broken levees and houses washed away that were downstream from a dam. With our in-creased concerns about climate change and with weather patterns proving to be progressively unpredictable, ignoring these problems is no longer an option. We must determine which programs can be most effectively implemented, with respect to costs and energy, to provide the labor and resources necessary to update America's infrastructure. The infrastructure wish-list should reflect an investment in light rail, energy-efficient LED (light-emitting diodes) lighting, embedded sensors to provide warnings for future catastrophes, green buildings, and community involvement, to name a few. Regional planners and the local community must coalesce to fully understand the needs of each area and to develop lasting, efficient, and effective solutions.

A FRAMEWORK FOR ASSESSMENT

The *Covenant* set forth "Assuring Environmental Justice for All" and "Ensur-ing Broad Access to Affordable Neighborhoods That Connect to Opportu-nity" as covenants dedicated to bringing to light the serious environmental challenges confronting our nation. At the end of these chapters, we imag-ine what individuals, all levels of government, and community leaders can do to impact such related issues. THE COVENANT *In Action* then provided a toolkit to equip citizens with the instruments to effect change on this and all of *The Covenant* issues. *ACCOUNTABLE* will help assess whether we have lived up to the aspirations put forward in *The Covenant* and give us a measuring tool for future evaluation.

During the 2008 presidential election, all of the major candidates agreed that U.S. energy policy was in dire need of a makeover. John McCain and Barack Obama both prioritized the need to address climate change and related environmental issues.

The key questions now are: what are the potential solutions to these dilemmas, and who should take part in crafting them? The stakeholders are widespread—the federal government; international governments; business and industry leaders from the oil, energy, and transportation sectors; environmentalists; small business owners; nonprofits; and citizens themselves. Finally, how will we know that these solutions are working?

Solutions for Government Reform

The federal government has long been active, most times unevenly so, in protecting and conserving the environment, although it was not until 1970 that it formally structured an agency—the U.S. Environmental Protection Agency (EPA)—to address comprehensive environmental issues. The EPA is charged with protecting human health and safeguarding the natural environment—air, water, and land—upon which life depends. But numerous federal agencies have a hand in addressing the issues relevant to the ninth and fifth Covenants, including energy, climate change, environmental justice, transportation, urban development, and infrastructure protection.

Climate change exemplifies where the federal government has done extensive work costing billions of dollars. But has the government offered any real solutions to one of the most vexing environmental problems of our time? Established in 2002, the U.S. Climate Change Science Program (CCSP) is an initiative of 15 federal agencies[201] overseen by the White House. CCSP coordinates the research results from the long-standing U.S. Global Change Research Program, which documented and characterized climate change, with the Climate Change Research Initiative, which has a short-term goal of evaluating optimal strategies to address global change risks.

The government's scientific findings on climate change are not in dispute. For example, the fiscal year 2009 edition of the CCSP's report, "Our Changing Planet," summarizes a massive array of scientific evidence that human activities are responsible for recent global warming.[202] We must hold our leaders accountable, however, because these incontrovertible facts have not yet led to a comprehensive plan to resolve these issues. And resolving the issues should not be that difficult. Solutions to deal with catastrophic climate change are well documented, such as reducing our use and consumption of fossil fuels, upgrading our infrastructure to inhabit green buildings, reducing our commuting times, and developing alternative energy sources.[203]

Among the success stories: The Department of Energy's (DOE) Energy Savers Program, which is geared to homeowners, informing them about energy-efficiency improvements that would save them 20 to 30 percent on their household energy bills and would reduce overall energy waste. Its companion program, EnergySTAR, is a voluntary labeling program whereby products adhering to strict energy-efficiency guidelines set by the EPA and DOE are promoted to consumers. EnergySTAR products include appliances such as dishwashers, clothes washers, and air conditioners; also promoted are heat and cooling elements, household electronics, windows and doors, office equipment, and other commercial products.[204]

Another success story is the federal government's implementing Executive Order 13123, "Greening the Government through Efficient Energy Management," stating that the federal government shall significantly improve its energy management in order to save taxpayer dollars and to reduce emissions that contribute to air pollution and global climate change. Other expressed goals include promoting energy efficiency, water conservation, decreased petroleum dependency, and using renewable energy products to help foster markets for emerging technologies. Federal facilities nationwide are striving to achieve these goals. Andrews Air Force Base outside of Washington, DC, is a strong case in point; it is on target to reduce energy consumption per gross square foot of its expansive facilities by 30 percent by 2005 and 35 percent by 2010, relative to 1985.[205]

Another federal solution has been employed in promoting environmental justice; it should be significantly strengthened. In 1994, President

Clinton issued Executive Order 12898, "Federal Actions and Environmental Justice," requiring each federal agency to make achieving environmental justice part of its mission by identifying and addressing, as appropriate, disproportionately high and adverse human health or environmental effects of its programs, policies, and activities on minority populations and low-income populations in the United States. This Executive Order resulted in no small measure because of the effective advocacy of the environmental justice movement, led by Professor Robert Bullard, whom we featured earlier. This Executive Order should be codified to establish an unequivocal mandate imposing federal responsibility for advancing equal protection under law when it comes to environmental matters. Because the Executive Order is an internal "housekeeping" measure, codification would affirm a right under Title VI of the Civil Rights Act for minority and low-income citizens to be free from discriminatory exposures to environmental toxins and would create a real remedy to redress any impact.[206]

States and their utilities commissions also offer successful solutions. For example, in the mid-1990s, the Texas State Legislature authorized the public utilities commission to seek public input to determine what energy options citizens preferred to meet future electric requirements. Between 1996 and 1998, eight of the state's electric utility companies used an innovative methodology known as Deliberative Polling™ to ensure that they obtained invaluable input from truly informed citizens. The process started with traditional telephone surveys, later utilizing briefing documents, a representative stakeholder advisory group, panels of experts, and town meetings. Two hundred to 300 survey participants—customers of utility companies—were invited to a weekend meeting to reflect on their environmental values and grapple with complex questions about renewable energy and energy efficiency. The public utilities commissioners were present, and the deliberative process was broadcast on public television to ensure transparency.[207]

The commissioners were astonished at the consumers' ability to comprehend such complex issues. Customers changed their minds based on the information they gained during the process, and both the utilities and their regulators increased their level of interest in and commitment to renewables and energy efficiency as a result of what they heard. The citizens praised the entire experience, noting that they felt like their opinions mattered. They also bridged gaps, forming lasting relationships with people they had originally thought of as "different." This process was repeated eight times in Texas, with the customers recommending an alternative energy combination of wind and gas. Subsequent to the polling, the Texas Legislature included a renewable portfolio standard in the state's electricity restructuring law, and more than 1,000 megawatts of new renewable capacity have been developed in Texas. Today, Texas leads the nation in its investment in wind power as a clean, renewable energy source.[208]

Solutions for Nonprofits

CREATING GREEN KIDS

Nonprofit organizations must participate in solving our nation's environmental and energy challenges. Organizations focusing on youth and underrepresented minorities have unique opportunities to win over the hearts and minds of the next generation with regard to how the decisions and actions they make every day impact the global environment. One such organization is New Haven, Connecticut–based Solar Youth, an environmental education organization; it enables community youth the opportunity to connect to the environment and to develop a positive sense of self and commitment through environmental exploration, leadership, and community service.[209] Solar Youth has taken children on numerous outdoor trips as part of its Kids Explore! program. Its Citycology program is compelling, training inner-city teens to teach younger school-aged children about water and watersheds. The Solar Youth model should be lifted up and replicated because it produces young adults who are more inclined to be actively engaged, environmentally aware, and globally prepared.

Organizations such as Solar Youth go a long way toward bridging the historical divide between mainstream environmental organizations—which usually focus on global warming—and environmental justice organizations, which tend to focus on local issues like air quality, hazardous wastes, and healthy communities. A broader framework is needed, and concerned citizens are coming to understand their common ground. The same companies responsible for locating oil refineries in communities of color are also responsible for the millions of dollars and dozens of years spent trying to disprove the fact that man's activities cause global warming. Both groups of environmental organizations are needed to resolve the issues of the new millennium, and nonprofit intermediaries such as PolicyLink are fostering the critically needed understanding in this area.[210]

PROMOTING GREEN BUILDING

Rebuilding New Orleans post-Katrina has generated valued nonprofit solutions. In 2006, actor and activist Brad Pitt joined forces with the organization Global Green to promote environmentally friendly building. They sponsored a sustainable design architectural competition for the areas of New Orleans devastated by Hurricane Katrina. The contest drew 3,000 registrants from all over the world. Six finalists were chosen who clearly understood the need to address rising electricity and energy costs and mounting health problems caused by exposure to unhealthy building practices.[211] Debunking the myth that low-income housing and cost-effective measures are incompatible with sustainable building design, more than 125 entrants competed to design a net-zero, energy-affordable housing and community center development in the Holy Cross neighborhood of the Lower 9th Ward. The jury selected the design by Matthew Berman and Andrew Kotchen of Workshop/apd, an innovative New York City firm. If 50,000 of the homes destroyed by Hurricane Katrina could be rebuilt according to the green standards set by the design competition, residents of New Orleans would annually save an estimated $38 million to $56 million in energy bills and eliminate over a half-million total tons of CO_2—the equivalent of taking 100,000 cars off the road.[212]

CREATING GREEN JOBS

Lincoln Park Coast Cultural District (LPCCD) is also illustrative of a nonprofit breaking ground and creating green solutions for the future. This innovative organization has forged the way to transform a blighted low-income neighborhood in Newark, NJ, into an urban eco-village and emerging arts and cultural district. According to its website, the project includes 300 U.S. Green Building Council Leadership in Energy and Environmental Design (LEED) certified housing units, green-collar jobs, music festivals, historic restoration projects, and the Museum of African American Music, a Smithsonian Affiliate.[213]

LPCCD also operates a Green Collar Apprenticeship Program (Green-CAP), which helps to create a local, skilled, green-collar workforce. Green-CAP trains Newark residents—reaching out to veterans, underserved young people, and formerly incarcerated men and women in the construction trades of HVAC, plumbing, and electrical, teaching them "green" skills and providing the know-how to earn a livable wage by participating in the emerging green economy. Newark's mayor, Cory A. Booker, approves LPCCD's successful ventures: "LPCCD's GreenCAP program is positioned to be a national best practice and provides an economic incentive for low-income people to join the green movement."[214]

EXPLORING ALTERNATIVE ENERGY

Recognizing America's annual $700 billion expense for oil and its reliance on importing 70 percent of that oil, T. Boone Pickens is in the vanguard to reorder America's renewable energy future. Ranked by *Forbes* magazine as the 117th richest person in America and 369th in the world, Thomas Boone Pickens, Jr., has an estimated net worth of $3 billion. Born in Oklahoma, he is the son of an oil and mineral landman who moved his family to Texas at the end of the oil boom in Oklahoma. After graduating from Oklahoma State University with a degree in geology, Pickens accepted a position with Phillips Petroleum and later founded Mesa Petroleum. Although renowned as a successful oilman at heart, Pickens is now preaching the gospel of alternative energy. The Pickens Plan promotes the use of wind power as a primary energy source. It relies heavily on a Stanford University study in 2005, the findings of which demonstrated that there is enough wind power to meet the global demand seven times over, even if only 20 percent of wind power is captured.[215] While wind power holds tremendous promise, a diverse portfolio of options will be necessary to sustain our current energy demands.

Pickens' plan has produced as many skeptics and critics as supporters. A *Los Angeles Times* article written by a senior fellow of the Cato Institute labeled it "Pickens' Plan to Rig the Market," purporting that Pickens was motivated by greed, corporate welfare, and tax breaks.[216] The criticism, however, was based on a view that is more sympathetic to drilling for oil and that has serious doubts about the viability of wind energy and natural gas technologies. On the other hand, some of Pickens' would-be supporters remain skeptical, finding it difficult to believe that a former financial backer of the Swift Boat Veterans for Truth campaign against former Democratic presidential hopeful John Kerry would visit the 2008 Democratic National Convention, share a stage with John Podesta and the executive director of the Sierra Club, and pitch a "politically neutral" energy plan to Barack Obama.[217] Yet, stranger things have happened. And the truth is that corporate energy giants and other privately owned companies are critically important partners in our country's environmental and energy maturation and independence.

Solutions for Individuals

Solving our energy, environmental, and infrastructure challenges need not wait for governmental and industry action. Every citizen must hold himself or herself accountable to create a future that is sustainable for future generations. We must understand the lessons that Al Gore sought to deliver in his Academy Award–winning documentary, *An Inconvenient Truth*. "If we allow this to happen, it is deeply, ethically immoral in every way." His talk of melting glaciers, rising sea levels, and the potential of New Orleans and Manhattan Island being under water reminds us that it is not only terrorists that should worry us.[218] Taking action is the responsibility of every American, and there are several strategies that we can adopt, many of which will save money and the environment.

ENERGY-EFFICIENCY TIPS[219]

1. Turn off the water while brushing your teeth and shaving.

2. Use cold water to wash clothes, and wash only full loads.

3. Set your refrigerator temperature to 36°F–39°F.

4. Insulate your water heater.

5. Cover pots and pans while cooking.

6. Preheat only the oven when you are baking.

7. Properly orient your curtains by opening them on the south side of the house during the day and keeping them closed on the north.

8. Dress in layers and use quilts and comforters to stay extra warm to avoid using unnecessary heat.

9. Install low-flow showerheads and faucet aerators.

10. Replace traditional light bulbs with compact fluorescent bulbs.

11. Use this book to advocate for renewable energy in your community by writing to your city council members, state legislators, and congressional members.

TRANSPORTATION AND CLIMATE CHANGE TIPS[220]

1. Learn your carbon footprint—the measure of the impact of your activities on the environment, in particular on climate change. Calculate yours at http://www.carbonfootprint.com/.

2. Buy a hybrid vehicle.

3. If you live in a city, get rid of your car and use a car-sharing arrangement such as Zipcar.

4. Carpool or rideshare. Websites such as http://www.erideshare.com/, http://www.dividetheride.com/, and http://carpoolconnect.com/ support your efforts.

5. Reduce commuting and travel time by working at home one day per week, if allowed. If possible, move closer to work.

6. Buy less and use reusable grocery bags.

7. Eat locally grown produce, cutting down on the barrels of oil for fertilizer and the diesel fuel for food transport.

8. Unplug. You spend more money on electricity to power devices when off than when on. Instead of turning them off, unplug televisions, stereo equipment, computers, battery chargers, and a host of other gadgets and appliances that consume more energy when seemingly switched off.

9. Recycle aluminum. The energy saved by recycling one aluminum beverage can is enough to power a television for three hours.

ACCOUNTABLE ASSESSMENT CHECKLIST

The most powerful tool we have as citizens to effect change is our vote. We should not allow our elected officials to make promises during their campaigns without fulfilling their obligations once in office. Use this list to hold our new president accountable on the environment.

Campaign Promises 2008: The Environment, Energy, and Infrastructure

BARACK OBAMA AS PROMISED . . .

- Will invest $150 billion over 10 years to spur private efforts toward clean energy, in the process creating 5 million green-collar jobs.

- Will ensure 10 percent of our electricity comes from renewable sources by 2012, and 25 percent by 2025.

- Will implement an economy-wide, cap-and-trade program to reduce greenhouse gas emissions 80 percent by 2050.

- Will enact a windfall profits tax to provide a $1,000 emergency energy rebate to American families.

- Will consider lifting oil-drilling bans in some offshore federal waters as part of a broader energy package.

- Will eliminate our current imports from the Middle East and Venezuela within 10 years.

- Will require all utilities to produce at least 10 percent of their electricity from renewable energy such as wind, solar, or biomass.

- Will overhaul appliance and other energy-efficiency standards with the goal of reducing building energy use by 25 to 50 percent.

Use this checklist to evaluate whether the entities that can make a difference are doing all that they can to help America realize the goal of the fifth and ninth Covenants: "Ensuring Broad Access to Affordable Neighborhoods That Connect to Opportunity" and "Assuring Environmental Justice for All." Reexamine this checklist every six months to assess progress.

OUR PRESIDENT

☐ Have you made environmental policies a priority during your first 100 days in office?

☐ Did you assemble a team of experts on environmental, climate, and infrastructure issues to consider short-term and long-term decision making?

☐ Have you explored responsibly using domestic oil and natural gases?

☐ Have you provided leadership in the international community on making climate change and environmental issues global priorities?

☐ Are you helping states and local communities to update their infrastructure?

☐ Will you make exploring and implementing "green" energy sources a national priority?

OUR U.S. CONGRESSMEN AND CONGRESSWOMEN

☐ Have you proposed legislation to explore alternative energy sources?

☐ Have you brought the concerns of citizens struggling with rising fuel costs to Congress?

☐ Have you supported aggressive goals for reducing greenhouse emissions?

☐ Do you know whether plans have been discussed or implemented by Congress to deal with emergencies such as Hurricane Katrina?

OUR GOVERNOR AND STATE LEGISLATORS

☐ Have you worked to strengthen our state's infrastructure, such as roads and bridges?

☐ Do you have a plan for providing citizens with incentives to reduce energy consumption?

☐   Have you improved local and state public transportation options?

☐   Have you worked to provide consumers and business owners relief from rising fuel prices?

☐   Do you have a plan to deal with a weather emergency such as Hurricane Katrina?

OUR COMMUNITY LEADERS
AND FAITH-BASED ORGANIZATIONS

☐   Have you offered members education about important environmental issues and how they may affect future generations?

☐   Will you promote small solutions to the energy crisis, such as ride sharing or energy-efficient light bulbs?

☐   Have you investigated or pushed government leaders to investigate areas of weak infrastructure in our community?

☐   Have you led local efforts to promote recycling?

YOU AND I

☐   Do I understand the issue of global climate change and how it will affect our world?

☐   Do I recycle at home and at work?

☐   Do I use public transportation and reduce driving to save money and help the environment?

☐   Do I use energy-efficient light bulbs?

☐   Do I own a hybrid or energy-efficient car?

☐   Do I sometimes ride a bike?

☐   Do I talk to neighbors, family, children, and friends about the importance of environmental issues?

6

Democracy

We the People in Order
to Form a More Perfect Union

To make democracy work, we must be a nation of participants, not
simply observers. One who does not vote has no right to complain.

—LOUIS L'AMOUR

Information is the currency of democracy.

—PRESIDENT THOMAS JEFFERSON

COVENANT SIX
Claiming Our Democracy

Imagine you are 18 years old and recently arrived at the college of your choice, far away from home, an entering freshman. You are excited. Except for a senior-class trip, you've never been away from home for longer than a few weeks and without adult supervision. Now, for the first time, you are on your own.

Mostly, anyway. Your parents took you to campus, met your roommate, and helped you settle in. They are partially paying for your education and have cosigned for your tuition loans. Still, for the first time, you are responsible for getting to class on time, taking care of yourself, and deciding what you'll study. You are taking your first real steps toward becoming a self-reliant adult.

It's an extraordinary time to enter college because it is also a presidential election year. For the first time, you are eligible to vote. You are politically aware, and you often engage in round-the-clock debates with classmates. You greatly anticipate exercising your right to vote, a bedrock right reserved for all adult citizens.

And what an election year! History has unfolded before your very eyes. Who could have imagined that a woman and an African American man would vie for the presidential nomination of the Democratic Party, that a woman would be the running mate on the GOP ticket, or that a record number of voters would decide the nominees? The presidency may no longer be the privileged burden of only one group of Americans. The reality sinks in: you can actually participate in the process. You are an adult. You are a citizen. You have the right to vote. And you can.

Now imagine going to register in the state where you attend college and being told by state election officials that if you register and vote in the state of your school as opposed to your home state, "you have declared your independence from your parents and can no longer be claimed as a dependent on their income tax filing. If you have a scholarship attached to your former residence, you could lose this funding. And if you change your registration . . . [the] Code requires you to change your driver's license and car registration to your present address within 30 days."[221]

Would you know this is misinformation? Would you question the state officials who told you this? Would you call home? Would you still register?

Being 18, are you likely to know that, in 1979, the U.S. Supreme Court ruled students have the right to register at their college addresses?[222] Although the flyers don't directly question your right to register or vote, would you recognize you are being subjected to voter suppression tactics? Or would you simply move on, trusting that state officials would never intentionally engage in voter suppression; would you tell yourself you will vote in the next election?

This scenario is exactly what happened to many students at Virginia Tech in August, just prior to the 2008 presidential election.[223] Out-of-state students were dissuaded from voting by a state-sponsored flyer stating, in language replicated above, they were risking their parents' income tax filings, their scholarships, and their insurance. Sujatha Jahagirdar, program director for the Student Public Interest Research Group's New Voters Project—a group dedicated to monitoring barriers to voter registration—said, "Virginia's warnings were profoundly misleading. . . . [W]e have been registering young voters for 25 years." Jahagirdar points out that the New Voters Project registered 500,000 young voters in 2004, the majority on college campuses. "We've never heard of a single one who lost health insurance, scholarships, or tax status because of where they registered to vote."[224]

Jon Greenbaum, director of the Voting Rights Project at the Lawyers' Committee for Civil Rights Under Law, agrees with Jahagirdar's assessment. What the Virginia Board of Elections has on its website, says Greenbaum, "sounds like it is discouraging students from registering at their school address." For Greenbaum, such unethical tactics are old hat, his having been involved in similar student registration cases throughout his career.[225]

Voter disenfranchisement is alive and well in this country despite our being widely heralded as "the foremost democracy in the world." What kind of impressions do we leave on our young citizens—the future of our country—when their first electoral experience is marred by the ugliness of voter suppression?

Who is accountable for ensuring our youth do not become part of the millions of Americans who have given up on the very rights that led the Founding Fathers of this nation to declare independence from the British Empire? Who is accountable when the self-proclaimed leader of the free world cannot guarantee the integrity of its election process for the highest office in the land?

■   ■   ■

In *The Covenant,* the chapter "Claiming Our Democracy" addresses the institutional processes by which we actually do the work of democracy. Central to that chapter was concern over whether several key provisions of the Voting Rights Act of 1965 would be renewed by Congress. Those provisions, which have served as bulwarks against discriminatory voting practices, were set to expire in August 2007. They were renewed on July 27, 2007, thanks to the tireless work of civil rights leaders like Wade Henderson, who authored the introductory essay on democracy in *The Covenant.* The work of claiming our democracy was not completed, however, with the renewal of key provisions of the Voting Rights Act of 1965. To quote poet Archibald MacLeish, "Democracy is never a thing done. Democracy is always something that a nation must be doing."

The Promise of Democracy

We must recognize how fragile democracy is despite its central role to the conceptual foundation of our nation. One of the tragedies of being human is we often stray from our beginnings, forgetting our roots, ignoring our origins. We gloss over the past at the peril of having to repeat its harsh mistakes.

Twice in the history of western civilization, democratic forms of government have existed; the time span between its first and second manifestations is more than 2,000 years. When democracy's light went out in Athens in the third century B.C.E., it did not come on again until the 18th century A.D., and in a very different form than that practiced by the Greeks. This second incarnation was the extraordinary revolution of New World colonists against the British Empire. They brought into existence the republican form of constitutional democracy that evolved into the United States of America. But, viewed through the long lens of history, democracy is a mere or occasional snapshot. Most of human history is replete with forms of government that subject the individual to the whims of a ruling class, a ruling elite, or brutal militaristic regimes where notions of individual rights are barely significant, if existing at all.

In the twentieth century—a century Dr. Cornel West calls "the most barbaric in human history"—democracy barely survived the rise of fascism and totalitarianism in Germany, Italy, and Russia. More chilling is the fact that, in the beginning at least, those nations turned toward fascism and totalitarianism willingly. World War II not only ripped apart a continent, but also pulled much of the rest of the world into the simmering cauldron of Europe's internal strife and failures. Democracy could have been lost in Europe. This is a significant and useful memory to keep.

Maybe democracy is but a brief moment of rest in an otherwise tumultuous human history. Maybe, 2,000 years from now, schools will regard democracy as an aberration, as a historic yet fleeting form of government employed in a few unique circumstances. Perhaps the best move we can make to reclaim and secure our democracy is to appreciate just how fragile and precious the notion is that everyday people can govern themselves.

"We *the people* in order to form a more perfect union . . . in order to secure the *blessings* of liberty to ourselves and our posterity . . ." Words more beautiful have never been spoken in expression of the desire for self-governance. Yet, democracy is more than a beautiful thought. It is a set of behaviors, a way of being in the world, and a daily practice.

Winston Churchill once famously quipped: "Democracy is the worst form of government, except for all those other forms that have been tried from time to time." His notion is that democracy is messy, incomplete, unfinished, and difficult in practice. People of all stripes come together with competing agendas, outlooks, ideologies, dispositions, and interests. Fortunately, democracy doesn't believe in perfection. Its messiness notwithstanding, democracy clearly stipulates that free, autonomous, responsible, community-minded citizens can govern themselves, and that this form of governing is reflective of the core tenet of our constitutional form, epitomized by "We hold these truths to be self-evident, that all men are created equal . . ."

Democracy affirms the belief that all of us are equal. Too often we lose sight of this animating principle and the democratic behaviors that arise from it. As the award-winning trumpeter, author, and master teacher Wynton Marsalis observes in his latest book, *Moving to Higher Ground*, "Balance is required to maintain something as delicate as democracy, a subtle understanding of how your power can be imagined through joining with and sharing the power of another person."[226]

Even with the recent, historic presidential election, we are not doing the work of democracy well, for many reasons. Some citizens have grown tired of the endless bickering and partisanship in government. Frustration over the tenor of our democracy, the corruption of its institutions, and the pernicious influence of money have caused many citizens to withdraw from any form of civic engagement.

The answer to a frustrated democracy is always more democracy. The cure is to commit ourselves over and over again to the fundamental principles that animate our democracy and to stand on those principles while moving toward more engaged roles of citizenship. When a democracy is in doubt, it's up to citizens to do more of its work.

Fear has caused many of us to turn our backs on democracy. Following the tragedy of 9/11, we bought into a false, opportunistic notion that promoted the sacrifice of our individual rights as a measure of "national security." We should have known better. After all, was not the very foundation of our American democracy forged by crisis? Our system of democracy was designed to account for best- and worst-case scenarios. Notions of fear and security can *never* be bigger than the concept and practice of democracy. If they are, then democracy itself ceases to exist.

Fear also plays a role in the naked partisanship that plagues American politics. Demonization of our fellow citizens simply for their political choices comes at the expense of the principles of our democratic society. Witness this past election; one example of such vile scare tactics was the "robo-calls" that disparaged candidates, often citing false information. A people who cannot rise above their political preferences long enough to defend those principles on which their democracy depends are a people flirting with anarchy. The promise of our democracy has always relied on an appeal to the better angels of our nature. But the process of democracy is always worked out "in the streets."

"Dreams have to be saddled before they can be ridden," observed Dr. Howard Thurman, the 20th-century theologian, mystic, and mentor to Dr. Martin Luther King, Jr. Our saddles must fit snugly before we can run with our dreams and achieve the promise of America.

The Process of Democracy

Michael Berman is not a household name, and he prefers it that way.[227] He is well known among California's political circles, both Democratic and Republican. A political consultant, Berman was hired by Democrats in 2001 to redraw voting district boundaries in California after the 2000 census.[228] He has participated in the process in every decade since 1970.[229]

Why is this important to our democratic process? Who cares who draws the lines that determine voter districts?

Every 10 years, after the U.S. Census is taken and updated, states are required to redraw their congressional boundaries so that each district contains roughly the same number of people and meets one person–one vote requirements. A parallel and similar process is undertaken to revise state legislative districts. This process frequently has an extraordinary impact on the outcome of elections. Say, for example, a Republican from the House of Representatives has held a seat by a slim two percent margin for the past four years due largely to an enclave of conservative, white Catholics that falls within her district boundaries. If boundaries are redrawn in such a way as to remove this voting bloc from her district, replacing it with several traditionally liberal suburbs, her chances for reelection become doomed. Consequently, whoever draws voter district lines has immense power.

We define this process of drawing lines at a disadvantage to one group over another as gerrymandering. And like voter disenfranchisement, suppression, and fraud, it threatens the democratic process.

It follows, then, in 2001, when California Democrats contracted Michael Berman to redraw the district lines for the state, it was to expand Democratic control in California. The Democrats certainly didn't pay Berman's hefty consulting fees to help out the other side.

Berman was faced that year with a voting district landscape that would not readily yield to his goal.[230] For any voter redistricting plan to advance in the state, it must have two-thirds approval from the legislature, and Democrats did not have the votes in 2001. Moreover, without two-thirds approval for any redistricting plan by the state legislature, any new plan could be challenged by the citizens of California, which meant that the plan would then be subject to the judgment of the courts.[231] Without some Republican votes, no radical redistricting plan could pass, and the idea that Republicans would sign off on losing control of their districts was unrealistic.

An alternative that made sense was surfacing. What was more threatening to both Republicans and Democrats than losing control of the redistricting process to each other was the prospect of losing control to the electorate and having the plan end up before the courts. Rather than risk a plan on which the people of California could deliberate, Democrats and Republicans found common ground to insulate both sides and maintain the status quo: they agreed to keep the current voter district lines, protecting Democrats and Republicans alike from new challengers.

This account might appear to be a political success story, given the practice of bipartisanship and compromise within the negotiations. It is not. The California legislature effectively found a way to ensure that those in power remained in power. Potential challengers to incumbent seats were largely locked out because the existing district lines were preserved. And we, the people, lost before the votes were even counted.

This unfortunate account is one of many that Spencer Overton— professor of law at George Washington University and Jamestown Project senior fellow—uses to illustrate threats posed to democratic processes in *Stealing Democracy: The New Politics of Voter Suppression*. Overton likens gerrymandering and voter suppression tactics to the movie *The Matrix*, by describing how these often hidden processes determine the outcome of elections before the first vote is even cast.[232] This is not a matter of conspiracy for Overton, but rather of pure, power politics and the control of mechanisms beyond the sight of ordinary citizens. Conspiracy or not, there is real danger here.

The growing gap between how we imagine our democracy and how our democracy actually functions is breeding ground for disillusionment, cynicism, and widespread mistrust in our way of governing. One need only consider the perceptions Americans have of their elected officials; they sense our democracy is in a deep crisis. But we can no longer believe that somehow our government is *them* and not *us*. *We* are the government. We elect our officials to work for us, and if they do not work for us, we are responsible for electing officials who will.

Recount: Elections and Democracy

Who can forget Florida and the presidential election of 2000? The entire world watched as our electoral mechanisms of democracy broke down. The election was plagued by irregularities and inconsistencies in the way votes were cast and counted, inaccurate and bogus voter purge lists, interventions by power brokers from each major party, conflicts between state officials and the highest court of Florida, and the assumption of the process by the U.S. Supreme Court. What a shot across the bow of democracy in America. Many of these problems still exist.

Consider Wisconsin and the actions taken by its state attorney general leading up to the 2008 presidential election.[233] On September 8, Attorney General J. B. Van Hollen filed a lawsuit calling for the removal of ineligible voters from state rolls. Their ineligibility was determined by cross-checking names against the rolls of Wisconsin's transportation, criminal, and death records, consistent with federal guidelines to protect against voter fraud.[234] Although Wisconsin's Government Accountability Board—the oversight mechanism responsible for checking voter registration in the state—has been operational only since August 6, 2008, the attorney general has called for cross-checks dating back to January 1, 2006, when the federal government implemented the Help America Vote Act, requiring states to cross-check against the above-mentioned databases.[235]

So what's the problem? After all, the attorney general is trying only to comply with a federal law, right? The problem is blatant partisanship, wherein an attorney general brought this lawsuit less than two months before the presidential election. Any discrepancies not resolved between the time of the lawsuit's being filed and the election would likely result in delays at the polling booths. In Wisconsin, a voter can register at the polls, but—as in 2008—when election-day traffic is predicted to be especially heavy, delays and potentially long lines may discourage some voters and they decide to stay home. The lawsuit was dismissed, fortunately; the presiding judge described it as unfounded 12 days prior to the election. This was a positive outcome, not only because of the rejection of the lawsuit's partisan nature, but also because such database checks are notoriously unreliable and usually result in purging legitimate voters from the rolls.

Democrats were outraged by these tactics; they had done all the hard work to get the majority of the new registrants on the roll—in the Democrat column.[236] But these tactics should not provoke outrage from only Democrats. Such tactics should outrage Americans of all political persuasions. When officials place their desired outcome ahead of their sworn duty to protect the integrity of the process, we place our fragile democracy in harm's way.

We've seen unchecked partisanship in other areas of American public life. The nomination and confirmation process of justices to the highest court in our land has become so partisan that the confirmation hearings of Robert Bork were the last time we actually heard a nominee answer questions pertinent to the responsibilities of a Supreme Court justice. Now the process is a shell game: Nominees deny having opinions about anything controversial. The process by which we nominate Supreme Court justices has been compromised and we, regrettably, seem to accept it.

Will we accept that we cannot prevent voter disenfranchisement in the same way we have accepted that Supreme Court nominees can refuse to answer honestly the questions we most want answered? Do we accept that party politics has gotten so divisive that the party in power will use any means to bar the participation of the challenging party?

Red State, Blue State?

President James Madison, the Founding Father widely regarded as the "father of the Constitution," asserted we are responsible for reining in partisanship like the kind that has recently divided America. Except Madison did not use the term "partisanship" to describe this threat to democracy. He preferred "the violence of faction."[237]

"Among the numerous advantages promised by a well-constructed Union, none deserves to be more accurately developed than its tendency to break and control the violence of faction," wrote Madison in *The Federalist Papers*. Urging his fellow Americans to support the new constitutional republic, he wrote: "By a faction I understand a number of citizens, whether amounting to a majority or a minority of the whole, who are united and actuated by some common impulse of passion, or of interest, adverse to the rights of other citizens, or to the permanent and aggregate interests of the community."[238] These words, written under the pen name Publius more than 200 years ago, are as relevant today as they were when written.

Everywhere in our democracy we find factions. We are divided by party, by red states and blue states, and even by media outlets. The most dire crises seem unable to keep us from dividing ourselves, placing party first, and placing our passions above the common good of the state. While "every man and woman for himself" is instinctive to all humans, this instinct is not the one on which democracy is predicated. Democracy is the coming together of a people to fashion a common good, and that requires a real concern for our collective well-being. If we continue to ignore the quest for the common good, we will undermine our democracy.

The answer to who is accountable for the current state of our democracy is the easiest answer we give in this book.

We, the people, are.

A FRAMEWORK FOR ASSESSMENT

The *Covenant* set forth "Claiming Our Democracy" as a covenant examining the health of the mechanisms and processes of our democracy. At the end of that chapter, we imagine what individuals, all levels of government, and community leaders can do to impact their related issues. THE COVENANT *In Action* next provided a toolkit to equip citizens with the instruments to effect change on this and all *The Covenant* issues. *ACCOUNTABLE* will help citizens assess whether we have lived up to the aspirations put forward in *The Covenant* books and give them a measuring tool for future evaluation.

During the 2008 presidential election, the major candidates agreed that our democracy is in desperate need of a change and a renewal of those core beliefs that animate our culture. We have yet to live up to the goal of reclaiming our democracy as set forth in *The Covenant*. What about potential solutions? And how will the American citizenry know if any implemented solutions are working?

Solutions for Government

In the 2008 presidential race, then-Senator Obama supported some electoral reforms, including a push to crack down on voter fraud and other means of voter tampering. He opposed the voter identification requirement for federal elections and spoke out against a Justice Department official's insensitive and inaccurate comments on the effect of these laws.[239] That official, John Tanner, subsequently stepped down after Obama called for his dismissal. Obama's campaign also filed a class-action lawsuit in Michigan in September 2008 to prevent local officials from barring citizens from voting whose homes are on foreclosure lists.[240]

As a senator, Obama introduced and helped to successfully navigate passage of the Deceptive Practices and Voter Intimidation Prevention Act, a measure prohibiting and punishing deceptive practices that seek to intimidate, mislead, or keep voters away from the polls on Election Day. Such practices have included distributing flyers falsely informing voters in urban neighborhoods that they can "vote on Saturday" if it rains on Election Day (Tuesday), and encouraging them to vote for their "favorite Democrat" while listing the name of his or her Republican opponent.

Obama cosponsored The Ballot Integrity Act of 2007, which provides safeguards to prevent errors and tampering at the polls, requires state voting systems to employ auditable and voter-verified paper records by 2010, and ensures voters are not denied the right to vote by faulty purges of voting rolls. He also was a primary sponsor of Yale Law professor Heather Gerken's Democracy Index, which ranks states based on how effectively they operate their election systems and allows for data collection in each state to identify deficiencies and provide incentives for improvement.

Election Day Registration

At the state and local levels, reforms have been achieved that provide models for our nation. Same-day voter registration is one such program. In eight states—Idaho, Iowa, Maine, Minnesota, Montana, New Hampshire, Wisconsin, and Wyoming—voters can go to the polls on Election Day, register, and vote in one visit. North Carolina has a similar program that allows voters to register and vote at one time up until three days before the election. Other benefits include eliminating such current electoral challenges as illegitimate voter purges and refusing provisional ballots from voters in the wrong polling location. While critics charge that voters could travel from polling place to polling place and vote multiple times, North Carolina state officials say this has not presented a problem thus far, and new legislation requiring computerized voter rolls would prevent any misconduct.

In October 2008, the U.S. Sixth Circuit Court of Appeals and the Ohio State Supreme Court upheld an Ohio law allowing same-day registration and vote by absentee ballot. George Cintron, a homeless Cleveland resident, voted for the first time since 1976 by taking advantage of this program. He explained that as someone who lives in a shelter, it is difficult to exercise his right to vote because he lacks the permanent residence that makes obtaining an absentee ballot, or finding the correct polling place, possible. Only federal legislation can require states to allow same-day registration, but states are free to conduct their elections as they choose. Organizations such as Demos—a nonpartisan public policy research and advocacy organization—are pushing for more states to adopt this election reform to get more people to the polls.[241]

Campaign Finance

In September 2008, candidate Obama raised an unprecedented $150 million in campaign contributions that, at the time, increased his fund-raising total to in excess of $600 million for the primaries and general election, surpassing the *combined* amount raised by President Bush and Sen. John Kerry in their 2004 contest. Obama's opponent, Sen. John McCain, chose to participate in the public financing program, allotting him $84 million to spend between September 1 and Election Day. This left Obama—who initially pledged to participate in public financing but later backed out of his promise—with a four-to-one spending advantage in the final month of the campaign. In future elections, there is little incentive for a candidate to follow in McCain's publicly-financed, second-rate shoes.

The Obama campaign raised part of its money through sizable private donations; equally successful was his Internet-based fund-raising campaign for small donors. By the general election, his campaign war chest exceeded $650 million. His campaign staff also coalesced with the Democratic National Committee and numerous state-level Democratic committees to create joint fund-raising bodies that attracted tens of millions more.

Obama's broken promise and subsequent electoral success highlight the need for meaningful campaign finance reform to rein in the influence of wealthy special interests in electing public officials. "One man, one vote" can hardly compete with "one man, $1 million." The implication is clear: democracy loses when our polling places become secondary to the size of our bank accounts.

The courts recently ruled that political parties and other organizations can independently spend any amount they want to on candidates, making it virtually impossible to control spending. A movement is growing among reform advocates, however, to require that all donors to parties, campaigns, and advocacy groups be clearly identified. Such transparency is necessary in a democracy to protect us citizens, our votes, and our trust.

Solutions for Business and Community Leaders

INCREASING VOTER TURNOUT

Given the significance of the 2008 election, community, business, and faith-based organizations engaged their memberships in get-out-the-vote programs to deliver as many constituents to the polls as possible. Some programs targeted increasing voter participation, while others sought to promote specific candidates or issues.

Hispanic Chambers of Commerce coordinated Hispanic businesses and Spanish-language media to increase Latino voting and civic engagement projects. For example, the Ayuda Business Coalition in Northern Virginia set up registration booths outside of grocery stores and at soccer games to register citizens. It sponsored demonstrations of how to use voting equipment and ran advertisements with the tagline, "Si no votas, no cuentas," or "If you don't vote, you don't count." By educating voters on issues key to Hispanic voters—especially immigration reforms central to the 2008 debate—organizers galvanized citizens who previously saw their vote as meaningless or not worth the effort; they stressed how important the Hispanic vote would be to the outcome in November.[242]

Exposing and preventing voter fraud and misinformation was a big part of organizational efforts leading up to the 2008 election. The *Tom Joyner Morning Show*, in conjunction with the NAACP National Voter Fund, operated the 1-866-MYVOTE1 campaign as a nonpartisan initiative to provide voter information, fraud prevention, and registration to the popular disc jockey's audience of more than 8 million mostly African American listeners. Twice-weekly "Trickery Updates" documenting instances of polling irregularities were broadcast to inform citizens about the electoral process and potential barriers to voting. Their collaboration added tens of thousands of registrants across America who planned to vote November 4.

Getting the youth vote to turn out on Election Day was an important goal of a number of organizations, as reflected by the work of Rock the

Vote and its affiliated Rap the Vote. Rock the Vote conducted the largest voter registration drive in history by way of online, mobile, and grassroots outreach efforts in 2008, resulting in more than 2.5 million registration form downloads. Its subsequent and extensive get-out-the-vote effort included in excess of 100,000 Election Day text message reminders and 13,300 phone-banking reminders. Rock the Vote activists also accompanied numerous college students to the polls at such institutions of higher learning as Ohio State and Drexel universities.[243]

Rap the Vote—through its collaborating with high-profile celebrities headlined by Russell Simmons, Sean "Diddy" Combs, and Jay-Z—steered a flood of hip-hop generation and first-time voters to the polls. Its initiative centered on education, registration, and get-out-the-vote, contributing to the more than 24 million 18- to 29-year-olds who cast a ballot on Election Day.[244]

FINDING COMMON GROUND

What do the 38-million-member Association for the Advancement of Retired People (AARP), the 2-million-member Service Employees International Union (SEIU), the 350,000-member National Federation of Independent Businesses (NFIB), and the powerful and conservative Business Roundtable have in common?

Launched in 2007, the Divided We Fail campaign is a collaboration of these prominent groups dedicated to "engaging the American people, businesses, nonprofit organizations, and elected officials in finding bipartisan solutions to ensure affordable, quality health care and long-term financial security for all of us. The need for health and financial security is something we all share, not just for ourselves, but for future generations. It is the promise of America."[245] With 362 members of Congress having already signed the Divided We Fail congressional pledge, and with the endorsement of more than 80 supporting organizations, Divided We Fail is a stellar example of a move away from partisan politics to a positive collaboration on issues that matter most.

By the way, have you ever heard of an elephonkey? Seen one? No?

It is the symbol of Divided We Fail: a cross between the Democratic Party's donkey and the Republican Party's elephant. Its purple color represents the desire to find common ground between "red" and "blue" issues. Look for it. Common-ground politics, we hope, will be indicative of a new era of democratic practices in our country.

Solutions for Individuals

RE-ENFRANCHISEMENT

During the heart—and heat—of the 2008 presidential campaign, community organizer Monica Bell strolled around the parking lot at a strip mall in Orlando, FL, asking shoppers if they had registered to vote. She asked Antonious Belton if he was registered. He replied that he was not allowed to because of prior felony drug convictions. Bell, however, had good news for Belton: The Florida legislature and Governor Charles Crist approved a measure in 2007 restoring voting rights to more than 100,000 former convicted felons.

Benton reflected on his situation: "After you go to prison—you do your time and they still take all your rights away. You can't get a job. You can't vote. You can't do nothing even 10 or 20 years later. You don't feel like a citizen. You don't even feel human."[246]

Citizens like Bell help spread the word about Florida's new law, trying to improve on the current rate of former felon voting. As of 2007, only 9,000 eligible voters had registered. Bell and other caring citizens like her are trying to help those who have paid their debts to society reclaim their civic rights and responsibilities. Theirs is an important task, given that de facto disenfranchisement—where former felons assume they can't vote when they really can—is a significant problem. In many states, former felons forgo their own right to vote out of a lack of information or embarrassment stemming from their prior conviction.[247]

KIDS AT THE POLLS

They may be too young to vote, but some American middle- and high-school students spend Election Day at the polls. Even though they can't yet cast a vote, they help others exercise their civic duty and, in so doing, learn about our electoral process. In Montgomery County, MD; St. Louis, MO; and other locations, thousands of students are trained on polling procedures, addressing citizens, and helping voters with special needs. On Election Day, students reach the polling places before dawn, prepared to instruct citizens on how to use voting machines, distribute voting-related literature, and provide logistical assistance. Julianne Martin, a student in Missouri participating in the state's Kids Voting Missouri program, commented, "I am also excited to help because, being 17 years old, I have never voted, so I want to see what the voting process is really like—the normal experience and behind the scenes." Students may also receive school service credit for their work; some even get paid for their long hours of Election Day service.[248]

ACCOUNTABLE ASSESSMENT CHECKLIST

The most powerful tool we have as citizens to effect change is our vote. We should not allow our elected officials to make promises during their campaigns without fulfilling their obligations once in office. Use this list to hold our new president accountable.

Campaign Promises 2008: Democracy

BARACK OBAMA AS PROMISED . . .

▪ Will establish harsh penalties for those who have engaged in voter fraud and provide voters who have been misinformed with accurate and full information so they can vote.

- Will create a database with lobbyist reports, ethics records, and campaign finance filings to enhance transparency.

- Will create an independent entity responsible for overseeing ethics investigations.

- Will expose, then eliminate, pork barrel spending.

- Will require federal agencies to work in public so citizens can understand and participate in their decision making.

Use this checklist to evaluate whether the entities that can make a difference are doing all they can to help America realize the goal of the sixth Covenant: "Claiming Our Democracy." Reexamine this checklist every six months to assess progress.

OUR PRESIDENT

- ☐ Can you put the best interests of the country first regardless of partisan politics or political pressure?

- ☐ Are you developing and enforcing laws that prevent unfair campaign funding?

- ☐ Are you ensuring citizens are allowed to exercise their votes freely and fairly?

- ☐ Have you implemented policies to ensure up-to-date voting equipment so that elections reflect the people's choice?

- ☐ Are you including a variety of viewpoints in your Cabinet, including some from outside the Democratic Party?

OUR U.S. CONGRESSMEN AND CONGRESSWOMEN

- ☐ Are you working to achieve campaign finance reform?

- ☐ Have you proposed or supported legislation to ensure that all citizens have access to the polls on Election Day?

- ☐ Have you "reached across the aisle" to work with members of other political factions when it benefited your constituents?

OUR GOVERNOR AND STATE LEGISLATORS

☐ Have you ensured that our state has up-to-date equipment to tally and count all votes correctly?

☐ Are you ensuring that polling places are managed fairly so that all citizens can participate in the democratic process?

☐ Are you representing the interests of your constituents rather than those of powerful lobbyists?

☐ Have you implemented campaign finance reforms in our state?

OUR LOCAL LEADERS

☐ Are you working with state and national officials to ensure fair electoral processes?

☐ Do you make decisions based on the best interests of our community, not on those of special interest groups?

☐ Have you organized or will you organize programs to educate and encourage citizens about their voting rights?

OUR COMMUNITY LEADERS
AND FAITH-BASED ORGANIZATIONS

☐ Do you have a plan or an initiative to monitor the progress of the democratic process, ensuring fair elections and political decision making?

☐ Do you have a plan or an initiative to educate your members about why voting is important and how to register?

☐ Have you worked with local government to manage fair polling places on Election Day?

☐ Do you educate members about the responsibilities of citizens?

☐ Will you help residents seeking citizenship in navigating the citizenship process?

☐ Will you educate young people about the importance of participating in our democracy?

YOU AND I

☐ Do I know the names of my elected officials?

☐ If possible, am I registered to vote?

☐ If possible, do I vote, even if voting requires obtaining an absentee ballot?

☐ Do I talk to my friends, family, children, and neighbors about the importance of voting?

☐ Do I educate myself about issues that matter to me and my community so that I can make an informed choice at the polls?

☐ Do I engage in honest discussion with others about the pluses and minuses of political issues and individual politicians and find ways to compromise?

☐ Have I volunteered to help my democracy through participating in a voter registration drive, helping those in my community to register, providing rides to the polls on Election Day, or helping to educate others about the importance of civic engagement?

☐ Have I served as a poll worker?

7

Retelling the American Story

Make up a story. Narrative is radical, creating us
at the very moment it is being created.

—TONI MORRISON

We recently experienced one of the most significant and hopeful elections in our nation's history. But America is still largely divided. Although the distinctions between red states and blue states are less pronounced, the divisions in the popular vote remain largely intact.

At the heart of these divisions, we believe, are competing stories about what it means to be an American. The "red" version of our identity and direction as a country differs markedly from the "blue" version. It oftentimes feels as though these versions will never find common ground.

Some people believe that America is at its best when individuals are allowed to pursue their ambitions with minimal government intervention. The 2008 economic meltdown tested this belief. On the other hand, some citizens feel the role of government should be to provide social safety nets to "catch" the more vulnerable among us.

Our global conceptions differ as well. Some believe we are a country obligated to no one except ourselves; others see an important role for the United States as bridge-builder and relationship manager.

■ ■ ■

Countless issues face our nation. On so many of them—from health care to the military—we seem split right down the middle. Behind each of these issues is a larger narrative that illuminates what America means. We can tell ourselves a story, with real consequences, that frames our nation as the authoritarian "policeman of the world" with a "divine mandate" to protect and spread democracy. Or we can tell ourselves that we are one nation among many working toward a more humane, interconnected existence. For each story, there will be different but very real results.

Though we cannot offer a perfect answer to the question of how we should understand our history, we do believe in casting a wide net. A grand narrative extolling our rich diversity might elude us, but we certainly can describe more representative narratives than we have in the past. If we hope to make America fulfill its promise to be a truly inclusive and accountable democracy, we must retell our collective story so that we can capture more of the flavor and richness of what it means to be an American.

If, for example, your vision of America cannot accommodate the reality of slavery and ignores the impact that our nation's slaveholding past continues to have on our nation, you have an incomplete version of who we are as Americans. If your vision of America explains the voting patterns of fellow citizens in the Rust Belt by considering them "ignorant, gun-toting Jesus freaks," then yours is an incomplete version of America. If you are a descendant of a family that passed through Ellis Island and yet have no sympathy for Hispanic Americans striving to bring their families here for better opportunity, then yours is an incomplete version of who we are.

If, on the other hand, you strive for a more complete version of the American story, then you will have your work cut out for you. You will have to engage not only your own family and community, but also communities outside of your comfort zone.

An active democracy is always a work in progress, an incomplete epic narrative that, in the profound words of Nobel laureate Toni Morrison, "is creating us as we are creating it." We get to choose. We can choose to create a radically individualistic American story in which our differences are held against us and every citizen "goes for self." Or we can create a common American story that recognizes the values of empathy, negotiation, and compromise.

ACCOUNTABLE is premised on the assumption that we want to create a common story. To do so, we must work harder than ever to understand the challenges faced by our fellow citizens. We fail to take up this challenge at our own peril. We must reject the conclusion that our differences will inevitably divide us and understand that when ideological positions substitute for inquiry and engagement, common ground escapes us. When we do not expand our own perspective on what it means to be an American, we leave ourselves open to classifying fellow citizens as *others*, as strangers, or worse yet, as enemies. The more we talk to each other and not at each other, the more we share our stories and gaze more deeply into the fabric of American history, the more likely it is that we will recognize the threads that bind us all.

Competing conceptions of our nation's history are at the heart of much that still divides us. For many Americans our story is simple, straightforward: brave, heroic, freedom-minded colonists unwilling to continue suffering the abuses of the British Empire banded together and struck a resounding blow for "life, liberty and the pursuit of happiness," forging the course of this nation and inspiring freedom, dignity, and democracy for ages to come. The heroes of this version are familiar—Washington, Jefferson, Franklin, and Hamilton. Monuments bear their names and currency bears their likeness. We learn about *The Federalist Papers* in school, with its brilliant discourses on why the Constitution should be ratified.

But there were other voices and heroes among the founders, often overlooked, but just as inspired and freedom-loving, with deep misgivings about the early course and direction of our country. Their concern and reasoning also helped to mold the final form our nation and our Constitution would take. Fitting examples are the Anti-Federalist writings of Revolution-era figures—George Clinton, Robert Yates, and Samuel Bryan—which led to the adoption of the Bill of Rights.

■   ■   ■

These few examples scratch the surface of competing narratives among founders and framers of our nation. But they say nothing about the numerous "other" Americans who contributed interlacing strands to our national fabric. Although the Founding Fathers were heroes of liberty, it was a liberty reserved for the few at the expense of the many. The Constitution, for all of its grand values and practical genius, was a document designed to protect, first and foremost, the interests of the landed gentry, the elite of the time: white male property owners. That same document barely refers to Native Americans; men and women of African descent were reduced to fractions of human beings; and the rights of white women to participate as full citizens were implicitly denied. The omission, reduction, and silencing of these groups in our original American story to this day limits our understanding and definition of ourselves.

The storied founders of this nation were certainly inspired and remarkable human beings. Against seemingly insurmountable odds, these courageous, visionary, and intelligent men forged a fledgling nation and bound it together with a Constitution that remains one of the most enduring and inspiring documents in human history. For all of their genius, several of these framers were flawed, hypocritical men unable or unwilling to see the yokes they placed on others even as they rebelled against the yokes the British placed on them. And the document they produced, inspiring though it is, reflected these flaws, as evidenced by the numerous amendments ratified to improve it and to hold our union together.

The founders held King George III and the British government accountable for their ruling transgressions, but failed to hold themselves accountable. How would our national story be different had the founders decided at our nation's inception that the enslavement of human beings was inconsistent with their deepest values? How would we understand ourselves if—rather than through force and treaty poisoned by mendacity or a conveniently "divine" mission to settle this land—the early settlers had found a way to respect and live peaceably with the country's native inhabitants? What if, from the outset, women had been regarded as equals to men in rights and duties under the laws of the land? In our history, there *were* voices every step of the way that opposed slavery, wanted to live peaceably and honorably with Native

Americans, and argued that women were every bit as capable as men of assuming the rights and obligations of citizenship.

We sometimes justify this country's troubled beginnings by convincing ourselves that this is "just the way things were back then." When we tell ourselves this story, we are not telling the whole truth. We are simply highlighting some aspects of it at the expense of others, covering up our flaws. We have concocted a less-than-true story that is reflected in the enduring divisions among races, genders, and classes and the marginalization of America's minorities.

W. E. B. DuBois, the renowned scholar and educator, once wrote that the great tragedy of racism is that "men know so little of men." Certainly, one of the tragedies of our nation at this moment is that we know so little about the hopes, experiences, and dreams of our fellow citizens. We have wrapped ourselves too tightly in private, familiar, regional, and racial security blankets. It is easy for a New Yorker to dismiss the concerns, dreams, and fears of a fellow citizen from Thurmond, WV, because the New Yorker may know nothing about Thurmond or West Virginia. He may lack the desire to know more about a rural place that exists far beyond his New York state of mind. But the big-city American who dismisses the small-town American loses an opportunity for a more complete understanding of what it means to be a citizen of our nation—what the challenges are, what richness we enjoy. And we, collectively, lose an opportunity to grow, and grow closer.

And growing *closer* as a nation—tightening our bonds with each other—is a critical step along the path to making democracy real. Today, we challenge you to ask yourself if you have given up on building relationships with unfamiliar neighbors. If we have given up, if we have failed to hold ourselves accountable for doing so, then the brutal, partisan, and ugly politics that characterize our political process are exactly what we deserve.

■   ■   ■

With so much hope and such good will generated by the election of President Barack Obama, we should use the spirit of this unique historical time to build bridges of understanding over the differences that separate us.

There is an adage that says, "You don't take out the garbage in another person's house." Too many people in America view our problems as taking place in someone else's house. We challenge you to view your fellow citizen's challenges and obligations as your own. After all, once the stench from that garbage reaches beyond the walls of your neighbor's home, it is no longer just your neighbor's problem. And indeed, as the economic crisis of 2008 has shown, those who are among the "haves" today can suddenly end up among the "have-nots" tomorrow.

We have shared the stories of some of our neighbors to deepen our understanding of the problems we face as a nation and to point the way to solutions. We have highlighted the problems posed by barriers to affordable and timely health care as tragically represented by the unnecessary death of Deamonte Driver. We have offered ideas for improving both accessibility and affordability.

We have argued that quality public education is essential to the preservation of our democracy. Education should prepare our youth for more than individual accomplishment. It should stress character development and teach our children the responsibilities of good citizenship as well. We examined the ways in which our nation's schools are failing our children, like the neglected 15-year-old girl who assaulted her teacher; but we also pointed to creative and effective educational initiatives such as Bob Moses' Algebra Project. We demonstrated the very real shortcomings of the No Child Left Behind Act in its overreliance on standardized testing, and we outlined a path to efficacy.

We have looked at a criminal justice system characterized by drastic racial, ethnic, and class disparities in the dispensation of justice that must be addressed. But we also pointed to model programs for improving that system such as the celebrated Community Court Initiatives that function as alternative programs for resolving quality-of-life matters without incarceration.

We have explored the ways in which the economic crisis is affecting our daily lives. We considered the struggles of Cynthia Porter, the hardworking and committed woman who walks to her low-wage job by herself in the dead of night because she can't afford a car. On the other hand, we pointed out the effectiveness of Small Business Development Centers in New York in assisting business owners like Jorge Rodriguez.

We have demonstrated how environmental issues are not just for stereotypically "green" types who buy organic produce and attach solar panels to their houses. Because of the interdependent nature of humans and the environment, it's a concern for us all. All our children suffer from polluted air and water. We're all endangered when the bridges and tunnels that connect our cities and states fall into disrepair. We presented evidence of environmental racism and classism, pointing out how hazardous waste treatment plants and oil refineries are commonly placed in minority and low-income communities. We also looked at exciting advances in renewable energy, including T. Boone Pickens' plan for wind power as an effective and plentiful source of alternative energy.

■　■　■

We began this book with a story about A. Philip Randolph, the powerful organizer who held President Franklin Delano Roosevelt accountable to ordinary citizens—black taxpayers who had been told by Roosevelt and other elected leaders that they were a part of this American democratic process. But when it came to the critical issue of economic empowerment, the reality did not match their rhetoric. Randolph held the most powerful leader in the world accountable. He forced the president to integrate black people more fully into the American story.

In his collection of essays, *Contingency, Irony and Solidarity*, Richard Rorty—arguably the most influential American philosopher of the past 50 years—introduced his readers to a concept called "We-Talk," the kind of talking or writing that promotes our interdependent nature, or our sense of *we*. Rorty suggests that big concepts such as humanity, democracy, and freedom don't always inspire people to action. He suggests that good works of fiction can often do a better job and cites as examples the novels written by Leslie Marmon Silko—novels that help us see Native Americans not as one of *them*, but as one of *us*. We-Talk is rich in the details and particularities that help us see ourselves in the lives of other people whom we might initially assume are nothing like us. We-Talk transforms once strange experiences into familiar ones.[249]

■ ■ ■

The United States of America remains one of the most improbable creations in human existence. That a small band of colonists could throw off the yoke of an empire; that we could survive a near apocalyptic Civil War; that we could expand the legal rights of women and minorities from virtual nothingness to near equality, is an improbable story indeed. That we could prevail in two cataclysmic world wars; land a man on the moon; and make breathtaking advances in medicine and the arts: truly amazing.

Yes, we have come far as a nation, yet we still have far to go. We are at a crossroad. We realize that we are a long way from full realization of our democratic ideals. And because we are conditioned by our consumer society to get everything we want and when we want it, we might be tempted to impatiently ask, "When will we get *there*?"

The answer in a democracy is as tragic as it is necessary. We never actually get *there*, but we do get closer, better at imagining *there*, better at bringing *there* to life.

But on our way *there*, shouldn't we—at this moment, at this crossroad—take time for an honest accounting of where we have been and what we have become? Should we not commit, once again, to making good on the promises that have made our American dream so sought after by people the world over?

ACCOUNTABLE aspires to help create a space for us to take a collective deep breath, to take that sober look at where we have been and who we are. We hope its stories—both inspiring and tragic—help you to historically exhale, then motivate you to take that next step with us as we continue our walk together along America's path. We have created a narrative that we hope, in turn, will create us.

8

Promises, Promises . . .

The *ACCOUNTABLE* Report Card

It is the job of politicians to make promises, but it is the job of the people who elect them to make sure they keep them. Presidential election seasons are the times in our politics when most promises are made. This was certainly the case in the run-up to the 2008 election, especially given the many crises our country continues to face.

That said, what follows are a series of easy-to-use charts that detail the promises made by President Barack Obama.

We hope these charts, in conjunction with the Frameworks for Assessment at the end of each chapter, will motivate all who read them to track the progress of the president's vision for our future.

Presidents alone do not shape our future. Congress and the courts can pass laws and hand down decisions that chip away at any president's promises. Nonetheless, citizens must always be prepared to hold the president accountable on what he (perhaps one day, she!) promised he'd fight for.

Never forget, we, the people, are *accountable* for making sure that promises made are promises kept.

HEALTH

"[M]y health care proposal will ask hospitals and providers
to collect, track, and publicly report measures of health
care quality. We'll provide the public with information
about preventable medical errors, nurse-to-patient ratios,
and hospital-acquired infections."[1]

Health Insurance

*Without health insurance, my kids and I won't be able to afford the care we need. How
will an Obama administration help us?*

PROVIDE UNIVERSAL HEALTH INSURANCE. "And we need to finally pass universal
health care so that every American has access to health insurance that they can afford, and our getting the preventive services that are the key to cutting health care
costs. That's what I pledge to do in my first term as president."[2] "I'll pass a universal health care bill that cuts a typical family's premiums by up to $2,500. And
mark my words—I will sign this bill by the end of my first term as president."[3]

MAKE INSURANCE AVAILABLE TO ALL WHO SEEK TO PURCHASE IT. "If
you are one of the 45 million Americans who don't have health insurance, you
will have it after this plan becomes law. No one will be turned away because of
a preexisting condition or illness. Everyone will be able to buy into a new health
insurance plan that's similar to the one that every federal employee . . . currently
has for themselves. It will cover all essential medical services, including preventive,
maternity, disease management, and mental health care. And it will also include
high standards for quality and efficiency."[4]

OFFER SUBSIDIES FOR THE UNINSURED. "If you cannot afford this insurance, you will receive a subsidy to pay for it. If you have children, they will be
covered. If you change jobs, your insurance will go with you. If you need to see
a doctor, you will not have to wait in long lines for one."[5]

SUPPORT THE ALREADY-INSURED. Under Obama's plan, "if you like your
current health insurance, nothing changes, except your costs will go down by as
much as $2,500 per year."[6]

EXPAND EXISTING PLANS. Obama will "expand eligibility for the SCHIP and Medicaid programs and ensure that these programs continue to serve their critical safety-net function."[7]

FOCUS ON PREVENTION. "Under my plan, we'll make sure insurance companies cover evidence-based, preventive care services—weight loss programs, smoking-cessation programs, and other efforts—to help people avoid costly, debilitating health problems in the first place."[8]

ESTABLISH A NATIONAL EXCHANGE. "Establish a National Health Insurance Exchange with a range of private insurance options as well as a new public plan based on benefits available to members of Congress that will allow individuals and small businesses to buy affordable health coverage."[9] "The Exchange will feature comprehensive benefits; affordable premiums, co-pays and deductibles, simplified paperwork, easy enrollment, and portability."[10]

MANDATE PAYROLL CONTRIBUTIONS. "Make employer contributions more fair by requiring large employers that do not offer coverage or make a meaningful contribution to the cost of quality health coverage for their employees to contribute a percentage of payroll toward the costs of their employees' health care."[11]

MAKE CHILD COVERAGE MANDATORY. Obama "will require that all children have health care coverage."[12]

SUPPORT MALPRACTICE INSURANCE. Obama will "strengthen antitrust laws to prevent insurers from overcharging physicians for their malpractice insurance."[13]

ACCOUNTABILITY:

☐ has fulfilled ALL his promises

☐ has fulfilled SOME promises

☐ FAILED to fulfill any promises

☐ has proceeded contrary to his promises

NOTE:

HEALTH

"[M]y health care proposal will ask hospitals and providers
to collect, track, and publicly report measures of health
care quality. We'll provide the public with information
about preventable medical errors, nurse-to-patient ratios,
and hospital-acquired infections."

Catastrophic Illness

*My Mom is more than sick—she has a chronic, terminal illness. How will President
Obama help her pay the bills?*

PAY FOR WORST ILLNESSES. "[W]e'll reduce costs for businesses and their
workers by picking up the tab for some of the most expensive illnesses. Right
now, the five percent of patients with the most serious illnesses like cancer and
heart disease account for nearly fifty percent of health care costs. Insurance companies devote the lion's share of their expenses to these patients, and then pass
the cost on to the rest of us in the form of higher premiums. Under my plan, the
federal government will pay for part of these catastrophic cases, which means that
your premiums will go down."[14]

REFORM BANKRUPTCY LAWS TO PROTECT FAMILIES FACING A MEDI-
CAL CRISIS. "We have to release people who are in bankruptcy as a consequence
of health care. We've got to give them a break."[15] Obama "will create an exemption in bankruptcy law for individuals who can prove they filed for bankruptcy
because of medical expenses. This exemption will create a process that forgives
the debt and lets the individuals get back on their feet."[16]

END CHERRY-PICKING. "Insurance companies spend $50 billion a year on
elaborate efforts to cherry-pick the healthiest patients and avoid covering everyone else. I intend to save them a whole lot of time and money by putting an end
to this practice once and for all."[17]

ACCOUNTABILITY:

☐ has fulfilled ALL his promises

☐ has fulfilled SOME promises

☐ FAILED to fulfill any promises

☐ has proceeded contrary to his promises

NOTE:

HEALTH

"[M]y health care proposal will ask hospitals and providers
to collect, track, and publicly report measures of health
care quality. We'll provide the public with information
about preventable medical errors, nurse-to-patient ratios,
and hospital-acquired infections."

Research Funding

How will an Obama administration advance medical science through research?

LIFT BAN ON STEM CELL RESEARCH. "I will lift the current administration's
ban on federal funding of research on embryonic stem-cell lines created after 9
August 2001 through executive order, and I will ensure that all research on stem
cells is conducted ethically and with rigorous oversight."[18]

SUPPORT STEM CELL RESEARCH ENHANCEMENT. "I am a proud supporter
of the Stem Cell Research Enhancement Act. The president was wrong to veto it,
and I will make sure that it is finally signed into law when I'm president."[19]

FUND DISEASE MANAGEMENT RESEARCH. "I will encourage the development of biological markers of disease that might simplify the evaluation of new
therapies, the use of genetic information to select patients most likely to benefit from new treatments, and the multidisciplinary efforts that are now possible
at many research centers. In addition, I will support increased attention to research that focuses on prevention, early detection, and improved management of
disease."[20]

Global Public Health

I hear a lot about the new "globalized economy," but I get the sense that health issues, too, know no borders. How will President Obama protect our nation's health, in the context of global health?

HELP ELIMINATE AIDS. Obama pledged to "increase spending on global HIV/ AIDS to $50 billion between 2009 and 2013, while at the same time increasing overall foreign assistance spending to $50 billion annually."[21]

FIGHT AGAINST DISEASE USED AS A WEAPON. "I will work with the international community to make any use of disease as a weapon declared a crime against humanity."[22]

COLLABORATE IN GLOBAL RESEARCH. "I will also encourage research collaboration in areas where multinational investments are essential, such as medical research on malaria and other diseases. These programs will be fully funded as a part of my strong commitment to double basic research budgets."[23]

ACCOUNTABILITY:

☐ has fulfilled ALL his promises

☐ has fulfilled SOME promises

☐ FAILED to fulfill any promises

☐ has proceeded contrary to his promises

NOTE:

HEALTH

"[M]y health care proposal will ask hospitals and providers to collect, track, and publicly report measures of health care quality. We'll provide the public with information about preventable medical errors, nurse-to-patient ratios, and hospital-acquired infections."

Lowering Costs

How will President Obama ensure that patients get the best bang for their buck?

PERMIT GENERIC IMPORTS. Obama promised to "lower drug costs by allowing the importation of safe medicines from other developed countries, increasing the use of generic drugs in public programs, and taking on drug companies that block cheaper generic medicines from the market."[24]

CONVERT PAPER RECORDS TO ELECTRONIC RECORDS. Obama will "invest $10 billion a year over the next five years to move the U.S. health care system to broad adoption of standards-based electronic health information systems, including electronic health records."[25]

REQUIRE THAT PLANS USE PROVEN METHODS. Obama will "require that plans that participate in the new public plan, Medicare, or the Federal Employees Health Benefits Program (FEHBP) utilize proven disease management programs. This will improve quality of care and lower costs as well."[26]

ALLOW DRUG PRICE NEGOTIATION. Obama will "repeal the ban on direct negotiation with drug companies and use the resulting savings, which could be as high as $30 billion, to further invest in improving health care coverage and quality."[27]

ACCOUNTABILITY:

☐ has fulfilled ALL his promises

☐ has fulfilled SOME promises

☐ FAILED to fulfill any promises

☐ has proceeded contrary to his promises

NOTE:

HEALTH

"[M]y health care proposal will ask hospitals and providers
to collect, track, and publicly report measures of health
care quality. We'll provide the public with information
about preventable medical errors, nurse-to-patient ratios,
and hospital-acquired infections."

Informing Patients

*While I'm no medical expert, I believe that knowledge is power. How will an Obama
administration encourage transparency among health care providers?*

ESTABLISH INSTITUTE ON COMPARATIVE EFFECTIVENESS. Obama will
"establish an independent institute to guide reviews and research on comparative
effectiveness, so that Americans and their doctors will have accurate and objective
information to make the best decisions for their health and well-being."[28]

PUBLICIZE HEALTH DATA. Obama will "require hospitals to collect and report health care cost and quality data. We'll provide the public with information
about preventable medical errors, nurse-to-patient ratios, and hospital-acquired
infections."[29] "Health plans will be required to disclose the percentage of premiums that actually goes to paying for patient care as opposed to administrative
costs."[30]

PUBLICIZE DISPARITY DATA. Obama will "challenge the medical system to
eliminate inequities in health care by requiring hospitals and health plans to collect, analyze, and report health care quality for disparity populations and holding
them accountable for any differences found: diversifying the workforce to ensure
culturally effective care . . . and supporting and expanding the capacity of safety-
net institutions, which provide a disproportionate amount of care for underserved
populations with inadequate funding and technical resources."[31]

PUBLICIZE MEDICAL ERRORS. Obama "will require providers to report preventable medical errors and support hospital and physician practice improvement
to prevent future errors."[32]

SHARE PROFITS. Obama will "prevent companies from abusing their monopoly power through unjustified price increases." In markets where the insurance business is not competitive, his plan will "force insurers to pay out a reasonable share of their premiums for patient care instead of keeping exorbitant amounts for profits and administration."[33]

ACCOUNTABILITY:

☐ has fulfilled ALL his promises

☐ has fulfilled SOME promises

☐ FAILED to fulfill any promises

☐ has proceeded contrary to his promises

NOTE:

EDUCATION

"As president, I will lead a new era of accountability in education. But see, I don't just want to hold our teachers accountable; I want to hold our government accountable. I want you to hold me accountable. And that's why every year I'm president, I will report back to you on the progress our schools are making because it's time to stop passing the buck on education and start accepting responsibility. And that's the kind of example I'll set as President of the United States."

Supporting Parents

President Obama has outlined his administration's support for schools and students. What about parents?

CREATE PARENTS' REPORT CARD. "I'll create a parents' report card that will show you whether your kid is on the path to college."[2]

EXPAND PAID MEDICAL LEAVE. "I'll expand the Family Medical Leave Act to include . . . millions more workers, to let parents participate in school activities with their kids. . . . [W]e'll . . . put federal support behind state efforts to provide paid . . . [l]eave."[3]

OFFER BETTER CHILD CARE. Obama will "provide affordable and high-quality child care to ease the burden on working families."[4] The Child Care Development Block Grant (CCDBG) program provides critical support to low-income families to pay for child care. Obama "will reverse this policy and ensure that CCDBG remains adequately funded every year."[5] He will also "double the resources for quality within CCDBG to support efforts such as developing quality rating systems for child care that reflect higher standards and supports for teacher training and professional development."[6]

EXPAND HOME VISITING PROGRAMS. Obama will "expand . . . home visiting programs to all low-income, first-time mothers, [programs that have empirically] improved women's prenatal health, . . . [reduced] childhood injuries, . . . increased maternal employment, and increased children's school readiness. The . . . plan will assist . . . 570,000 first-time mothers each year."[7]

PRESENT ANNUAL REPORT. Obama will "make federal education programs more performance-based and report results to the public and Congress at least once a year."[8]

ACCOUNTABILITY:

☐ has fulfilled ALL his promises

☐ has fulfilled SOME promises

☐ FAILED to fulfill any promises

☐ has proceeded contrary to his promises

NOTE:

EDUCATION

"As president, I will lead a new era of accountability in education. But see, I don't just want to hold our teachers accountable; I want to hold our government accountable. I want you to hold me accountable. And that's why every year I'm president, I will report back to you on the progress our schools are making because it's time to stop passing the buck on education and start accepting responsibility. And that's the kind of example I'll set as President of the United States."

Affording College

How will an Obama administration help me pay for college?

OFFER TAX CREDIT: $4K FOR 100 HOURS. "I want to give tax breaks to young people, in the form of an annual $4,000 tax credit"[9] that will be "available . . . at the time of enrollment by using prior year's tax data to deliver the credit at the time that tuition is due."[10] "Recipients of this credit will be required to conduct 100 hours of public service a year."[11]

PROVIDE 40,000 TEACHING SERVICE SCHOLARSHIPS: $25K EACH. These scholarships "cover four years of undergraduate or two years of graduate teacher education . . . for those who are willing to teach in a high-need field or location for at least four years."[12]

FUND PELL GRANTS. Obama will "ensure that the award keeps pace with the rising cost of college tuition."[13]

FUND VETERANS. "[F]or those who serve in our military, we'll cover all of your tuition with an even more generous 21st Century GI Bill."[14]

ELIMINATE FAFSA FORMS. Obama will "streamline the financial aid process by eliminating the current federal financial aid application [FAFSA—Free Application for Federal Student Aid] and enabling families to apply simply by checking a box on their tax form, authorizing their tax information to be used, and eliminating the need for a separate application."[15]

ELIMINATE FFEL PROGRAM. Obama will "eliminate the FFEL [Federal Family Education Loan] program that provides wasteful subsidies to banks and mandate that all federal student loans be provided through the direct loan program."[16]

CONSOLIDATE DIRECT LOAN PROGRAM. "It's really important that we revamp our college loan programs to free up more money for students. The direct loan program works extremely well—there doesn't appear to be a need for these student loan programs to be managed through banks and other private lenders. If we consolidate programs under the Direct Loan program, we would save $4.5 billion."[17]

ACCOUNTABILITY:

☐ has fulfilled ALL his promises

☐ has fulfilled SOME promises

☐ FAILED to fulfill any promises

☐ has proceeded contrary to his promises

NOTE:

EDUCATION

"As president, I will lead a new era of accountability in education. But see, I don't just want to hold our teachers accountable; I want to hold our government accountable. I want you to hold me accountable. And that's why every year I'm president, I will report back to you on the progress our schools are making because it's time to stop passing the buck on education and start accepting responsibility. And that's the kind of example I'll set as President of the United States."

Empowering Teachers

How will President Obama help teachers help students?

MANDATE ACCREDITATION. Obama will "require professional accreditation of all programs preparing teachers, with a focus on evidence regarding how well teachers are prepared."[18]

TRACK TEACHERS' PROGRESS. "Colleges of education and alternative licensure programs will track their graduates' entry and retention in teaching and their contributions to growth in student learning."[19]

OFFER CHALLENGE GRANTS. "Challenge grants will encourage the adoption of successful practices across the entire enterprise of teacher preparation."[20]

REFORM TEACHER EDUCATION: $100 MILLION. Obama will "provide $100 million to stimulate teacher education reforms built on school-university partnerships."[21]

OFFER BONUSES. "[W]e've got to provide bonuses for certain areas like math and science instruction where we just don't have enough teachers as well as bonuses for teachers who are willing to teach in tough settings."[22]

EXPAND TEACHER RESIDENCY PROGRAMS. Obama will expand the number of Teacher Residency Programs, especially in math and science, by providing funding for 200 new programs serving an average of 150 candidates each year. The plan will annually "supply 30,000 exceptionally well-prepared recruits to high-need schools to provide long-term commitment and leadership in these districts."[23]

SUPPORT CAREER LADDER INITIATIVE. "[W]e've got to have career ladders for teachers, so that if they become nationally board-certified, if they're learning new subject matter, if they are serving as a master teacher to help younger teachers, you know, that they get increased pay for those things that they're doing."[24] The program "provide[s] federal resources to states and districts to leverage state efforts to create strong mentoring that supports beginning teachers. It will provide $1 billion in funding for grants to create mentoring programs and reward veteran teachers for becoming mentors."[25]

DEVELOP CLASSROOM CORPS. Obama will establish a "Classroom Corps to help teachers and students, with a priority placed on high-need and underserved schools. The Corps will enlist retired or mid-career engineers and scientists to provide support for math and science teachers in the form of mentoring, student tutoring, curriculum development, and technology support. It will recruit neighborhood civic, business, and faith leaders to offer after-school programs and community service opportunities."[26]

PROVIDE TEACHING SERVICE SCHOLARSHIPS. Obama will "create substantial, sustained Teaching Service Scholarships that completely cover training costs in high-quality teacher preparation or alternative certification programs . . . for those who are willing to teach in a high-need field or location for at least four years. The scholarships will cover four years of undergraduate or two years of graduate teacher education, including programs for mid-career recruits in exchange for teaching for at least four years in a high-need field or location."[27]

ACCOUNTABILITY:

- ☐ has fulfilled ALL his promises
- ☐ has fulfilled SOME promises
- ☐ FAILED to fulfill any promises
- ☐ has proceeded contrary to his promises

NOTE:

EDUCATION

"As president, I will lead a new era of accountability in education. But see, I don't just want to hold our teachers accountable; I want to hold our government accountable. I want you to hold me accountable. And that's why every year I'm president, I will report back to you on the progress our schools are making because it's time to stop passing the buck on education and start accepting responsibility. And that's the kind of example I'll set as President of the United States."

Strengthening Our K–12 Schools

How will President Obama ensure that all children have access to an excellent, 21st-century education?

EXTEND LEARNING TIME. Longer school days or longer school years can help provide additional learning time for students to close the achievement gap. Obama will "create a $200 million grant program for states and districts that want to provide additional learning time for students in need."[28]

EXPAND SUMMER PROGRAMS. Obama called for expanding summer programs "so young people have a place to do homework and are not on the street getting into trouble."[29]

DOUBLE THE NUMBER OF CHARTER SCHOOLS. "[A]s president, I'll double the funding for responsible charter schools."[30]

CREATE INNOVATIVE SCHOOLS FUND. Obama will "create an Innovative Schools Fund to provide funds to states and school districts to implement plans to create a 'portfolio' of successful public school types, including charters, nonprofit schools, Montessori schools, career academies, and theme-focused schools."[31]

FOSTER COLLABORATION. Obama will "establish a competitive grant process open to existing or proposed public/private partnerships or entities that are pursuing evidence-based models that work—such as Diploma Plus or Teacher Advisor programs. These grants will decrease the dropout rate by increasing the capacity of state and district leaders as well as outside leaders—foundations, politicians, entrepreneurs, and community leaders—to collaborate on improving graduation rates."[32]

BE WARY OF VOUCHERS. "What I do oppose is using public money for private school vouchers. We need to focus on fixing and improving our public schools, not throwing our hands up and walking away from them."[33]

IMPROVE STEM EDUCATION. "I will support research to understand the strategies and mechanisms that bring lasting improvements to STEM [Science, Technology, Engineering, and Mathematics] education and ensure that promising practices are widely shared. This includes encouraging the development of cutting-edge STEM instructional materials and technologies, and working with educators to ensure that assessments measure the range of knowledge and skills needed for the 21st century. I will bring coherency to STEM education by increasing coordination of federal STEM education programs and facilitating cooperation among state efforts."[34]

DOUBLE R&D FUNDING. Obama promised to "double our investment in early education and educational R&D [Research and Development]" by the end of his first term in office. "Part of this investment will involve an R&D program for improving science education. This new program will build knowledge about strategies and mechanisms that can bring lasting improvements to science and math and technology education."[35]

INVEST IN INTERVENTION STRATEGIES. Obama will address the dropout crisis by pushing for his legislation "to provide funding to school districts to invest in intervention strategies in middle school—strategies such as personal academic plans, teaching teams, parent involvement, mentoring, intensive reading and math instruction, and extended learning time."[36]

DOUBLE AFTER-SCHOOL PROGRAMS. Obama will "double funding for the main federal support for after-school programs—the 21st Century Learning Centers program—to serve one million more children."[37]

SUPPORT COLLEGE READINESS: AP CLASSES. Obama will "create a national 'Make College A Reality' initiative that has a bold goal to increase students taking AP or college-level classes nationwide [to] 50 percent by 2016, and will build on [my] bipartisan proposal in the U.S. Senate to provide grants for students seeking college-level credit at community colleges if their school does not provide those resources."[38] "I'm calling for the creation of innovative—an Innovative Schools Fund. This fund will invest in schools like the Austin Polytechnical Institute, which is located in a part of Chicago that's been hard hit by the decline in manufacturing over the past few decades. . . . That's the kind of model we'll replicate across the country when I'm President of the United States."[39]

INVEST IN EARLY ASSESSMENT. Obama will "provide $25 million annually in matching funds for states to develop Early Assessment Programs. These funds will also promote state efforts to raise awareness about the availability of federal and state financial aid programs. . . . This program will increase college readiness and is voluntary."[40]

INVEST IN TECHNOLOGY. Obama will "build on existing federal education technology programs and create a $500 million matching fund to ensure technology is fully integrated throughout schools." He will also "create new technology-based curricula with leaders in the technology industry so schools can create courses around developing high-demand technology skills and working on authentic projects."[41]

REFORM NCLB. Obama pledged to "fix the failures of No Child Left Behind [NCLB] by providing the funding that was promised."[42] He will "reform NCLB, which starts by funding the law . . . [to] improve the assessments used to track student progress to measure readiness for college and the workplace, and improve student learning in a timely, individualized manner." He will also "improve NCLB's accountability system so that we are supporting schools that need improvement, rather than punishing them."[43]

ACCOUNTABILITY:

☐ has fulfilled ALL his promises

☐ has fulfilled SOME promises

☐ FAILED to fulfill any promises

☐ has proceeded contrary to his promises

NOTE:

EDUCATION

"As president, I will lead a new era of accountability in education. But see, I don't just want to hold our teachers accountable; I want to hold our government accountable. I want you to hold me accountable. And that's why every year I'm president, I will report back to you on the progress our schools are making because it's time to stop passing the buck on education and start accepting responsibility. And that's the kind of example I'll set as President of the United States."

Contributing to a College Education

How will President Obama support colleges?

ESTABLISH A COMMUNITY COLLEGE PARTNERSHIP PROGRAM. Obama will "create a Community College Partnership Program to strengthen community colleges by providing grants to (a) conduct more thorough analysis of the types of skills and technical education that are in high demand from students and local industry; (b) implement new associate of arts degree programs that cater to emerging industry and technical career demands; and (c) reward those institutions that graduate more students and also increase their numbers of transfer students to four-year institutions."[44]

OFFER NOT JUST WORK-STUDY, BUT *SERVE*-STUDY. Obama "believe[s] we need to move now to raise the service threshold to 25 percent so that more students can afford to engage in public service. This will help more than 200,000 college students a year complete part-time public service while they are in school. [I] will work to help colleges and universities reach the goal of 50 percent in serve-study."[45]

SUPPORT THE ROTC. Presidential debate moderator Tim Russert: "Senator Obama . . . [w]ill you vigorously enforce a statute which says colleges must allow military recruiters on campus and provide ROTC programs?" Senator Obama: "Yes."[46]

SUPPORT VIRTUAL LEARNING. Obama will "support efforts to allow students to take advantage of virtual learning opportunities for college credit, particularly in rural areas."[47]

CONTINUE AFFIRMATIVE ACTION. "So I still believe in affirmative action as a means of overcoming both historic and potentially current discrimination, but I think that it can't be a quota system and it can't be something that is simply applied without looking at the whole person, whether that person is black or white or Hispanic, male or female."[48] "At the college level, I will work to increase our number of science and engineering graduates, encourage undergraduates studying math and science to pursue graduate studies, and work to increase the representation of minorities and women in the science and technology pipeline, tapping the diversity of America to meet the increasing demand for a skilled workforce."[49]

ACCOUNTABILITY:

☐ has fulfilled ALL his promises

☐ has fulfilled SOME promises

☐ FAILED to fulfill any promises

☐ has proceeded contrary to his promises

NOTE:

EDUCATION

"As president, I will lead a new era of accountability in education. But see, I don't just want to hold our teachers accountable; I want to hold our government accountable. I want you to hold me accountable. And that's why every year I'm president, I will report back to you on the progress our schools are making because it's time to stop passing the buck on education and start accepting responsibility. And that's the kind of example I'll set as President of the United States."

Immigrant Education

I live in America, but I'm not an American citizen. Are my children included in your plan?

FOSTER BILINGUAL EDUCATION. Obama "support[s] transitional bilingual education and will help Limited English Proficient students get ahead by supporting and funding English Language Learner (ELL) classes." He will "support development of appropriate assessments for ELL students, monitor the progress of students learning English, and hold schools accountable for making sure these students complete school."[50]

ENCOURAGE TEACHING FOREIGN LANGUAGES. Obama maintains that teaching "[f]oreign languages is one of those areas that I think has been neglected. I want to put more resources into it."[51] "Something that we can do immediately that I think is very important is to pass the Dream Act, which allows children who through no fault of their own are here but have essentially grown up as Americans, allow them the opportunity for higher education."[52]

ACCOUNTABILITY:

☐ has fulfilled ALL his promises

☐ has fulfilled SOME promises

☐ FAILED to fulfill any promises

☐ has proceeded contrary to his promises

NOTE:

DIGITAL DIVIDE

"As president, I will set a simple goal: every American should have the highest-speed broadband access—no matter where you live, or how much money you have."[1]

Closing the Digital Divide

How will President Obama ensure that everyone has access to 21st-century technology?

EXPAND BROADBAND IN URBAN AMERICA. "Getting broadband Internet access into every home and business in urban America at an affordable rate could give low-income people increased opportunities to start businesses and engage actively in our communities."[2]

OFFER HIGHEST-SPEED BROADBAND FOR ALL. "We'll connect schools, libraries, and hospitals. And we'll take on special interests to unleash the power of wireless spectrum for our safety and connectivity."[3]

EQUIP SCHOOLS WITH SUPPLEMENTARY RESOURCES. "I will . . . make sure that there are adequate training and other supplementary resources to allow every school, library, and hospital to take full advantage of the broadband connectivity."[4]

REFORM UNIVERSAL SERVICE FUND. "I will reform the two major programs which can drive broadband into underserved communities. . . . [M]y administration will establish a multi-year plan with a date certain to change the Universal Service Fund program from one that supports voice communications to one that supports affordable broadband, with a specific focus on reaching previously unserved communities."[5]

ENCOURAGE COLLABORATION. "I will encourage innovation at the local level through federal support of public/private partnerships that deliver broadband to communities without real broadband."[6]

DEPLOY MODERN COMMUNICATIONS INFRASTRUCTURE. Obama believes "we can get true broadband to every community in America through a combination of . . . better use of the nation's wireless spectrum; promotion of next-generation facilities, technologies, and applications; and new tax and loan incentives."[7]

ACCOUNTABILITY:

☐ has fulfilled ALL his promises

☐ has fulfilled SOME promises

☐ FAILED to fulfill any promises

☐ has proceeded contrary to his promises

NOTE:

ECONOMY

"I think everybody understands at this point that we are experiencing the worst financial crisis since the Great Depression. And the financial rescue plan that Senator McCain and I supported is an important first step. . . . But what we haven't yet seen is a rescue package for the middle class. . . . So [from jobs to middle-class tax cuts for people making less than $200,000], I've proposed . . . specific things that I think can help."[1]

Taxes

Once President Obama is inaugurated, who will be eligible for tax relief? Which income brackets will be taxed more heavily after 2008 than before?

FAMILIES

REWARD WORKING FAMILIES. "I will reward work through a 'Making Work Pay' tax credit of $500 for American workers and $1,000 for working families. . . . What I've called for is a tax cut for 95 percent of working families."[2]

SUPPORT MIDDLE-INCOME FAMILIES. "If you're making less than $75,000 a year, we are proposing that we offset the payroll tax to give you relief, $1,000 for the average family."[3]

HELP FAMILIES EARNING LESS THAN $250K. "And if you make less than $250,000, less than a quarter-million dollars a year, then you will not see one dime's worth of tax increase."[4] "I can make a firm pledge: under my plan, no family making less than $250,000 will see their taxes increase—not your income taxes, not your payroll taxes, not your capital gains taxes, not any of your taxes."[5]

ENHANCE CHILD CARE CREDIT. Obama will "reform the Child and Dependent Care Tax Credit by making it refundable and allowing low-income families to receive up to a 50 percent credit for their child care expenses."[6]

BUSINESSES

SUPPORT START-UP COMPANIES. "I've also proposed exempting all start-up companies from capital gains taxes."[7] Obama would also "provide small businesses a refundable credit of up to 50 percent on premiums for employees."[8]

RESTRAIN COMPANIES THAT OUTSOURCE. Obama believes that "companies should not get billions of dollars in tax deductions for moving their operations overseas."[9]

TAX EXCESSIVE PROFITS OF OIL COMPANIES. "What I will do as president is tax the record profits of oil companies and use the money to help struggling families pay their energy bills."[10] Specifically, Obama will "enact a windfall profits tax on excessive oil company profits to give American families an immediate $1,000 emergency energy rebate to help families pay rising bills."[11]

RAISE CEO TAXES. "I will raise CEO taxes, no doubt about it."[12]

SHUT DOWN TAX HAVENS. "My opponent supports tax havens that let companies avoid paying taxes here in America—tax havens that cost $100 billion every year. But what will work is shutting those tax havens."[13]

EXTEND PRODUCTION TAX CREDIT. Obama will also "extend the Production Tax Credit, a credit used successfully by American farmers and investors to increase renewable energy production and create new local jobs."[14]

ACCOUNTABILITY:

☐ has fulfilled ALL his promises

☐ has fulfilled SOME promises

☐ FAILED to fulfill any promises

☐ has proceeded contrary to his promises

NOTE:

ECONOMY

"I think everybody understands at this point that we are experiencing the worst financial crisis since the Great Depression. And the financial rescue plan that Senator McCain and I supported is an important first step. . . . But what we haven't yet seen is a rescue package for the middle class. . . . So [from jobs to middle-class tax cuts for people making less than $200,000], I've proposed . . . specific things that I think can help."

Taxes

THE WEALTHY

END TAX BREAKS FOR WEALTHY AMERICANS. "[We'll save] money . . . by ending George Bush's tax breaks for people making more than $250,000 a year. They'll go back to paying similar rates to what they paid when Bill Clinton was president."[15]

REWORK FORMULA FOR PAYROLL TAXES. "What I have proposed is that we raise the cap on the payroll tax, because right now millionaires and billionaires don't have to pay beyond $97,000 a year."[16]

CAP FARM SUBSIDIES. "Congress subsidizes these big mega farms and hurts family farmers oftentimes in the process. And we've got to cap those subsidies so that we don't have continued concentration of agriculture in the hands of a few large agribusiness interests."[17]

RELIEF FOR ORDINARY FOLK

PROTECT SENIORS. "[I]f you're a senior citizen who is making less than $50,000 a year, or getting less than $50,000 in Social Security benefits, then you shouldn't have to pay taxes on that Social Security income."[18]

EXPAND EITC. "I'll expand the Earned Income Tax Credit—because it's one of the most successful anti-poverty measures we have"[19] to "benefit 12 million Americans."[20]

PROVIDE REBATE CHECKS. "What I can do—and what I will do—is push for a second stimulus package that will send out another round of rebate checks to the American people."[21]

FOR EVERYONE

SIMPLIFY TAX FORMS. Obama will "dramatically simplify tax filings so that millions of Americans will be able to do their taxes in less than five minutes." . . . He will "ensure that the IRS uses the information it already gets from banks and employers to give taxpayers the option of prefilled tax forms to verify, sign, and return."[22]

REVISE TAX CODE. "Right now, we have a tax code that gives incentives for companies to move offshore. Instead, we must have a tax code that rewards companies that are doing the right thing by investing in American workers and investing in research and development here in the United States."[23]

OFFER R&D TAX CREDIT. "I'll double federal funding for basic research and make the R&D tax credit permanent."[24]

DEFER 401(K) TAXES. "If they have a 401(k), then they are going to see those taxes deferred, and they're going to pay ordinary income when they finally cash out."[25]

BAN INTERNET-ONLY TAXES. "I support the moratorium on Internet-only taxes and will support all efforts to keep the Internet tax free."[26]

ACCOUNTABILITY:

☐ has fulfilled ALL his promises

☐ has fulfilled SOME promises

☐ FAILED to fulfill any promises

☐ has proceeded contrary to his promises

NOTE:

ECONOMY

"I think everybody understands at this point that we are
experiencing the worst financial crisis since the Great
Depression. And the financial rescue plan that Senator
McCain and I supported is an important first step. . . .
But what we haven't yet seen is a rescue package for the
middle class. . . . So [from jobs to middle-class tax cuts
for people making less than $200,000], I've proposed . . .
specific things that I think can help."

International Trade

How will an Obama administration improve America's international economic status?

ENFORCE TRADE AGREEMENTS. "Well . . . in a year's time, it'll be me who's
enforcing [the environmental and labor regulations associated with the Peru trade
agreement]. And so we're going to make sure that the right thing is being done."[27]
Obama will "pressure the World Trade Organization to enforce trade agreements
and stop countries from continuing unfair government subsidies to foreign export-
ers and nontariff barriers on U.S. exports."[28]

AMEND NAFTA. "There's no doubt that NAFTA needs to be amended. I've already said I would contact the president of Mexico and the prime minister of
Canada to make sure that labor agreements are enforceable. But I did want to just
go back briefly to the issue of trade and human rights that you had mentioned. We
have to stand for human rights, and that should be part of the trade equation."[29]

OPPOSE CAFTA. "I will fight against trade agreements that undermine American
competitiveness, and use trade as a tool to grow American jobs. I will use trade
agreements to spread good labor and environmental standards around the world
and stand firm against agreements like the Central American Free Trade Agreement (CAFTA) that fail to live up to those important benchmarks."[30]

ACCOUNTABILITY:

☐   has fulfilled ALL his promises

☐   has fulfilled SOME promises

☐   FAILED to fulfill any promises

☐   has proceeded contrary to his promises

NOTE:

ECONOMY

"I think everybody understands at this point that we are experiencing the worst financial crisis since the Great Depression. And the financial rescue plan that Senator McCain and I supported is an important first step. . . . But what we haven't yet seen is a rescue package for the middle class. . . . So [from jobs to middle-class tax cuts for people making less than $200,000], I've proposed . . . specific things that I think can help."

Credit Crisis

How will President Obama protect consumers from predatory lenders?

CAP OUTLANDISH INTEREST RATES ON PAYDAY LOANS; IMPROVE DIS-CLOSURE. Obama will "extend a 36-percent interest cap to all Americans. [He] will require lenders to provide clear and simplified information about loan fees, payments, and penalties, which is why [he]'ll require lenders to provide this information during the application process."[31]

INSTITUTE NATIONAL RATING SYSTEM. "To make sure that Americans know what they're signing up for, I'll institute a five-star rating system to inform consumers about the level of risk involved in every credit card."[32]

ESTABLISH CONSUMERS' BILL OF RIGHTS. Obama will "create a Credit Card Bill of Rights to protect consumers. The Obama plan will:

- Ban Unilateral Changes
- Apply Interest Rate Increases Only to Future Debt
- Prohibit Interest on Fees
- Prohibit 'Universal Defaults'
- Require Prompt and Fair Crediting of Cardholder Payments"[33]

ACCOUNTABILITY:

☐ has fulfilled ALL his promises

☐ has fulfilled SOME promises

☐ FAILED to fulfill any promises

☐ has proceeded contrary to his promises

NOTE:

ECONOMY

"I think everybody understands at this point that we are experiencing the worst financial crisis since the Great Depression. And the financial rescue plan that Senator McCain and I supported is an important first step. . . . But what we haven't yet seen is a rescue package for the middle class. . . . So [from jobs to middle-class tax cuts for people making less than $200,000], I've proposed . . . specific things that I think can help."

Social Security

How will President Obama handle Social Security?

PRIVATIZATION. "Number one, no privatization of Social Security, no privatization."[34]

Minimum Wage

I make barely enough money to support my family. Will President Obama fight for a living wage?

RAISE MINIMUM WAGE ANNUALLY. "I won't wait 10 years to raise the minimum wage—I'll guarantee that it goes up every single year."[35]

INDEX IT FOR INFLATION. "I will ensure that the minimum wage is indexed for inflation."[36]

ACCOUNTABILITY:

☐ has fulfilled ALL his promises

☐ has fulfilled SOME promises

☐ FAILED to fulfill any promises

☐ has proceeded contrary to his promises

NOTE:

ECONOMY

"I think everybody understands at this point that we are
experiencing the worst financial crisis since the Great
Depression. And the financial rescue plan that Senator
McCain and I supported is an important first step. . . .
But what we haven't yet seen is a rescue package for the
middle class. . . . So [from jobs to middle-class tax cuts
for people making less than $200,000], I've proposed . . .
specific things that I think can help."

Supporting Domestic Workers

How will President Obama create, and keep, jobs here at home?

CREATE MANUFACTURING STRATEGIES. To produce new products and new
jobs, Obama will "create an Advanced Manufacturing Fund to identify and invest
in the most compelling advanced manufacturing strategies."[37]

LIMIT OUTSOURCING. To help all workers adapt to a rapidly changing economy, Obama would "update the existing system of Trade Adjustment Assistance
by extending it to service industries, creating flexible education accounts to help
workers retrain, and providing retraining assistance for workers in sectors of the
economy vulnerable to dislocation before they lose their jobs."[38]

CREATE JOBS THROUGH INVESTMENT IN INFRASTRUCTURE. "As presi-
dent, I will launch a National Infrastructure Reinvestment Bank that will invest $60
billion over 10 years—a bank that can leverage private investment in infrastructure
improvements, and create nearly two million new jobs. The work will be determined by what will maximize our safety and security and ability to compete."[39]
"[W]e'll not only invest in rebuilding our crumbling roads and bridges, and our
outdated electricity grid, we'll strengthen the auto industry that built the middle
class in this country."[40]

PROTECT EXISTING JOBS THROUGH TWO $25 BILLION FUNDS. Obama will create a "$25 billion State Growth Fund to prevent state and local cuts in health, education, housing, and heating assistance or counterproductive increases in property taxes, tolls, or fees. . . . [It] will also include $25 billion in a Jobs and Growth Fund to prevent cutbacks in road and bridge maintenance and fund school repair—all to save more than 1 million jobs in danger of being cut."[41]

EXPAND FLEXIBLE WORK ARRANGEMENTS. Obama will "create a program to inform businesses about the benefits of flexible work schedules; help businesses create flexible work opportunities; and increase federal incentives for telecommuting." He will also "make the federal government a model employer in terms of adopting flexible work schedules and permitting employees to request flexible arrangements."[42]

SUPPORT WORKERS' RIGHTS. Obama supports "the right of workers to bargain collectively and strike if necessary. [I] will work to ban the permanent replacement of striking workers, so workers can stand up for themselves without worrying about losing their livelihoods."[43]

ADVOCATE FOR EFCA. Obama cosponsored and is a strong advocate for the Employee Free Choice Act [EFCA], a bipartisan effort to assure that workers can exercise their right to organize. He will "continue to fight for EFCA's passage and sign it into law."[44]

DOUBLE MEP FUNDING. Obama will "double funding for the Manufacturing Extension Partnership (MEP) . . . which works with manufacturers across the country to improve efficiency, implement new technology, and strengthen company growth. This highly successful program has engaged in more than 350,000 projects across the country and in 2006 alone, helped create and protect over 50,000 jobs."[45]

INCREASE FEDERAL WORKFORCE TRAINING FUNDING. Obama will "increase funding for federal workforce training programs and direct these programs to incorporate green technologies training, such as advanced manufacturing and weatherization training, into their efforts to help Americans find and retain stable, high-paying jobs. [He] will also create an energy-focused youth jobs program to invest in disconnected and disadvantaged youth."[46]

ACCOUNTABILITY:

- ☐ has fulfilled ALL his promises
- ☐ has fulfilled SOME promises
- ☐ FAILED to fulfill any promises
- ☐ has proceeded contrary to his promises

NOTE:

ECONOMY

"I think everybody understands at this point that we are
experiencing the worst financial crisis since the Great
Depression. And the financial rescue plan that Senator
McCain and I supported is an important first step. . . .
But what we haven't yet seen is a rescue package for the
middle class. . . . So [from jobs to middle-class tax cuts
for people making less than $200,000], I've proposed . . .
specific things that I think can help."

Supporting Domestic Workers

CREATE RPS. Obama will "create a federal Renewable Portfolio Standard (RPS)
that will require 25 percent of American electricity be derived from renewable
sources by 2025, which has the potential to create hundreds of thousands of new
jobs on its own."[47]

CREATE NATIONAL NETWORK OF BUSINESS INCUBATORS. Obama will
support entrepreneurship and spur job growth by creating a national network of
public/private business incubators. Business incubators facilitate the critical work
of entrepreneurs in creating start-up companies. Obama will "invest $250 million
per year to increase the number and size of incubators in disadvantaged communities throughout the country."[48]

ACCOUNTABILITY:

☐   has fulfilled ALL his promises

☐   has fulfilled SOME promises

☐   FAILED to fulfill any promises

☐   has proceeded contrary to his promises

NOTE:

ECONOMY

"I think everybody understands at this point that we are
experiencing the worst financial crisis since the Great
Depression. And the financial rescue plan that Senator
McCain and I supported is an important first step. . . .
But what we haven't yet seen is a rescue package for the
middle class. . . . So [from jobs to middle-class tax cuts
for people making less than $200,000], I've proposed . . .
specific things that I think can help."

Keeping Our Homes

How will an Obama administration help ordinary people pay for and stay in their homes?

URGE GOVERNMENT TO PURCHASE MORTGAGES DIRECTLY. "[W]e should consider giving the government the authority to purchase mortgages directly instead of simply purchasing mortgage-backed securities." Obama will "encourage Treasury to study the option of buying individual mortgages like we did successfully in the 1930s."[49]

MANDATE ACCURATE LOAN DISCLOSURE. Obama will "create a Homeowner Obligation Made Explicit (HOME) score, which will provide potential borrowers with a simplified, standardized borrower metric (similar to APR) for home mortgages. The HOME score will allow individuals to easily compare various mortgage products and understand the full cost of the loan."[50]

CLOSE BANKRUPTCY LOOPHOLE FOR MORTGAGE COMPANIES. Obama will "work to eliminate the provision that prevents bankruptcy courts from modifying an individual's mortgage payments."[51]

CREATE UNIVERSAL MORTGAGE CREDIT. Obama will "create a 10 percent universal mortgage credit to provide tax relief to homeowners who do not itemize. This credit will provide an average of $500 to 10 million homeowners, the majority of whom earn less than $50,000 per year."[52]

ESTABLISH FORECLOSURE FUND. "For homeowners facing foreclosure through no fault of their own, we'll create a fund and reform bankruptcy laws to give them a shot at avoiding foreclosure."[53]

MANDATE MORTGAGE OPTION INFORMATION. "We'll mandate that prospective homebuyers have access to accurate and complete information about their mortgage options."[54]

ACCOUNTABILITY:

☐ has fulfilled ALL his promises

☐ has fulfilled SOME promises

☐ FAILED to fulfill any promises

☐ has proceeded contrary to his promises

NOTE:

AFFORDABLE HOUSING

"Yes, we need to fight poverty, . . . fight crime. But we also
need to stop seeing our cities as the problem and start
seeing them as the solution. Because strong cities are the
building blocks of strong regions, and strong regions are
essential for a strong America."[1]

Strengthening Infrastructure

How will an Obama administration help repair our inner cities' buildings and roads?

STRENGTHEN CITY INFRASTRUCTURE. Obama will "open a national bank,
seeded with $60 billion over 10 years, to finance road, bridge, airport, and other
public works projects in metropolitan areas. The bank would be modeled on the
Federal Deposit Insurance Corp., with an independent board of directors."[2]

REPAIR AND IMPROVE TRANSPORTATION. Obama "believes that we must
devote substantial resources to repairing our roads and bridges. [I] also believe that
we must devote significantly more attention to investments that will make it easier
for us to walk, bicycle, and access other transportation alternatives. [I am] committed to reforming federal transportation funding and leveling employer incentives
for driving and public transit."[3]

ACCOUNTABILITY:

☐   has fulfilled ALL his promises

☐   has fulfilled SOME promises

☐   FAILED to fulfill any promises

☐   has proceeded contrary to his promises

NOTE:

AFFORDABLE HOUSING

"Yes, we need to fight poverty, . . . fight crime. But we also
need to stop seeing our cities as the problem and start
seeing them as the solution. Because strong cities are the
building blocks of strong regions, and strong regions are
essential for a strong America."

Offer Real Opportunity to Our Youth

How will an Obama administration create opportunities for our young people?

CREATE PROMISE NEIGHBORHOODS. Obama will "create 20 Promise Neighborhoods in areas that have high levels of poverty and crime and low levels of student academic achievement in cities across the nation. The Promise Neighborhoods
will be modeled after the Harlem Children's Zone, which provides a full network of
services, including early childhood education, youth violence prevention efforts, and
after-school activities, to an entire neighborhood from birth to college."[4]

END THE DANGEROUS CYCLE OF YOUTH VIOLENCE. Obama will "sup-
port innovative local programs, such as the CeaseFire program in Chicago, that
have been proven to work. Such programs implement a comprehensive public
health approach that implements a community-based strategy to prevent youth
violence. [I] will also double funding for federal after-school programs and invest
in 20 Promise Neighborhoods across the country to ensure that urban youth have
meaningful opportunities to succeed."[5]

ACCOUNTABILITY:

☐   has fulfilled ALL his promises

☐   has fulfilled SOME promises

☐   FAILED to fulfill any promises

☐   has proceeded contrary to his promises

NOTE:

AFFORDABLE HOUSING

"Yes, we need to fight poverty, . . . fight crime. But we also need to stop seeing our cities as the problem and start seeing them as the solution. Because strong cities are the building blocks of strong regions, and strong regions are essential for a strong America."

Create White House Office of Urban Policy

In what ways will President Obama institutionalize his commitment to urban policy reform?

CREATE A WHITE HOUSE OFFICE OF URBAN POLICY. "I will also create a White House Office of Urban Policy and have the Director of that Office report directly to me."[6] The office will "develop a strategy for metropolitan America and ensure that all federal dollars targeted to urban areas are effectively spent on the highest-impact programs."[7]

Supporting Local Businesses

How will an Obama administration encourage rich retail options?

STRENGTHEN BUSINESS CLIMATE. "When I'm president, I'll make sure that every community has the access to the capital and resources it needs to create a stronger business climate by providing more loans to small businesses and setting up the financial institutions that can help get them started. I'll also create a national network of business incubators, which are local services that help first-time business owners design their business plans, find the best location, and receive expert advice on how to run their businesses whenever they need it."[8]

ACCOUNTABILITY:

☐   has fulfilled ALL his promises

☐   has fulfilled SOME promises

☐   FAILED to fulfill any promises

☐   has proceeded contrary to his promises

NOTE:

RURAL AREAS

"Legalized discrimination—where blacks were prevented, often through violence, from owning property, or loans were not granted to African American business owners, or black homeowners could not access FHA mortgages, or blacks were excluded from unions or the police force or the fire department—meant that black families could not amass any meaningful wealth to bequeath to future generations. That history helps explain the wealth and income gap between blacks and whites, and the concentrated pockets of poverty that persist in so many of today's urban and rural communities."[1]

Rural Education

How will President Obama ensure that his education plan reaches rural areas?

ENCOURAGE ADVANCED PLACEMENT CREDITS. "I've worked with Republican Senator Jim DeMint [of South Carolina] on a bill that would challenge high school students to take college-level courses and make sure low-income neighborhoods and rural communities have access to those courses, and I'll make it the law of the land when I'm president."[2]

ESTABLISH TEACHING SERVICE SCHOLARSHIPS. Obama will "create . . . [s]cholarships that completely cover training costs . . . for those who are willing to teach in a high-need field or location for at least four years."[3]

EMPLOY 21ST CENTURY TECHNOLOGY. Obama will "establish a multi-year plan with a date certain to [ensure that the] Universal Service Fund program . . . supports affordable broadband [in] unserved communities."[4]

IMPROVE RURAL EDUCATION. Obama will "provide . . . increased pay for teachers who work in rural areas. [I] will create a Rural Revitalization Program to attract and retain young people to rural America. [I] will [also] increase research and educational funding for Land Grant colleges."[5]

ACCOUNTABILITY:

☐   has fulfilled ALL his promises

☐   has fulfilled SOME promises

☐   FAILED to fulfill any promises

☐   has proceeded contrary to his promises

NOTE:

RURAL AREAS

"Legalized discrimination—where blacks were prevented,
often through violence, from owning property, or loans
were not granted to African American business owners,
or black homeowners could not access FHA mortgages,
or blacks were excluded from unions or the police force
or the fire department—meant that black families could
not amass any meaningful wealth to bequeath to future
generations. That history helps explain the wealth
and income gap between blacks and whites, and the
concentrated pockets of poverty that persist in so many
of today's urban and rural communities."

Agribusiness

President Obama will work with our urban areas, but what will he do for farmers?

PROTECT FAMILY FARMERS. Obama will "implement a $250,000 payment limitation so that we help family farmers—not large corporate agribusiness. [I] will close the loopholes that allow mega farms to get around the limits by subdividing their operations into multiple paper corporations."[6]

CAP FARM SUBSIDIES. Obama will "cap mega farm subsidies so that we don't have continued concentration of agriculture in the hands of a few large agribusiness interests."[7]

PROMOTE COMPETITION. Obama "support[s the] . . . packer ban. . . . [I] . . . will strengthen antimonopoly laws and . . . producer protections to ensure independent farmers have fair access to markets, control over their production decisions, and transparency in prices."[8]

DEVELOP THE NEXT GENERATION OF FARMERS. Obama will "establish a new program to identify and train the next generation of farmers. [I] will also provide tax incentives to make it easier for new farmers to afford their first farm."[9]

INCREASE INCENTIVES. Obama will "increase incentives for farmers . . . to conduct sustainable agriculture and protect wetlands, grasslands, and forests."[10]

ACCOUNTABILITY:

☐   has fulfilled ALL his promises

☐   has fulfilled SOME promises

☐   FAILED to fulfill any promises

☐   has proceeded contrary to his promises

NOTE:

RURAL AREAS

"Legalized discrimination—where blacks were prevented, often through violence, from owning property, or loans were not granted to African American business owners, or black homeowners could not access FHA mortgages, or blacks were excluded from unions or the police force or the fire department—meant that black families could not amass any meaningful wealth to bequeath to future generations. That history helps explain the wealth and income gap between blacks and whites, and the concentrated pockets of poverty that persist in so many of today's urban and rural communities."

Rural Economic Development

How will an Obama administration grow the rural economy?

SUPPORT SMALL BUSINESS DEVELOPMENT. Obama will "provide capital for farmers to create value-added enterprises, like cooperative marketing initiatives and farmer-owned processing plants. [I] also will establish a small business and micro-enterprise initiative for rural America."[11]

CONNECT RURAL AMERICA. Obama will "ensure that rural Americans have access to a modern communications infrastructure. [I] will modernize an FCC program that supports rural phone service so that it promotes affordable broadband coverage across rural America as well."[12]

UPGRADE RURAL INFRASTRUCTURE. Obama will "invest in the core infrastructure, roads, bridges, locks, dams, water systems, and essential air service that rural communities need."[13]

Miscellaneous

COMBAT METHAMPHETAMINE. "As president, I will continue the fight to rid our communities of meth and offer support to help addicts heal."[14]

IMPROVE HEALTH CARE. Obama will "work to ensure a more equitable Medicare and Medicaid reimbursement structure. [I] will attract providers to rural America by creating a loan forgiveness program for doctors and nurses who work in underserved rural areas. [I] support increasing rural access to care by promoting health information technologies like telemedicine."[15]

ACCOUNTABILITY:

☐   has fulfilled ALL his promises

☐   has fulfilled SOME promises

☐   FAILED to fulfill any promises

☐   has proceeded contrary to his promises

NOTE:

CRIMINAL JUSTICE

"We will have to confront the biases in our criminal justice
system, but we will also have to acknowledge the deep-
seated violence that still resides in our own communities
and marshal the will to break its grip."[1]

Reducing Crack or Cocaine Abuse

*How will an Obama administration rectify the sentencing disparities between crack
and cocaine?*

ELIMINATE CRACK/COCAINE SENTENCING DISPARITY. Obama "believes
the disparity between sentencing crack and powder-based cocaine is wrong and
should be completely eliminated"[2] and "will work in a bipartisan way to eliminate
these disparities."[3]

RECONSIDER SENTENCING FOR FIRST-TIME OFFENDERS. Obama "will
also repeal the mandatory minimum sentence for first-time offenders convicted of
simple possession of crack, as crack is the only drug that a nonviolent first-time
offender can receive a mandatory minimum sentence for possessing."[4]

Reviewing Mandatory Minimums

Are mandatory minimums here to stay under President Obama?

REVIEW SENTENCING GUIDELINES. Obama "will immediately review . . .
sentences to see where we can be smarter on crime and reduce the ineffective
warehousing of nonviolent drug offenders."[5]

ACCOUNTABILITY:

☐   has fulfilled ALL his promises

☐   has fulfilled SOME promises

☐   FAILED to fulfill any promises

☐   has proceeded contrary to his promises

NOTE:

CRIMINAL JUSTICE

"We will have to confront the biases in our criminal justice
system, but we will also have to acknowledge the deep-
seated violence that still resides in our own communities
and marshal the will to break its grip."

Ending Drug Abuse

Will President Obama regard drug abuse as a crime or an illness?

OFFER REHAB FOR FIRST-TIME OFFENDERS. "And we will give first-time,
nonviolent drug offenders a chance to serve their sentence, where appropriate, in
the type of drug rehabilitation programs that have proven to work better than a
prison term in changing bad behavior. So let's reform this system. Let's do what's
smart. Let's do what's just."[6]

EXPAND DRUG COURTS. Obama will "replicate [drug courts] within the federal
criminal justice system by signing a law that would authorize federal magistrates
to preside over drug courts and federal probation officers to oversee the offenders'
compliance with drug treatment programs."[7]

FIGHT METHAMPHETAMINE. "As president, I will continue the fight to rid
our communities of meth and offer support to help addicts heal and to reduce the
demand for the drug. I will work to cut off drug lab supplies by restricting global
imports of precursor chemicals, and I will take on the Mexican drug cartels in
partnership with Mexico and other nations in the region."[8]

PROMOTE ANTIDRUG HEMISPHERIC PACT. "I will direct my attorney general and homeland security secretary to meet with their Latin American and Caribbean counterparts in the first year of my presidency to produce a regional
strategy to combat drug trafficking, domestic and transnational gang activity, and
organized crime. A hemispheric pact on security, crime, and drugs will permit the
United States, Latin America, and the Caribbean to advance serious and measurable drug demand reduction goals, while fostering cooperation on intelligence and
investigating criminal activity."[9]

PROMOTE ANTICORRUPTION, POLICE REFORM. "The United States will also work to strengthen civilian law enforcement and judicial institutions in the region by promoting anticorruption safeguards and police reform."[10]

SUPPORT CROSS-BORDER AGREEMENTS. "I will . . . support the efforts of our border states to foster cooperation and constructive engagement with the region. . . . The . . . partnership[s]—based on information sharing, technical assistance, and training—provide an excellent model for regional cooperation on security issues. An Obama and Biden administration will support these initiatives and will work to integrate these efforts into the region's coordinated security pact."[11]

FUND BYRNE-JAG PROGRAM. "As president, I will restore funding to this critical program."[12] "Funding the Byrne Justice Assistance Grant (Byrne-JAG) Program is essential to avoid law enforcement layoffs and cuts to hundreds of antidrug and antigang efforts across the country. . . . Byrne-JAG also funds prevention and drug treatment programs that are critical to reducing the U.S. demand for drugs."[13]

ADVOCATE FOR ADDITIONAL REFORM EFFORTS. "I would . . . ensure that Congress robustly funds prevention and treatment programs like the Second Chance Act, Drug Courts, and the Drug Free Communities Support Program. . . . I will continue to support (and, in the case of drug courts, expand) these programs as president."[14]

BAR MEDICAL MARIJUANA RAIDS. "I would not have the Justice Department prosecuting and raiding medical marijuana users. It's not a good use of our resources."[15]

ACCOUNTABILITY:

☐ has fulfilled ALL his promises

☐ has fulfilled SOME promises

☐ FAILED to fulfill any promises

☐ has proceeded contrary to his promises

NOTE:

CRIMINAL JUSTICE

"We will have to confront the biases in our criminal justice
system, but we will also have to acknowledge the deep-
seated violence that still resides in our own communities
and marshal the will to break its grip."

Recruiting Public Defenders

*I read recently that public defenders' offices are understaffed and overburdened. How
will President Obama ease the load?*

FORGIVE LOANS. "We'll recruit more public defenders to the profession by for-
giving college and law school loans."[16] "[We] will work to improve the quality
of our nation's public defenders by creating loan-forgiveness programs for law
students who enter this field."[17]

Ending Racial Profiling

*I've been stopped driving while black, shopping while black—and seemingly breathing
while black! What will an Obama administration do to halt this unfair practice?*

BAN RACIAL PROFILING. As president, Obama will "continue his decades-long
fight against racial profiling and sign legislation that will ban the practice of racial
profiling by federal law enforcement agencies and provide federal funding to state
and local police departments if they adopt policies to prohibit the practice."[18]

COORDINATE WITH CIVIL RIGHTS DIVISION. "We know that in our criminal justice system, African Americans and whites, for the same crime, are arrested
at very different rates, are convicted at very different rates, receive very different
sentences . . . [t]hat is something that we have to talk about. But that's a substantive issue and it has to do with how do we pursue racial justice. If I am president, I
will have a civil rights division that is working with local law enforcement so that
they are enforcing laws fairly and justly."[19]

ACCOUNTABILITY:

☐   has fulfilled ALL his promises

☐   has fulfilled SOME promises

☐   FAILED to fulfill any promises

☐   has proceeded contrary to his promises

NOTE:

CRIMINAL JUSTICE

"We will have to confront the biases in our criminal justice system, but we will also have to acknowledge the deep-seated violence that still resides in our own communities and marshal the will to break its grip."

Fighting Hate Crimes

Violence seems worse somehow when it's perpetrated in the name of racial hatred. Will President Obama acknowledge that hate crimes deserve special, separate recognition?

EXPAND HATE CRIMES LEGISLATION. Obama "will strengthen federal hate crimes legislation [and] expand hate crimes protection by passing the Matthew Shepard Act [named for the gay Wyoming student murdered in 1998]."[20]

PRIORITIZE PROSECUTION OF HATE CRIME. "As president, [I] will ensure that the Criminal Section of the Civil Rights Division makes hate crime a priority."[21]

Supporting Ex-Offenders

How will an Obama administration prepare convicts to reenter society as rehabilitated, productive citizens?

PROVIDE JOB TRAINING. "[W]e'll provide job training for ex-offenders [so that] . . . they don't return to a life of crime."[22]

CREATE JOBS. Obama will "create a prison-to-work incentive program, modeled on the Welfare-to-Work Partnership, to create ties with employers, third-party agencies that provide training and support services to ex-offenders, and to improve ex-offender employment and job retention rates."[23]

REDUCE INSTITUTIONAL BARRIERS. Obama will "reduce bureaucratic barriers at state correctional systems that prevent former inmates from finding . . . employment."[24]

FUND TRANSITIONAL WORK. "I will increase funding for transitional jobs and career pathways programs, and I'll provide greater supports for ex-offenders and their families."[25]

FUND COUNSELING. Obama "will provide . . . substance abuse and mental health counseling to ex-offenders so that they are successfully reintegrated into society."[26]

ACCOUNTABILITY:

☐ has fulfilled ALL his promises

☐ has fulfilled SOME promises

☐ FAILED to fulfill any promises

☐ has proceeded contrary to his promises

NOTE:

CRIMINAL JUSTICE

"We will have to confront the biases in our criminal justice system, but we will also have to acknowledge the deep-seated violence that still resides in our own communities and marshal the will to break its grip."

Reducing Gun Violence

How will President Obama get guns out of our neighborhoods?

SUPPORT GUN TRACEABILITY. Obama will "repeal the Tiahrt Amendment, which restricts the ability of local law enforcement to access important gun trace information, and give police officers across the nation the tools they need to solve gun crimes and fight the illegal arms trade."[27]

CLOSE LOOPHOLES. Obama "support[s] closing the gun show loophole."[28] He believes local communities can "take those illegal handguns off the streets . . . and crack down on the various loopholes that exist in terms of background checks for children [and] the mentally ill."[29]

MAKE ASSAULT WEAPONS BAN PERMANENT. Obama also supports "making the expired federal Assault Weapons Ban permanent, as such weapons belong on foreign battlefields and not on our streets."[30]

MAKE GUNS CHILDPROOF. Obama supports "making guns in this country childproof."[31]

ENFORCE EXISTING GUN LAWS. "We've got to enforce the gun laws that are on the books. We've got to make sure that unscrupulous gun dealers aren't loading up vans and dumping guns in our communities, because we know they're not made in our communities."[32]

Miscellaneous

HELP ESTABLISH NCCIPS. Obama "fully support[s] . . . establishing a National Commission on Crime Intervention and Prevention Strategies (NCCIPS). . . . [It] will investigate approaches that are successful and help state and local law enforcement implement these effective strategies to fight and prevent crime. [It] will also tackle the new 21st-century crime and homeland security challenges the country faces."[33]

END THE DANGEROUS CYCLE OF YOUTH VIOLENCE. As president, Obama will "support innovative local programs such as the CeaseFire program in Chicago that have been proven to work. Such programs implement a comprehensive public health approach that implements a community-based strategy to prevent youth violence. [I] will also double funding for federal after-school programs and invest in 20 Promise Neighborhoods across the country to ensure that urban youth have meaningful opportunities to succeed."[34]

ACCOUNTABILITY:

☐ has fulfilled ALL his promises

☐ has fulfilled SOME promises

☐ FAILED to fulfill any promises

☐ has proceeded contrary to his promises

NOTE:

COMMUNITY POLICING

"If I am president, I will reestablish the federal
partnership with state, local, and tribal law enforcement
by funding the Byrne Justice Assistance Grants [and]
the COPS program."[1]

COPS Program

How will an Obama administration help local communities and law enforcement officials trust each other and collaborate on reducing crime in their communities?

RESTORE FUNDING TO COPS PROGRAM. Obama is "committed to fully funding the COPS [Community Oriented Policing Services] program to combat crime and help address police brutality and accountability issues in local communities. [In addition to putting 50,000 officers on the street,[2] it] . . . provides local law enforcement funding for:

- hiring and training law enforcement officers;

- procuring equipment and support systems;

- paying officers to perform intelligence, anti-terror, or homeland security duties; and

- developing new technologies, including inter-operable communications and forensic technology."[3]

INVEST IN COMMUNITY POLICING. "[W]e must stand for more than force; we must support the rule of law from the bottom up. That means more investments in prevention and prosecutors; in community policing and an independent judiciary."[4]

CREATE "COPS FOR KATRINA." "[I]nstead of unsafe streets and shocking crimes, we will help New Orleans rebuild its criminal justice system. We'll start a new 'COPS for Katrina' program to put more resources into community policing, so that heroic officers . . . have more support."[5]

ACCOUNTABILITY:

☐   has fulfilled ALL his promises

☐   has fulfilled SOME promises

☐   FAILED to fulfill any promises

☐   has proceeded contrary to his promises

NOTE:

ENERGY

"I consider energy to be one of the three most important issues that we're facing domestically."[1]

Carbon

What are President Obama's positions on carbon?

IMPOSE CARBON TAXES. "I believe that, depending on how it is designed, a carbon tax accomplishes much of the same thing that a cap-and-trade program accomplishes. . . . So as I roll out my proposals for a cap-and-trade system, I will price permits so that [they have] much of the same effect as a carbon tax."[2]

FIGHT FOR LCFS. "I believe I am the only candidate who has proposed a National Low Carbon Fuel Standard [LCFS]. . . . My LCFS provides a way for us to better understand the impacts of an advanced biofuels industry on the environment, so that as we move forward on cellulosics and other domestic fuels, we do so responsibly."[3] "The standard requires fuels suppliers in 2010 to begin to reduce the carbon of their fuel by 5 percent within five years and 10 percent within 10 years."[4]

ACCOUNTABILITY:

☐ has fulfilled ALL his promises

☐ has fulfilled SOME promises

☐ FAILED to fulfill any promises

☐ has proceeded contrary to his promises

NOTE:

ENERGY

"I consider energy to be one of the three most important
issues that we're facing domestically."

Emissions

How will an Obama administration keep greenhouse gas emissions under control?

REDUCE GREENHOUSE GASES. Obama has committed to "setting a goal of an 80 percent reduction in greenhouse gas emissions"[5] . . . "below 1990 levels"[6] . . . by 2050.[7] "I will start reducing emissions immediately by establishing strong annual reduction targets with an intermediate goal of reducing emissions to 1990 levels by 2020."[8]

MAKE POLLUTERS PAY. "All polluters will have to pay based on the amount of pollution they release into the sky. . . . [N]o business will be allowed to emit any greenhouse gases for free."[9]

ENFORCE CAP AND TRADE. "My cap-and-trade system will require all pollution credits to be auctioned [100 percent of them]."[10] "A small portion of the receipts generated by auctioning allowances ($15 billion per year) will be used to support the development of clean energy and energy efficiency. All remaining receipts will be used for rebates and other transition relief to ensure that families and communities are not adversely impacted by the transition to a new energy, low-carbon economy."[11]

SUPPORT CLIMATE SCIENCE. "I will fully support scientific efforts to understand climate change and [its] effects. . . . I will depoliticize climate science in the federal government and ensure that our policymakers rely on the best scientifically based evidence available. I will also expand on existing federal efforts to examine climate science, ensure that there is greater cooperation across the relevant federal agencies that already analyze aspects of climate science, and seek to bolster U.S. engagement in international climate science initiatives."[12]

ACHIEVE CARBON NEUTRALITY BY 2030. Obama will "establish a goal of making all new buildings carbon neutral, or produce zero emissions, by 2030."[13]

ENGAGE AGAIN WITH THE UNFCC. Obama will "re-engage with the U.N. Framework Convention on Climate Change (UNFCC), the main international forum dedicated to addressing the climate problem."[14]

CONVENE EMITTING NATIONS. Obama will "invigorate the Major Economies (MEM) effort and bring all the major emitting nations together to develop effective emissions reduction efforts."[15]

ACCOUNTABILITY:

☐ has fulfilled ALL his promises

☐ has fulfilled SOME promises

☐ FAILED to fulfill any promises

☐ has proceeded contrary to his promises

NOTE:

ENERGY

"I consider energy to be one of the three most important
issues that we're facing domestically."

Collaboration

*Energy problems are global, and we'll need an international team to combat them.
How will President Obama ensure that when it comes to the environment, the United
States doesn't go it alone?*

CREATE GLOBAL ENERGY FORUM. "I will . . . engage China and India in
global climate-change reduction efforts, and I will create a 'global energy forum'—
[that] will include the world's highest emitters . . . to apply pressure to developed
and developing nations alike to meaningfully reduce their carbon emissions. I will
also re-engage the United States with the post-Kyoto international climate negotiations to restore U.S. leadership and pressure on the rest of the world to take
similar steps to combat this truly global problem."[16]

WORK WITH REPUBLICANS—AND EVERYBODY ELSE. "From the moment
I take office as president, I will call together scientists and entrepreneurs; heads of
industry and labor; Democrats, Republicans, and Americans from all walks of life
to help develop and deploy the next generation of energy that will allow us to
build the next generation's economy."[17]

INFORM THE PUBLIC. "I will report to the American people every year on the
State of Our Energy Future and let you know the progress we've made toward an
80 percent emissions reduction by 2050, toward replacing over a third of our oil
consumption by 2030, and toward improving our energy efficiency 50 percent
by 2030."[18]

ACCOUNTABILITY:

☐ has fulfilled ALL his promises

☐ has fulfilled SOME promises

☐ FAILED to fulfill any promises

☐ has proceeded contrary to his promises

NOTE:

ENERGY

"I consider energy to be one of the three most important
issues that we're facing domestically."

Investing in New Technologies

*How will an Obama administration keep us on the cutting edge of environmentally
protective technologies?*

INVEST $150 BILLION IN CLEAN ENERGY R&D. "I've talked about spending $150 billion over 10 years in an Apollo Project, a Manhattan Project to create the alternative energy strategies"[19] that "will generate five million new jobs that pay well and can't ever be outsourced."[20] "This research will cover:

- Basic research to develop alternative fuels and chemicals;

- Equipment and designs that can greatly reduce energy use in residential and commercial buildings—both new and existing;

- New vehicle technologies capable of significantly reducing our oil consumption;

- Advanced energy storage and transmission that would greatly help the economies of new electric-generating technologies and plug-in hybrids;

- Technologies for capturing and sequestering greenhouse gases produced by coal plants; and

- A new generation of nuclear electric technologies that address cost, safety, waste disposal, and proliferation risks."[21]

LAUNCH VENTURE CAPITAL FUND. "I will launch a Clean Technologies Venture Capital Fund that will provide $10 billion a year for five years to get the most promising clean energy technologies off the ground. This venture capital fund will get new technologies from the lab to the marketplace so that in the next few years, the American economy can benefit from America's innovations."[22]

PRIORITIZE BROAD ENERGY MIX. "We have to have a broad energy mix, and I as president intend to make this one of my number-one domestic priorities and to put in the resources needed in order to make it happen."[23]

Electricity

How will President Obama limit our reliance on electricity?

REDUCE DEMAND BY 2020. Obama will "set an aggressive energy efficiency goal—to reduce electricity demand 15 percent from projected levels by 2020."[24]

INCREASE RENEWABLE SOURCES BY 2025. "Ensure 10 percent of our electricity comes from renewable sources by 2012, and 25 percent by 2025."[25]

ACCOUNTABILITY:

☐ has fulfilled ALL his promises

☐ has fulfilled SOME promises

☐ FAILED to fulfill any promises

☐ has proceeded contrary to his promises

NOTE:

ENERGY

"I consider energy to be one of the three most important
issues that we're facing domestically."

Renewable Energy

*So many of us drive cars to work every day. How will an Obama administration
ensure that not only his White House, but our America, uses fuel efficiently? And will
he invest in renewable energy?*

REPEAL 2005 ENERGY BILL. Obama opposes "a 2005 energy bill that represented the largest-ever investment in renewable sources of energy. That bill certainly wasn't perfect . . . contained irresponsible tax breaks for oil companies that
I consistently opposed, and that I will repeal as president."[26]

BY 2012, INCREASE RENEWABLE SOURCES OF ENERGY. "I'll . . . require
that 10 percent of our energy comes from renewable sources by the end of my
first term—more than double what we have now."[27]

EXTEND PTC. "I'll . . . extend the Production Tax Credit [PTC] for five years to
encourage the production of renewable energy like wind power, solar power, and
geothermal energy."[28]

INCREASE BIOFUELS BY 2022. Obama aims "to have 6 billion gallons of . . .
fuel come from sustainable . . . biofuels, and we'll make sure that we have the infrastructure to deliver that fuel in place."[29]

MODERNIZE NATIONAL UTILITY GRID. "[W]e will . . . need to modernize
our national utility grid so that it's accommodating to new sources of power, more
efficient, and more reliable. That's an investment that will also create hundreds of
thousands of jobs, and one that I will make as president."[30]

ACCOUNTABILITY:

☐   has fulfilled ALL his promises

☐   has fulfilled SOME promises

☐   FAILED to fulfill any promises

☐   has proceeded contrary to his promises

NOTE:

ENERGY

*"I consider energy to be one of the three most important
issues that we're facing domestically."*

GENERAL GOALS

INCREASE FUEL EFFICIENCY STANDARDS. "I will increase fuel efficiency
standards by 4 percent per year, lift the 60,000-per-manufacturer cap on buyer tax
credits to encourage more Americans to buy ultra-efficient vehicles, and encourage
automakers to make fuel-efficient hybrid vehicles."[31]

UPDATE FUEL EFFICIENCY STANDARDS. Obama will "overhaul th[e] process for appliances and provide more resources to [the] Department of Energy
so it implements regular updates for efficiency standards. [I] will also work with
Congress to ensure that it continues to play a key role in improving our national
efficiency codes."[32]

FOSTER PRODUCTION OF FUEL EFFICIENT CARS. "I'll provide $4 billion
in loans and tax credits to American auto plants and manufacturers so that they
can retool their factories and build these cars."[33]

SPUR PURCHASES OF FUEL EFFICIENT CARS. "[O]ne of the things I want
to do is make sure that we're providing incentives so that you can buy a fuel efficient car that's made right here in the United States of America, not in Japan
or South Korea."[34] Obama will therefore "create a New $7,000 Tax Credit for
Purchasing Advanced Vehicles."[35]

WEATHERIZE HOMES. Obama will "make a national commitment to weatherize
at least one million low-income homes each year for the next decade, which can
reduce energy usage across the economy and help moderate energy prices for all."[36]

SPECIFIC TARGETS

BY 2010, INCREASE WHITE HOUSE PLUG-IN VEHICLES. "Within one year
of [my] becoming president, the entire White House fleet will be converted to
plug-ins as security permits; and half of all cars purchased by the federal government will be plug-in hybrids or all electric by 2012."[37]

BY 2012, ENSURE NEW BUILDINGS WILL BE 50 PERCENT MORE EF-
FICIENT. "We will set a goal of making our new buildings 50 percent more efficient over the next four years. And we'll follow the lead of California and change
the way utilities make money so that their profits aren't tied to how much energy
we use, but how much energy we save."[38]

BY 2013, REQUIRE ALL NEW VEHICLES BE FLEXIBLE FUEL VEHICLES.
Obama will "work with Congress and auto companies to ensure that all new vehicles have FFV capability . . . by the end of my first term in office."[39]

BY 2013, MANDATE BETTER FUEL EFFICIENCY IN FEDERAL BUILD-
INGS. Within five years, Obama will "achiev[e] a 40 percent increase in efficiency
in all new federal buildings" and "invest in cost-effective retrofits to achieve a 25
percent increase in efficiency of existing federal buildings."[40]

BY 2015, HAVE 1 MILLION PLUG-IN HYBRID CARS ON THE ROAD.
"These vehicles can get up to 150 miles per gallon. [I] believe we should work to
ensure these cars are built here in America, instead of factories overseas."[41]

ACCOUNTABILITY:

☐ has fulfilled ALL his promises

☐ has fulfilled SOME promises

☐ FAILED to fulfill any promises

☐ has proceeded contrary to his promises

NOTE:

ENERGY

"I consider energy to be one of the three most important
issues that we're facing domestically."

Drilling for Oil and Natural Gas

Does President Obama support drilling?

USE IT OR LOSE IT. "[W]e should start by telling the oil companies to drill on the 68 million acres they currently have access to but haven't touched. And if they don't, we should require them to give up their leases to someone who will."[42]

SAY YES TO LIMITED OFFSHORE DRILLING. "I believe in the need for increased oil production. We're going to have to explore new ways to get more oil, and that includes offshore drilling. It includes telling the oil companies, [which] currently have 68 million acres that they're not using, that either you use them or you lose them."[43]

SAY NO TO ARCTIC DRILLING. "I strongly reject drilling in the Arctic National Wildlife Refuge because it would irreversibly damage a protected national wildlife refuge."[44]

PRIORITIZE ALASKA PIPELINE. "We should also tap more of our substantial natural gas reserves and work with the Canadian government to finally build the Alaska Natural Gas Pipeline, delivering clean natural gas and creating good jobs in the process."[45] "As president, [I] will work with stakeholders to facilitate construction of the pipeline. Not only is this pipeline critical to our energy security, it will create thousands of new jobs."[46]

Oil

How will President Obama manage our petroleum reserves?

SHUT SPECULATION LOOPHOLES. "Current loopholes in Commodity Futures Trading Commission regulations have contributed to the skyrocketing price of oil on world markets. . . . [I] will enact simple legislation to close these loopholes and increase transparency on the market to help bring oil prices down and prevent traders from unfairly lining their pockets at the expense of the American people."[47]

LEASE NATIONAL PETROLEUM RESERVE. "Over the next five years, we should also lease more of the National Petroleum Reserve in Alaska for oil and gas production."[48]

SELL SOME OIL FROM STRATEGIC PETROLEUM RESERVE. "We should sell 70 million barrels of oil from our Strategic Petroleum Reserve for less expensive crude, which in the past has lowered gas prices within two weeks."[49] Our current "economic emergency . . . requires a limited, responsible swap of light oil from the Strategic Petroleum Reserve (SPR) for heavy crude oil to help bring down prices at the pump."[50]

ACCOUNTABILITY:

☐   has fulfilled ALL his promises

☐   has fulfilled SOME promises

☐   FAILED to fulfill any promises

☐   has proceeded contrary to his promises

NOTE:

ENERGY

"I consider energy to be one of the three most important
issues that we're facing domestically."

Nuclear Energy

What role does nuclear energy play in President Obama's energy policy?

SAFELY STORE NUCLEAR ENERGY. "I think that with nuclear power, we have
got to see if there are ways for us to store the radioactive material in a safe, environmentally sound way, and if we can do that and deal with some of the safety
and security issues, [nuclear power] is something that we should look at."[51]

BAN NEW NUKES. "I will not authorize the development of new nuclear weapons. And I will make the goal of eliminating nuclear weapons worldwide a central
element of U.S. nuclear policy."[52]

DON'T DUMP AT YUCCA. "I will end the notion of Yucca Mountain because
it has not been based on the sort of sound science that can assure the people of
Nevada that they're going to be safe. And that, I think, was a mistake."[53]

Coal

How will President Obama ensure that American coal is more cleanly mined?

PRIORITIZE LOW-CARBON COAL TECHNOLOGIES. "As president, I will
significantly increase the resources devoted to the commercialization and deploy-
ment of low-carbon coal technologies and use a broad range of mechanisms to
commercialize clean-coal technology. I will direct my Secretary of Energy to enter
into public/private partnerships to develop five 'first-of-a-kind' commercial-scale,
coal-fired plants with carbon capture and sequestration."[54] "If we are using coal in
the absence of these clean technologies, then we are going to be worsening the
trend of global warming, and that is something that we can't do."[55]

ACCOUNTABILITY:

☐   has fulfilled ALL his promises

☐   has fulfilled SOME promises

☐   FAILED to fulfill any promises

☐   has proceeded contrary to his promises

NOTE:

ENERGY

"I consider energy to be one of the three most important
issues that we're facing domestically."

Sacrifice and Service

*Will President Obama call upon ordinary Americans to help create a better, greener
America?*

ENCOURAGE MASS TRANSIT. "I will . . . encourage communities around the
nation to design and build sustainable communities that cut energy use with walk-
able community designs and expanded investment in mass transit."[56]

CREATE ENVIRONMENTAL SERVICE CORPS. "I will . . . create the 5-E (Energy Efficiency, Environmental Education and Employment) Disconnected Youth
Service Corps. This program will directly engage disconnected and disadvantaged
youth in energy efficiency and environmental service opportunities to strengthen
their communities while also providing them with practical skills and experience in important career fields of expected high-growth employment. The program will engage private-sector employers and unions to provide apprenticeship
opportunities."[57]

LINK VETS WITH GREEN JOBS. Obama will "ensure that more of our veterans
can enter the new energy economy. [I] will create a new 'Green Vet Initiative' that
will have two missions: first, it will offer counseling and job placement to help
veterans gain the skills to enter this rapidly growing field: second, it will work
with industry partners to create career pathways and educational programs."[58]

SACRIFICE—IT'S A GOOD THING. "Everybody's going to have to change
their light bulbs. Everybody's going to have to insulate their homes. And that will
be a sacrifice, but it's a sacrifice that we can meet. Over the long term, it will generate jobs and businesses and can drive our economy for many decades."[59]

Green Products and Technologies

Will President Obama help bring green products and technologies to market at reasonable prices?

INVEST IN GREEN PRODUCTS: $1 BILLION. Obama will "establish a federal investment program to help manufacturing centers modernize and help Americans learn new skills to produce green products. This . . . grant program will allocate money to the states to identify and support local manufacturers with the most compelling plans for modernizing existing or closed manufacturing facilities to produce new, advanced clean technologies. This $1 billion per year investment will help spur sustainable economic growth in communities across the country."[60]

FUND GREEN TECHNOLOGIES. Obama will "increase funding for federal workforce training programs and direct these programs to incorporate green technologies training—advanced manufacturing and weatherization training—into their efforts to help Americans find and retain stable, high-paying jobs."[61]

ACCOUNTABILITY:

☐ has fulfilled ALL his promises

☐ has fulfilled SOME promises

☐ FAILED to fulfill any promises

☐ has proceeded contrary to his promises

NOTE:

ENERGY

"I consider energy to be one of the three most important
issues that we're facing domestically."

Miscellaneous

CONSIDER ENERGY REBATE. "I believe we should immediately give every
working family in America a $1,000 energy rebate, and we should pay for it with
part of the record profits that the oil companies are making right now."[62]

STRIVE FOR ENERGY INDEPENDENCE. "[W]e want to free ourselves from
Middle Eastern oil in ten years. And that's something that we can accomplish."[63]

RESTORE THE GREAT LAKES. "I promise to make restoring the Great Lakes a
top priority of [my administration] . . . and [will] push for a $5 billion trust fund
to help get it done."[64]

CONSERVE PRIVATE LANDS. "As president, in addition to protecting federal
public lands, I will put an unprecedented level of emphasis on the conservation
of private lands, including increased funding for the Conservation Security Program and the Conservation Reserve Program and creating additional incentives
for private landowners to protect and restore wetlands, grasslands, forests, and
other wildlife habitat."[65]

ACCOUNTABILITY:

☐ has fulfilled ALL his promises

☐ has fulfilled SOME promises

☐ FAILED to fulfill any promises

☐ has proceeded contrary to his promises

NOTE:

DEMOCRACY

"And just to wrap up, part of the change that's desperately needed is to enlist the American people in the process of self-government."[1]

Self-Government

How will President Obama keep me abreast of his, and our, progress?

CALL FOR TRANSPARENCY. "My administration will open up the doors of democracy. We'll put government data online, and use technology to shine a light on spending. We'll invite the service and participation of American citizens, and cut through the red tape to make sure that every agency is meeting cutting-edge standards. We'll make it clear to the special interests that their days of setting the agenda in Washington are over, because the American people are not the problem in this 21st century; they are the answer."[2]

PROMOTE ELECTORAL REPRESENTATION IN DC. "The first thing I would do would be to move forward with an agenda to make sure that we give DC the opportunity to elect its own representatives and have some political power on Capitol Hill."[3]

MOTIVATE POOKIE. "I also know that if cousin Pookie would vote, get off the couch and register some folks, and go to the polls, we might have a different kind of politics. That's what the Moses generation teaches us. Take off your bedroom slippers. Put on your marching shoes. Go do some politics. Change this country! That's what we need."[4]

Taxes and Investments

What do my tax dollars entitle me to?

REINVIGORATE TAXPAYERS. "I will create a High-Performance Team of experts [that] evaluates every agency and every office based on how well they're serving the American taxpayer."[5]

EXPECT A RETURN ON YOUR INVESTMENT. "If American taxpayers are financing this solution, you should be treated like investors. That means that Wall Street and Washington should give you every penny of your money back once this economy recovers."[6]

ACCOUNTABILITY:

☐ has fulfilled ALL his promises

☐ has fulfilled SOME promises

☐ FAILED to fulfill any promises

☐ has proceeded contrary to his promises

NOTE:

DEMOCRACY

"And just to wrap up, part of the change that's desperately
needed is to enlist the American people in the process of
self-government."

Voting Rights

How will President Obama curb voting fraud?

PREVENT VOTER FRAUD. As president, Obama will "sign into law [a bill that
enables investigations into deceptive and fraudulent practices and will] charge the
Voting Rights Section with vigorously enforcing that law and the provisions of
the Voting Rights Act."[7]

END DECEPTIVE VOTING PRACTICES. Obama will "sign into law ... legislation that establishes harsh penalties for those who have engaged in voter fraud and
[that] provides voters who have been misinformed with accurate and full information so they can vote."[8]

ACCOUNTABILITY:

☐   has fulfilled ALL his promises

☐   has fulfilled SOME promises

☐   FAILED to fulfill any promises

☐   has proceeded contrary to his promises

NOTE:

DEMOCRACY

"And just to wrap up, part of the change that's
desperately needed is to enlist the American
people in the process of self-government."

Service

*This book has informed me of what my country can do for me. What can I do for
my country?*

EXPAND THE PEACE CORPS. Obama will "double the Peace Corps to 16,000
by 2011 . . . [and] will work with the leaders of other countries to build an international network of overseas volunteers so that Americans work side-by-side with
volunteers from other countries."[9]

SHOW THE WORLD AMERICA'S BEST FACE. Obama will "set up an America's
Voice Initiative to send Americans who are fluent speakers of local languages to
expand our public diplomacy. [I] also will extend opportunities for older individuals such as teachers, engineers, and doctors to serve overseas."[10]

EXPAND SERVICE-LEARNING IN OUR SCHOOLS. Obama will "set a goal
that all middle and high school students do 50 hours of community service a year.
[I] will develop national guidelines for service-learning and will give schools better tools both to develop programs and to document student experience."[11]

CREATE GREEN JOB CORPS. Obama will "create an energy-focused youth
jobs program to provide disadvantaged youth with service opportunities weather-
izing buildings and getting practical experience in fast-growing career fields."[12]

EXPAND YOUTHBUILD PROGRAM. Obama will "expand the YouthBuild program, which gives disadvantaged young people the chance to complete their high
school education, learn valuable skills, and build affordable housing in their communities. [I] will grow the program so that 50,000 low-income young people a
year get a chance to learn construction job skills and complete high school."[13]

EXPAND CORPORATION FOR NATIONAL AND COMMUNITY SERVICE. Obama will "expand AmeriCorps from 75,000 slots today to 250,000, and [we] will focus this expansion on addressing the great challenges facing the nation. [We] will establish a Classroom Corps to help teachers and students, with a priority placed on underserved schools: a Health Corps to improve public health outreach; a Clean Energy Corps to conduct weatherization and renewable energy projects; a Veterans Corps to assist veterans at hospitals, nursing homes, and homeless shelters; and a Homeland Security Corps to help communities plan, prepare for, and respond to emergencies."[14]

ENGAGE RETIRING AMERICANS IN SERVICE ON A LARGE SCALE. "Older Americans have a wide range of skills and knowledge to contribute. [We] will expand and improve programs that connect individuals over the age of 55 to quality volunteer opportunities."[15]

ACCOUNTABILITY:

□ has fulfilled ALL his promises

□ has fulfilled SOME promises

□ FAILED to fulfill any promises

□ has proceeded contrary to his promises

NOTE:

NOTES

INTRODUCTION

1 Peter Block, "Building Accountability and Commitment," http://www.designedlearning.com/workshops.htm.

1. HEALTH CARE AND WELL-BEING

2 *Carol Ann Reyes v. Kaiser Foundation Hospitals*, "Civil Complaint," Superior Court of the State of California, County of Los Angeles. Filed November 16, 2006.

3 Los Angeles Homeless Services Authority, "2007 Greater Los Angeles Homeless Count," http://www.lahsa.org/2007homelesscountreport.asp.

4 Andrew Blankstein and Richard Winton, "Paraplegic Allegedly 'Dumped' on Skid Row," *Los Angeles Times*, February 9, 2007, http://articles.latimes.com/2007/feb/09/local/medumping.

5 Tavis Smiley, *Covenant with Black America* (Chicago: Third World Press, 2006), 3.

6 Tom Daschle, *Critical: What We Can Do About the Health Care Crisis* (New York: St. Martin's Press, 2008), 47.

7 Ibid., 47–49.

8 Ibid., 49; David Blumenthal, M.D. M.P.P., "Employer-Sponsored Health Insurance in the United States: Origins and Implications," *New England Journal of Medicine* 355 (2006): 82–88.

9 Ibid.

10 Ibid., 62.

11 Jonathan Cohn, *Sick: The Untold Story of America's Health care Crisis—And the People Who Paid the Price* (New York: HarperCollins, 2007), 65.

12 Ibid., 60.

13 Daschle, *Critical*, 65–71.

14 H.R. 3600, The Health Security Act of 1993, http://thomas.loc.gov/cgi-bin/query/z?c103:H.R.3600.

15 Daschle, *Critical*, 71–72.

16 Cohn, *Sick*, 56–57.

17 Ibid., 57–58.

18 Hillary Clinton, *Living History* (New York: Simon & Schuster, 2003), 143–55.

19 Lisa Girion, "Sick But Insured? Think Again," *Los Angeles Times*, September 17, 2006.

20 Ibid.

21 Eric Cohen and Yuval Levin, "Health Care in Three Acts" *CommentaryMagazine.com*, February 2007, http://www.commentarymagazine.com/viewarticle.cfm/health-care-in-three-acts-10826.

22 Smiley, *Covenant*, 3–19.

23 National Urban League, "The State of Black America 2008: In the Black Woman's Voice" (paper presented at the Legislative Policy Conference, Washington, DC, March 2008).

24 Dr. Doris Browne, "The Impact of Health Disparities in African-American Women," in *The State of Black America 2008* (New York: National Urban League, 2008), 163.

25 National Institutes of Health, "Health Disparities Defined," Center to Reduce Cancer Health Disparities, http://crchd.cancer.gov/definitions/defined.html.

26 U.S. Department of Health and Human Services, "Access to Quality Services," *Healthy People 2010: Objectives for Improving Health*, http://www.healthypeople.gov/Publications/, 1-7 to 1-9.

27 Centers for Disease Control, "Health of Mexican American Population," National Center for Health Statistics, http://www.cdc.gov/nchs/FASTATS/mexican_health.htm.

28 Browne, *The State of Black America 2008*.

29 Mary Otto, "For Want of a Dentist," *Washington Post*, February 28, 2007, B01.

30 U.S. Department of Health and Human Services, "SCHIP Dental Coverage," Centers for Medicare & Medicaid Services, http://www.cms.hhs.gov/SCHIPDentalCoverage/.

31 Otto, "For Want of a Dentist."

32 Ibid.

33 Ibid.

34 Robyn Fleming, "Response to the Death of Young Deamonte Driver," Washington Area Women's Foundation, posted on March 1, 2007, http://thewomensfoundation.org/2007/response-to-the-death-of-young-deamonte-driver/.

35 Ibid.

36 U.S. Census Bureau, "Census Bureau Revises 2004 and 2005 Health Insurance Coverage Estimates," March 23, 2007, http://www.census.gov/Press-Release/www/releases/archives/health_care_insurance/009789.html.

37 The Commonwealth Fund, "Massachusetts Health Care Reform—On the Second Anniversary of Passage, What Progress Has Been Made?" April 28, 2008, http://www.commonwealthfund.org/innovations/innovations_show.htm?doc_id=682731.

38 Alice Dembner, "Success Could Put Health Plan in the Red: Mass. Program May Come Up $147M Short," *Boston Globe*, November 18, 2007, http://www.boston.com/news/local/articles/2007/11/18/success_could_put_health_plan_in_the_red/.

39 Consumer Watchdog, "Overview of Massachusetts' Insurance Mandate," http://www.consumerwatchdog.org/resources/masshealth.pdf.

40 YouTube, "Obama disses Massachusetts health care," Democratic Presidential Primary Debate, Myrtle Beach, SC, January 21, 2008, http://www.youtube.com/watch?v=0foRt63g100.

41 Barack Obama for President Campaign website, "Issues: Health care," http://origin.barackobama.com/issues/healthcare/; Jay Newton-Small and Aliza Marcus, "Obama, Following Rivals, Unveils Health Care Plan," *Bloomberg.com*, May 29, 2007.

42 Barack Obama for President Campaign website, "Issues, Health care."

43 Paul Steinhauser and Candy Crowley, "Clinton unveils mandatory health care insurance plan," CNN, September 18, 2007, http://www.cnn.com/2007/POLITICS/09/17/health.care/index.html.

44 Hillary Clinton for President Campaign website, "Issues: Health care" [website no longer active].

45 John McCain for President Campaign website, "Issues: Health Care," http://www.johnmccain.com/Informing/Issues/19ba2flc-c03-4ac2-8cd5-5cf2edb527cf.htm.

46 Cathy Schoen, Karen Davis, and Sara R. Collins, "Building Blocks For Reform: Achieving Universal Coverage With Private And Public Group Health Insurance," *Health Affairs* 27 (May–June 2008): 646–57.

47 Skyrocketing health care costs are the most common cause for bankruptcy filings in the United States. David U. Himmelstein, Elizabeth Warren, Deborah Thorne, and Steffie Woolhandler, "Market Watch: Illness and Injury as Contributors to Bankruptcy," *Health Affairs*, February 2, 2005, http://content.healthaffairs.org/cgi/content/full/hlthaff.w5.63/DC1.

48 Cohn, *Sick*, 3.

49 Ibid., 11–12.

50 Ibid., 13–25.

51 Jim Jubak, "Let Wal-Mart Fix U.S. Health Care," *MSN Money*, May 27, 2008, http://articles.moneycentral.msn.com/Investing/JubaksJournal/LetWalMartFixUSHealthCare.aspx.

52 Ibid.

53 Ibid.

54 Ibid.

55 Ibid.

56 America's Health Insurance Plans, "Estimates of the Potential Reduction in Health Care Costs from AHIP's Affordability Proposals," AHIP Center for Policy and Research, http://www.ahipresearch.org/PDFs/TechnicalMemo06.11.08.pdf.

57 Association of Black Cardiologists Inc., "Association of Black Cardiologists," http://www.abcardio.org.

58 The Cristo Rey Community Center partners with the Capital Area United Way to provide the Prescription Assistance Program to seniors. For more information: http://www.msucc.msu.edu/PDFs/Campaign_2007_2008/SuccessStories.pdf. For more information about the Cristo Rey model, visit http://www.cristoreynetwork.org.

2. EDUCATION

59 Sara Neufeld, "School violence appalls officials," *Baltimore Sun*, April 10, 2008, http://www.baltimoresun.com/news/local/baltimore_city/bal-te.md.ci.teacher10sapr10,0,601646.story.

60 Ibid.

61 Mike Celizic, "Teacher 'petrified' after being attacked by student," MSNBC, April 10, 2008, http://www.msnbc.msn.com/id/24047456/.

62 Neufeld, "School violence appalls officials."

63 Lisa Delpit, *Other People's Children: Cultural Conflict in the Classroom* (New York: The New Press, 1995).

64 University of Virginia Library, "Thomas Jefferson on Politics and Government," Thomas Jefferson Digital Archive, http://etext.virginia.edu/jefferson/quotations/jeff1350.htm.

65 The National Commission on Excellence in Education, *A Nation at Risk: The Imperative for Educational Reform* (Washington, DC: U.S. Government Printing Office, 1983).

66 Samuel G. Freedman, "A Teacher Grows Disillusioned After a 'Fail' Becomes a 'Pass,'" *New York Times*, August 1, 2007, http://www.nytimes.com/2007/08/01/education/01education.html.

67 Ibid.

68 Ibid.

69 Pioneer Institute for Public Policy Research, "Transforming Children's Lives," *Dialogue* Number 27, September 1998.

70 Alan Borsuk, "Committed to MPS Despite Attack," *Milwaukee Journal Sentinel*, Tuesday, May 6, 2007.

71 Sarah Carr, "Behind Knockout of Principal Lies a Sad Tale," *Milwaukee Journal Sentinel*, Tuesday, May 6, 2007.

72 Ibid.

73 Ibid.

74 Ibid.

75 Ibid.

76 Ibid.

77 Ibid.

78 Colbert I. King, "A Battlefield Called Wilson High," *Washington Post*, March 29, 2008.

79 Ibid.

80 Ibid.

81 Dan Keating and V. Dion Hayes, "Can D.C. Schools Be Fixed?" *Washington Post*, June 10, 2007.

82 Ibid.

83 Theola Labbe and Dan T. Keating, "Modest Gains in D.C. Schools," *Washington Post*, August 18, 2007.

84 Ibid.

85 Ibid.

86 Ibid.

87 Dan Keating and V. Dion Hayes, "Can D.C. Schools Be Fixed?"

88 John McCain for President Campaign website, "Issues: Education," http://www
.johnmccain.com/Informing/Issues/19ce50b5-daa8-4795-b92d-92bd0d985bca.htm.

89 Barack Obama for President Campaign website, "Issues: Education," http://www
.barackobama.com/issues/education/.

90 Microsoft Corporation, "Microsoft Links Classrooms Coast-to-Coast," PressPass, http://
www.microsoft.com/presspass/features/2000/jun00/06-06w2w.mspx.

91 The Algebra Project, Inc., "Who we are: History," http://www.algebra.org/history.php.

92 Jodi Wilgoren, "Algebra Project: Bob Moses Empowers Students," *New York Times*, January 7, 2001.

93 Marie Alice Garrett, "Turning Challenges into Success Stories," *The News Journal* (Wilmington, Delaware), June 19, 2008, http://www.delawareonline.com/apps/pbcs.dll/ article?AID=/20080619/NEWS03/806190303/1006/NEWS.

94 Uncommon Schools, Inc., "Uncommon Schools," http://www.uncommonschools.org.

95 Katie Lovell, "Charter School Grows to Elementary Level—North Star Academy's first class of kindergarteners shows lots of promise," *Newark Star Ledger*, November 29, 2007.

3. UNEQUAL JUSTICE

96 Stanton Peele, "McCain Has Two Standards on Drug Abuse," *Los Angeles Times*, February 14, 2000, B5, http://www.peele.net/lib/mccain.html.

97 Ibid.

98 Lauren Ruben, "McCain Wife Tells of Her Addiction," (New York) *DAILY NEWS*, April 2, 2001.

99 U.S. Department of Justice, "Controlled Substances in Schedule II," Drug Enforcement Administration, http://www.deadiversion.usdoj.gov/schedules/listby_sched/sched2.htm.

100 Consider New York, which, like many states, boasts mandatory disqualification of prospective adoptive parents for current abuse of alcohol or drugs (18 N.Y.C.R.R. §421.16[p]). See Michael A. Neff, "Applying to Adopt," New York State Citizens' Coalition for Children, http://www.nysccc.org/Neff/applyadopt.html.

101 See Dan Steinberg and Shelly Gehshan, "State Responses to Maternal Drug and Alcohol Use: An Update," National Conference of State Legislatures, http://www.ncsl.org/programs/health/forum/maternalabuse.htm ("In cases where the screening reveals drug use, the infant may be placed in foster care and the mother is referred to treatment. . . . If the mother fails to complete addiction treatment, child protective services may permanently remove the children from the home.")

102 Peele, "McCain Has Two Standards on Drug Abuse."

103 Ibid.

104 Ibid.

105 Supreme Court of the United States, "The Supreme Court Building," http://www.supremecourtus.gov/about/courtbuilding.pdf.

106 Associated Press, "War on Drugs Held Burdening Justice," *New York Times*, December 5, 1988.

107 Victoria Harker, "No Lockups for First-Time Drug Offenders: State High Court Cites '96 Ballot Proposition," *The Arizona Republic*, December 21, 1999. ("It's a reflection of . . . wise minds realizing that the war on drugs, when it comes to low-level offenders, is costing us a whole lot more than what it's worth," defense lawyer Al Flores said about the ruling. "Simply warehousing drug offenders is not solving the problem.")

108 Courtland Milloy, "Hardline Drug Law Threatens a Pillar of the Community," *Washington Post*, May 28, 2008, http://www.washingtonpost.com/wp-dyn/content/article/2008/05/27/AR2008052703153.html.

109 Stewart M. Powell, "Clinton Aims for Safer Public Housing," *The Times Union* (Albany), March 29, 1996.

110 "Clinton Announces Plan to Discourage Drugs in Housing," CNN Transcript #1470-2, March 28, 1996.

111 The Sentencing Project, "The Sentencing Project: Research and Advocacy for Reform," http://www.sentencingproject.org/.

112 Tamar Lewin, "Crime Costs Black Men the Vote, Study Says," *New York Times*, October 23, 1998, http://query.nytimes.com/gst/fullpage.html?res=9402EFDF1E3DF930A15753C 1A96E958260.

113 Human Rights Watch and The Sentencing Project, "Current Impact of Disenfranchisement Laws," http://www.hrw.org/reports98/vote/usvot980-01 .htm#P101_2428.

114 Jeff Manza and Christopher Uggen, *Locked Out: Felon Disenfranchisement and American Democracy* (New York: Oxford University Press USA, 2006).

115 *Reynolds v. Sims*, 377 U.S. 533 (1964). The phrase actually first appeared in *Gray v. Sanders*, 372 U.S. 368, 381 (1963).

116 See generally S. David Mitchell, "Undermining Individual and Collective Citizenship: the Impact of Exclusion Laws on the African-American Community," *Fordham Urban Law Journal* 34 (April 1, 2007), 833.

117 "Federal Drug Law Could Use a Fix," *The Ledger* (Lakeland,FL), April 10, 2004.

118 Colorado Department on Public Safety, "Colorado Commission on Criminal and Juvenile Justice," http://cdpsweb.state.co.us/cccjj/PDF/July%202008/LAC%20Report%20Card%20 -%20Colorado.pdf.

119 Legal Action Center, "After Prison: Roadblocks to Reentry," http://www.lac.org/ roadblocks-to-reentry/.

120 Ibid., 8.

121 Ibid., 9.

122 Ryan Handwerk, "DNA Frees Death Row Inmates, Brings Others to Justice," *National Geographic*, April 8, 2005, http://news.nationalgeographic.com/ news/2005/04/0408_050408_tv_dnadeath.html.

123 *People v. Cahill*, 777 N.Y.S. 2d 332, at n10 (New York, 2003).

124 U.S. Department of Justice, "Community Policing Topics," Office of Community Oriented Policing Services, http://www.cops.usdoj.gov/files/RIC/Publications/e05060064 .pdf.

4. THE ECONOMY

125 Beth Shulman, "Working and Poor in the USA," *The Nation*, January 22, 2004, http:// www.thenation.com/doc/20040209/shulman/print.

126 Ibid.

127 Ibid.

128 Ibid.

129 Ibid.

130 Ibid.

131 Charlie Rose, "Interview with Warren Buffett: I Haven't Seen As Much Economic Fear in My Adult Lifetime," PBS, October 1, 2008, http://www.cnbc.com/id/26982338/page/2/.

132 George Soros, *The New Paradigm For Financial Markets: The Credit Crisis Of 2008 And What It Means* (New York: PublicAffairs, 2008).

133 David Yergin and Joseph Stanislaw, *The Commanding Heights* (New York: Touchstone, 2002); Naomi Klein, *The Shock Doctrine: The Rise of Disaster Capitalism* (NY: Metropolitan Books, 2007).

134 Danny Hakim, "For a G.M. Family, the American Dream Vanishes," *New York Times*, Saturday, November 19, 2005.

135 "The Death of American Manufacturing," the Trumpet.com, December 15, 2005, http://www.thetrumpet.com/index.php?q=2011.878.0.0.

136 Ibid.

137 Hakim, "For a G.M. Family."

138 Ibid.

139 United for a Fair Economy, *Foreclosed: State of the American Dream 2008*, http://faireconomy.org/dream.

140 Kai Wright, "Mortgage Industry Bankrupts Black America," *The Nation*, July 14, 2008, http://www.thenation.com/doc/20080714/wright/print.

141 Ibid.

142 Ibid.

143 Ibid.

144 Ibid.

145 Ibid.

146 Ibid.

147 Stephanie Armour, "Foreclosures' financial strains take toll on kids," *USA Today*, July 9, 2008, http://www.usatoday.com/money/economy/housing/2008-07-08-children-foreclosure-homeless_N.htm.

148 New York State Small Business Development Center, "Education. Entrepreneurship. Development," http://www.nyssbdc.org/.

149 Jeff Bennett, "Class Act: Educate and they will come," *Wall Street Journal*, July 28, 2008, http://online.wsj.com/article/SB121676435398175079.html?mod=2_1593_topbox.

150 Capital Public Radio, "Buyers, Sellers Seek Help Dealing with Housing Crisis," April 1, 2008, http://www.mutualhousing.com/SMHA_news/articles/SMHA_NPRApril08_P3.pdf.

5. THE ENVIRONMENT, ENERGY, AND OUR AGING INFRASTRUCTURE

151 "Tour Spotlights Effect of Water Contamination on Dickson Family," NewsChannel 5 (Nashville, TN), http://www.newschannel5.com/Global/story.asp?S=7430002.

152 John Collins Rudolf, "The Warming of Greenland," *New York Times*, January 16, 2007, http://www.nytimes.com/2007/01/16/science/earth/16gree.html?pagewanted=1&_r=2.

153 "Bullard: Green issue is black and white," CNN, July 17, 2007, http://www.cnn.com/2007/US/07/17/pysk.bullard/index.html.

154 Ibid.

155 Van Jones and Ariane Conrad, *The Green Collar Economy: How One Solution Can Fix Our Two Biggest Problems* (New York: HarperOne, 2008).

156 Smiley, *Covenant*, 106–107.

157 See Smart Growth America, "What is Smart Growth?" http://www.smartgrowthamerica.org/whatissg.html.

158 Robert Bullard, Glenn S. Johnson, and Angel Torres, "Race, Equity & Smart Growth: Why People of Color Must Speak for Themselves," Smart Growth America, http://www.ejrc.cau.edu/raceequitysmartgrowth.htm.

159 Southern Piping Company website, "History of Southern Piping Company," http://southernpiping.com/index.php?option=com_content&task=view&id=25&Itemid=103.

160 House Small Business Committee, Subcommittee on Investigations and Oversight, Testimony of Tim Williford, April 9, 2008, http://www.house.gov/smbiz/hearings/hearing-04-09-08-gas-sub/testimony-04-09-08-williford.pdf.

161 Ibid.

162 T. Boone Pickens, "Pickens Plan," http://www.pickensplan.com/index.php.

163 Natural Gas Vehicles for America, "NGVAmerica Fact Sheet," http://www.ngvc.org/media_ctr/fact_ngv.html.

164 Ibid.

165 Serena W. Lin, *Understanding Climate Change: An Equitable Framework* (Oakland, CA: PolicyLink, 2008), http://www.policylink.com.

166 Andrew Martin, "U.S. Faces Criticism over Biofuel Policy," *International Herald Tribune*, May 30, 2008, http://www.iht.com/articles/2008/05/30/business/food.php. See also Pickens, "Pickens Plan," 2.

167 Pickens, "Pickens Plan," 1.

168 Rhone Resch and Noah Kaye, "The Promise of Solar Energy," *United Nations Chronicle* Volume XLIV, no. 2 (2007), http://www.un.org/Pubs/chronicle/2007/issue2/0207p63.htm.

169 Committee on Surface Temperature Reconstructions for the Last 2,000 Years, *Surface Temperature Reconstructions for the Last 2,000 Years* (Washington, DC: National Academies Press, 2006), http://www.nap.edu/catalog.php?record_id=11676.

170 Contribution of Working Group I to the Fourth Assessment Report of the Intergovernmental Panel on Climate Change, "Climate Change 2007: The Physical Science Basis," National Center for Atmospheric Research, http://ipcc-wg1.ucar.edu/wg1/docs/WG1AR4_SPM_PlenaryApproved.pdf.

171 "Report says global warming very likely man-made, to continue 'for centuries,'" *USA Today*, March 1, 2007, http://www.usatoday.com/weather/climate/globalwarming/2007-02-01-ipcc-report_x.htm.

172 Jeffrey Kluger, "Is Global Warming Fueling Katrina?" *Time*, August 29, 2005, http://www.time.com/time/nation/article/0.8599.1099102.00.html.

173 Ibid., citing a Massachusetts Institute of Technology study.

174 Thomas R. Knutson, "Global Warming and Hurricanes: An Overview of Current Research Results," Geophysical Fluid Dynamics Laboratory, National Oceanic and Atmospheric Administration, U.S. Department of Commerce, http://www.gfdl.noaa.gov/~tk/glob_warm_hurr_webpage.html#section1.

175 Shaila Dewan, "HURRICANE KATRINA: MISSISSIPPI; Face to Face With Death and Destruction in Biloxi," *New York Times*, August 31, 2005, http://query.nytimes.com/gst/fullpage.html?res=9500E1D61631F932A0575BC0A9639C8B63&sec=&spon=&pagewanted=all.

176 Ibid.; Edward S. Fink, "Biloxi's Tivoli Hotel After Hurricane Katrina," http://geoimages.berkeley.edu/worldwidepanorama/wwp1205/html/EdwardFink.html.

177 Fink, "Biloxi's Tivoli Hotel."

178 Dewan, "HURRICANE KATRINA: MISSISSIPPI."

179 Joby Warrick, "White House Got Early Warning on Katrina," *Washington Post*, January 23, 2006, http://www.washingtonpost.com/wp-dyn/content/article/2006/01/23/AR2006012301711.html.

180 Ibid.

181 Final Report of the Select Bipartisan Committee to Investigate the Preparation for and Response to Hurricane Katrina, "A Failure of Initiative," U.S. House of Representatives, February 15, 2006, http://www.gpoaccess.gov/katrinareport/fullreport.pdf.

182 Ibid.

183 Faye Fiore, "FEMA says it's applying Hurricane Katrina lessons to Gustav," *Los Angeles Times*, September 2, 2008. http://www.latimes.com/news/la-na-fema2-2008sep02,0,2578586.story.

184 Jay Root and Angela K. Brown, "Cities House Hundreds of Pets After Gustav, Ike," *Washington Post*, September 18, 2008.

185 Philip Rucker, "Charities Unprepared for Major Disaster, GAO Says," *Washington Post*, September 18, 2008, http://www.washingtonpost.com/wp-dyn/content/article/2008/09/17/AR2008091703628.html.

186 Ibid., referencing the GAO report, "Voluntary Organizations: FEMA Should More Fully Assess Organizations' Mass Care Capabilities and Update the Red Cross Role in Catastrophic Events."

187 John Podesta and Peter Ogden, "The Security Implications of Climate Change," *Washington Quarterly*, Winter 2007–08, http://www.twq.com/08winter/docs/08winter_podesta.pdf, 115–16.

188 National Weather Service, "NHC Archive of Hurricane Seasons," National Hurricane Center, http://www.nhc.noaa.gov/pastall.shtml.

189 Associated Press, "Bangladesh cyclone relief effort hampered," November 17, 2007, http://www.msnbc.msn.com/id/12784349/.

190 "After Major Cyclone, Bangladesh Worries about Climate Change," PBS, March 28, 2008, http://www.pbs.org/newshour/bb/environment/jan-june08/bangladesh_03–28.html.

191 Jo Tuckman, "Global warming brings busy year for UN disaster teams," *The Guardian*, December 27, 2007, http://www.guardian.co.uk/world/2007/dec/27/weather.environment.

192 Amy Wilentz, "Hurricanes and Haiti," *Los Angeles Times*, September 13, 2008, http://www.latimes.com/news/opinion/la-oe-wilentz13-2008sep13,0,7909229.story.

193 Marc Lacey, "Meager Living of Haitians Is Wiped Out by Storms," *New York Times*, September 10, 2008, http://www.nytimes.com/2008/09/11/world/americas/11haiti.html.

194 Jason Beaubien, "Relief Operations Under Way in Devastated Haiti," *All Things Considered*, National Public Radio, September 12, 2008, http://www.npr.org/templates/story/story.php?storyId=94561093.

195 Lauren Radomski, "Mercedes rises from chaos: Victim of bridge collapse turns to Fergus Falls fiancée for love, support," *Fergus Falls Journal*, September 22, 2007, http://www.fergusfallsjournal.com/news/2007/sep/22/mercedes-rises-chaos/.

196 Ibid.

197 Ibid.

198 Minnesota Legislative Reference Library, "Resources on Minnesota Issues: Minneapolis Interstate 35W Bridge Collapse," http://www.leg.state.mn.us/LRL/Issues/bridges.asp.

199 "Deadline approaches quickly for 35WBridge Victims Fund," *Fox Twin Cities*, September 15, 2008, http://www.myfoxtwincities.com/myfox/pages/Home/Detail?contentId=74370 12&version=1&locale=EN-US&layoutCode=TSTY&pageId=1.1.1.

200 Mercedes Gorden, "Caring Bridge Journal," http://www.caringbridge.org/cb/viewJournal.do?method=executeInit.

201 The 15 agencies are the U.S. Agency for International Development, Department of Agriculture, Department of Commerce (National Oceanic & Atmospheric Administration and the National Institute of Standards and Technology), Department of Defense, Department of Energy, Department of Health and Human Services (National Institutes of Health), Department of State, Department of Transportation, Department of the Interior (U.S. Geological Survey), Environmental Protection Agency, National Aeronautics & Space Administration, National Science Foundation, Office of Science and Technology Policy, Office of Management and Budget, and the Smithsonian Institution.

202 U.S. Global Change Research Program, "Our Changing Planet: The U.S. Climate Change Science Program," FY 2009, http://www.usgcrp.gov/usgcrp/Library/ocp2009/.

203 David Biello, "10 Solutions for Climate Change," *Scientific American*, November 26, 2007, http://www.sciam.com/article.cfm?id=10-solutions-for-climate-change.

204 See Environmental Protection Agency and U.S. Department of Energy, "Energy Star," http://www.energystar.gov/index.cfm?fuseaction=find_a_product, and U.S. Department of Energy, "Energy Efficiency and Renewable Energy," http://apps1.eere.energy.gov/consumer/.

205 Statmats Business Media, "5 Success Stories in Energy Management: Andrews Air Force Base in Buildings," November 2007, http://www.buildings.com/articles/detail.aspx?contentID=3575.

206 Deeohn Ferris, "Environmental Justice: Heck of a Job Ahead," *National Housing Institute Publication ShelterForce*, Fall 2008, http://www.shelterforce.org/article/1116/environmental_justice_heck_of_a_job_ahead/.

207 The Center for Deliberative Democracy, "Listening to Customers: How Deliberative Polling Helped Build 1,000 MW of New Renewable Energy Projects in Texas," http://cdd.stanford.edu/polls/energy/2003/renewable_energy.pdf; Stephanie Robinson telephone interview with James Fishkin, Director, Center for Deliberative Democracy, Stanford University, on September 16, 2008.

208 Ibid.

209 Solar Youth, Inc., "About Solar Youth, Inc.," http://www.solaryouth.com/.

210 Lin, *Understanding Climate Change: An Equitable Framework*, 16–18.

211 "Rebuilding a better, greener New Orleans," *Today*, MSNBC, July 18, 2006, http://www.msnbc.msn.com/id/13892600/.

212 Global Green USA, "Rebuilding New Orleans," http://globalgreen.org/neworleans/about/.

213 Lincoln Park Coast Cultural District, "Who We Are," http://www.lpccd.org/.

214 "Lincoln Park Coast Cultural District's Green Collar Apprenticeship Program Leads Newark To A Greener Future," *Business Wire,* February 20, 2008, http://findarticles.com/p/articles/mi_mOEIN/is_/ai_n24269062.

215 Stanford News Service, "New Global Wind Map may lead to cheaper power supply," *Stanford Report,* May 20, 2005, http://news-service.stanford.edu/news/2005/may25/wind-052505.html.

216 Jerry Taylor, "Pickens' Plan to Rig the Market," *Los Angeles Times,* August 19, 2008, http://www.cato.org/pub_display.php?pub_id=9613.

217 Matt Cooper, "Picket Pitches Platform in Denver," Seeking Alpha, http://seekingalpha.com/article/92988-picket-pitches-platform-in-denver.

218 Cecilia M. Vega, "Warning from Gore on future: Global warming called an emergency," *San Francisco Chronicle,* June 5, 2005, http://www.sfgate.com/cgi-bin/article.cgi?f=/c/a/2005/06/05/GORE.TMP.

219 See PowerSaver Program, "Energy Efficiency Tips," http://www.austinenergy.com/Energy%20Efficiency/Tools%20and%20Tips/residential/Energy%20Efficiency%20Tips/index.htm; U.S. Department of Energy, "Energy Savers," http://www1.eere.energy.gov/consumer/tips; and Energy Star, "Home Improvement," http://www.energystar.gov/index.cfm?c=home_improvement.hm_improvement_index.

220 Biello, "10 Solutions for Climate Change."

6. DEMOCRACY

221 Elizabeth Redden, "Warning College Student Voters," *Inside Higher Ed,* September 3, 2008, http://www.insidehighered.com/news/2008/09/03/voting.

222 Tamar Lewin, "Voter Registration by Students Raises Cloud of Consequences," *New York Times,* Monday, September 8, 2008.

223 Ibid.

224 Ibid.

225 Ibid.

226 Wynton Marsalis with Geoffrey C. Ward, *Moving to Higher Ground: How Jazz Can Change Your Life* (New York: Random House, 2008), 38.

227 Spencer Overton, *Stealing Democracy: The New Politics of Voter Suppression* (New York: W. W. Norton, 2006).

228 Ibid.

229 Ibid.

230 Ibid.

231 Ibid.

232 Ibid.

233 Steven Elbow, "Van Hollen's lawsuit will muck up election, voting officials say," *The Capital Times Madison*, September 13, 2008, http://www.madison.com/tct/news/304606.

234 Ibid.

235 Ibid.

236 Ibid.

237 James Madison, "Federalist No. 10," *The Federalist Papers*, http://www.constitution.org/fed/federa00.htm.

238 Ibid.

239 Nick Juliano, "Obama says voting rights official should be sacked for racially insensitive comments," *The Raw Story*, October 19, 2007, http://rawstory.com/news/2007/Obama_says_voting_rights_officials_should_1019.html.

240 Kathy Barks Hoffman, "Michigan Dems file lawsuit against Macomb Co. GOP," *ABC News*, ABC, September 16, 2008, http://abcnews.go.com/Politics/wireStory?id=5816419.

241 Mhari Saito, "Same Day Early Voting and Voter Registration Goes Smoothly," WCPN (Cleveland, NPR), October 1, 2008, http://www.wcpn.org/index.php/WCPN/news/14607/.

242 Alejandro Lazo, "Hispanic Businesses Get Out the Vote," *Washington Post*, September 15, 2008, D01, http://www.washingtonpost.com/wp-dyn/content/article/2008/09/14/AR2008091401570.html.

243 Martha Irvine, "Young voters could rock the polls this year," Associated Press, October 26, 2008.

244 Nekesa Mumbi Moody, "Diddy, Pete Wentz, other celebs rock their vote," Associated Press, November 4, 2008. For extensive details describing the national youth turnout, see http://www.rockthevote.org.

245 AARP (formerly the American Association of Retired Persons), "Divided We Fail," http://www.aarp.org/issues/dividedwefail/about_us/.

246 Solomon Moore, "States Restore Voting Rights for Ex-Convicts," *New York Times*, September 14, 2008, A22 (New York edition).

247 Ibid.

248 http://www/kidsvotingmissouri.org.

7. RETELLING THE AMERICAN STORY

249 Richard Rorty, *Contingency, Irony and Solidarity* (Cambridge, England: Cambridge University Press, 1989).

8. PROMISES, PROMISES . . .

Health

1 "Cutting Costs and Covering America: A 21st Century Health Care System." 2007. http://www.barackobama.com/2007/05/29/cutting_costs_and_covering_ame.php (accessed November 1, 2008).

2 "Remarks of Senator Barack Obama: Renewing American Competitiveness." 2008. http://www.barackobama.com/2008/06/16/remarks_of_senator_barack_obama_79.php (accessed November 1, 2008).

3 "Remarks of Senator Barack Obama: Reclaiming the American Dream." 2007. http://www.barackobama.com/2007/11/07/remarks_of_senator_barack_obama_31.php (accessed November 1, 2008).

4 "Cutting Costs and Covering America: A 21st Century Health Care System." 2007. http://www.barackobama.com/2007/05/29/cutting_costs_and_covering_ame.php (accessed November 1, 2008).

5 Ibid.

6 "Barack Obama and Joe Biden's Plan to Lower Health Care Costs and Ensure Affordable, Accessible Health Coverage for All." 2008. http://www.barackobama.com/pdf/issues/HealthCareFullPlan.pdf (accessed November 1, 2008).

7 Ibid.

8 "Remarks of Senator Barack Obama: Health Care." 2008. http://www.barackobama.com/2008/10/04/remarks_of_senator_barack_obama_129.php (accessed November 1, 2008).

9 "Health Care." 2008. http://www.barackobama.com/issues/healthcare/ (accessed November 1, 2008).

10 "Barack Obama and Joe Biden's Plan to Lower Health Care Costs and Ensure Affordable, Accessible Health Coverage for All." 2008. http://www.barackobama.com/pdf/issues/HealthCareFullPlan.pdf (accessed November 1, 2008).

11 Ibid.

12 Ibid.

13 Ibid.

14 "Remarks of Senator Barack Obama: Health Care." 2008. http://www.barackobama
.com/2008/10/04/remarks_of_senator_barack_obam_129.php (accessed November 1,
2008).

15 "FACTBOX: Democratic Candidates on Financial Issues." 2008. Reuters. http://www
.reuters.com/article/bondsNews/idUSN15565034200801 16?sp=true (accessed November
1, 2008).

16 "Economy." 2008. http://www.barackobama.com/issues/economy/ (accessed November
1, 2008).

17 "Remarks of Senator Barack Obama: Health Care." 2008. http://www.barackobama.
com/2008/10/04/remarks_of_senator_barack_obam_129.php (accessed November 1,
2008).

18 Witze, Alexandra. 2008. "U.S. election: Questioning the Candidates." *Nature.* http://www
.nature.com/news/2008/080903/full/455446a.html (accessed November 1, 2008).

19 "The Presidential Field: Barack Obama on the Issues." 2008. *Washington Post.* http://
projects.washingtonpost.com/2008-presidential-candidates/issues/candidates/barack-
obama/ (accessed November 2, 2008).

20 Witze, Alexandra. 2008. "U.S. election: Questioning the Candidates." *Nature.* http://www
.nature.com/news/2008/080903/full/455446a.html (accessed November 1, 2008).

21 "Barack Obama pledges to increase spending on global HIV/AIDS to $50 billion." 2007.
http://www.news-medical.net/?id=32046 (accessed November 1, 2008).

22 Witze, Alexandra. 2008. "U.S. election: Questioning the Candidates. Part 2." *Nature.*
http://www.nature.com/news/2008/080923/full/news.2008.1125.html (accessed
November 1, 2008).

23 Ibid.

24 "Health Care." 2008. http://www.barackobama.com/issues/healthcare/ (accessed
November 1, 2008).

25 Ibid.

26 Ibid.

27 "Barack Obama and Joe Biden's Plan to Lower Health Care Costs and Ensure Affordable,
Accessible Health Coverage for All." 2008. http://www.barackobama.com/pdf/issues/
HealthCareFullPlan.pdf (accessed November 1, 2008).

28 Ibid.

29 "Cutting Costs and Covering America: A 21st Century Health Care System." 2007.
http://www.barackobama.com/2007/05/29/cutting_costs_and_covering_ame.php
(accessed November 1, 2008).

30 "Barack Obama and Joe Biden's Plan to Lower Health Care Costs and Ensure Affordable, Accessible Health Coverage for All." 2008. http://www.barackobama.com/pdf/issues/ HealthCareFullPlan.pdf (accessed November 1, 2008).

31 Ibid.

32 Ibid.

33 Ibid.

Education

1 Sweet, Lynn. 2008. "Obama Education Speech in Ohio." Transcript. *Chicago Sun-Times.* http://blogs.suntimes.com/sweet/2008/09/obama_education_speech_in_ohio.html (accessed November 1, 2008).

2 Ibid.

3 "Remarks of Senator Obama: Reclaiming the American Dream." 2008. http://www .barackobama.com/2007/11/07/remarks_of_senator_barack_obam_31.php (accessed November 1, 2008).

4 "Education." 2008. http://www.barackobama.com/issues/education/ (accessed November 1, 2008).

5 "Barack Obama and Joe Biden's Plan for Lifetime Success through Education." 2008. http://www.barackobama.com/pdf/issues/PreK-12EducationFactSheet.pdf (accessed November 1, 2008).

6 Ibid.

7 Ibid.

8 "Reforming and Strengthening America's Schools for the 21st Century." 2008. http:// www.barackobama.com/pdf/issues/education/Fact_Sheet_Education_Reform_Speech_ FINAL.pdf (accessed November 1, 2008).

9 "Remarks of Barack Obama: Renewing American Competitiveness." 2008. http://www .barackobama.com/2008/06/16/remarks_of_senator_barack_obam_79.php (accessed November 1, 2008).

10 "Barack Obama and Joe Biden: Making College Affordable for Everyone." 2008. http:// www.barackobama.com/pdf/issues/CollegeAffordabilityFactSheet.pdf (accessed November 1, 2008).

11 Ibid.

12 "Barack Obama and Joe Biden's Plan for Lifetime Success through Education." 2008. http://www.barackobama.com/pdf/issues/PreK-12EducationFactSheet.pdf (accessed November 1, 2008).

13 "Barack Obama and Joe Biden: Making College Affordable for Everyone." 2008. http:// www.barackobama.com/pdf/issues/CollegeAffordabilityFactSheet.pdf (accessed November 1, 2008).

14 "Remarks of Barack Obama: Renewing American Competitiveness." 2008. http://www .barackobama.com/2008/06/16/remarks_of_senator_barack_obam_79.php (accessed November 1, 2008).

15 "Education." 2008. http://www.barackobama.com/issues/education/ (accessed November 1, 2008).

16 "Obama Calls for Elimination of Subsidies to Student Loan Providers." 2007. http:// www.barackobama.com/2007/05/15/obama_calls_for_elimination_of.php (accessed November 1, 2008).

17 "Barack Obama on Education." 2008. http://www.ontheissues.org/2008/Barack_ Obama_Education.htm (accessed November 1, 2008).

18 "Barack Obama and Joe Biden's Plan for Lifetime Success through Education." 2008. http://www.barackobama.com/pdf/issues/PreK-12EducationFactSheet.pdf (accessed November 1, 2008).

19 Ibid.

20 Ibid.

21 Ibid.

22 "Mashup Transcript: Barack Obama." 2007. http://www.huffingtonpost .com/2007/09/13/mashup-transcript-barack_n_64321.html (accessed November 1, 2008).

23 Sweet, Lynn. 2008. "Obama Education Speech in Ohio." Transcript. *Chicago Sun-Times.* http://blogs.suntimes.com/sweet/2008/09/obama_education_speech_in_ohio.html (accessed November 1, 2008).

24 "Barack Obama and Joe Biden's Plan for Lifetime Success through Education." 2008. http://www.barackobama.com/pdf/issues/PreK-12EducationFactSheet.pdf (accessed November 1, 2008).

25 "Helping All Americans Serve Their Country." 2008. http://www.barackobama.com/pdf/ NationalServicePlanFactSheet.pdf (accessed November 1, 2008).

26 "Barack Obama and Joe Biden's Plan for Lifetime Success through Education." 2008. http://www.barackobama.com/pdf/issues/PreK-12EducationFactSheet.pdf (accessed November 1, 2008).

27 Ibid.

28 "Obama Gives His Take on Education at Rally." 2008. http://edelection.blogspot .com/2008/07/obama-gives-his-take-on-education-at.html (accessed November 1, 2008).

29 Sweet, Lynn. 2008. "Obama Education Speech in Ohio." Transcript. *Chicago Sun-Times.*
http://blogs.suntimes.com/sweet/2008/09/obama_education_speech_in_ohio.html
(accessed November 1, 2008).

30 "Reforming and Strengthening America's Schools for the 21st Century." 2008. http://
www.barackobama.com/pdf/issues/education/Fact_Sheet_Education_Reform_Speech_
FINAL.pdf (accessed November 1, 2008).

31 "Barack Obama and Joe Biden's Plan for Lifetime Success through Education." 2008.
http://www.barackobama.com/pdf/issues/PreK-12EducationFactSheet.pdf (accessed
November 1, 2008).

32 Obama, Barack. 2008. "Obama's Speech to the Urban League." http://www
.realclearpolitics.com/articles/2008/08/obamas_speech_to_the_urban_lea.html (accessed
November 1, 2008).

33 Obama, Barack. 2008. "Barack Obama (Presidential Candidate): Candidate
Questionnaire." http://sharp.sefora.org/people/presidential-candidates/barack-obama-
presidential-candidate/ (accessed November 1, 2008).

34 "Barack Obama and Joe Biden's Plan for Lifetime Success through Education." 2008.
http://www.barackobama.com/pdf/issues/PreK-12EducationFactSheet.pdf (accessed
November 1, 2008).

35 "Education." 2008. http://www.barackobama.com/issues/education/ (accessed
November 1, 2008).

36 Ibid.

37 Ibid.

38 Sweet, Lynn. 2008. "Obama Education Speech in Ohio." Transcript. *Chicago Sun-Times.*
http://blogs.suntimes.com/sweet/2008/09/obama_education_speech_in_ohio.html
(accessed November 1, 2008).

39 "Barack Obama and Joe Biden: Making College Affordable for Everyone." 2008. http://
www.barackobama.com/pdf/issues/CollegeAffordabilityFactSheet.pdf (accessed November
1, 2008).

40 "Reforming and Strengthening America's Schools for the 21st Century." 2008. http://
www.barackobama.com/pdf/issues/education/Fact_Sheet_Education_Reform_Speech_
FINAL.pdf (accessed November 1, 2008).

41 "Remarks of Barack Obama: 80th Convention of the American Federation of Teachers."
2008. http://www.barackobama.com/2008/07/13/remarks_of_senator_barack_obam_94
.php (accessed November 1, 2008).

42 "Education." 2008. http://www.barackobama.com/issues/education/ (accessed
November 1, 2008).

43 Ibid.

44 "Helping All Americans Serve Their Country." 2008. http://www.barackobama.com/pdf/ NationalServicePlanFactSheet.pdf (accessed November 1, 2008).

45 "Jan. 15 Democratic Debate Transcript." 2008. MSNBC. http://www.msnbc.msn.com/ id/22682821/print/displaymode/1098/ (accessed November 1, 2008).

46 "Reforming and Strengthening America's Schools for the 21st Century." 2008. http:// www.barackobama.com/pdf/issues/education/Fact_Sheet_Education_Reform_Speech_ FINAL.pdf (accessed November 1, 2008).

47 "Democratic Debate Transcript, Philadelphia." 2008. http://www.cfr.org/ publication/16044/ (accessed November 1, 2008).

48 Arrington, Michael. 2007. "Q&A with Senator Barack Obama on Key Technology Issues." *TechCrunch.* http://www.techcrunch.com/2007/11/26/qa-with-senator-barack-obama-on-key-technology-issues/ (accessed November 1, 2008).

49 "Barack Obama and Joe Biden's Plan for Lifetime Success through Education." 2008. http://www.barackobama.com/pdf/issues/PreK-12EducationFactSheet.pdf (accessed November 1, 2008).

50 Russo, Alexander. 2008. "Obama Rips NCLB—For Lack of Foreign Language Instruction." http://scholasticadministrator.typepad.com/thisweekineducation/2008/02/ obama-rips-nclb.html (accessed November 1, 2008).

51 Sweet, Lynn. 2008. "Obama Education Speech in Ohio." Transcript. *Chicago Sun-Times.* http://blogs.suntimes.com/sweet/2008/09/obama_education_speech_in_ohio.html (accessed November 1, 2008).

52 Ibid.

Digital Divide

1 "Remarks of Senator Barack Obama: Renewing American Competitiveness." 2008. http:// www.barackobama.com/2008/06/16/remarks_of_senator_barack_obam_79.php (accessed November 1, 2008).

2 "The Presidential Field: Barack Obama on the Issues." 2008. *Washington Post.* http:// projects.washingtonpost.com/2008-presidential-candidates/issues/candidates/barack-obama/ (accessed November 2, 2008).

3 "Remarks of Senator Barack Obama: Renewing American Competitiveness." 2008. http:// www.barackobama.com/2008/06/16/remarks_of_senator_barack_obam_79.php (accessed November 1, 2008).

4 Arrington, Michael. 2007. "Q&A with Senator Barack Obama on Key Technology Issues." *TechCrunch.* http://www.techcrunch.com/2007/11/26/qa-with-senator-barack-obama-on-key-technology-issues/ (accessed November 1, 2008).

5 Ibid.

6 Ibid.

7 "Technology." 2008. http://www.barackobama.com/issues/technology/ (accessed November 2, 2008).

Economy

1 "The Third Presidential Debate." 2008. *New York Times.* http://elections.nytimes .com/2008/president/debates/transcripts/third-presidential-debate.html (accessed November 1, 2008).

2 "Remarks of Senator Barack Obama: On Taxes." 2008. http://www.barackobama .com/2008/09/12/remarks_of_senator_barack_obam_112.php (accessed November 1, 2008).

3 "Jan. 15 Democratic Debate Transcript." 2008. http://www.msnbc.msn.com/ id/22682821/print/1/displaymode/1098/ (accessed November 1, 2008).

4 "Transcript of First Presidential Debate." 2008. CNN. http://www.cnn.com/2008/ POLITICS/09/26/debate.mississippi.transcript/ (accessed November 1, 2008).

5 "Remarks of Senator Barack Obama: On Taxes." 2008. http://www.barackobama .com/2008/09/12/remarks_of_senator_barack_obam_112.php (accessed November 1, 2008).

6 "Barack Obama and Joe Biden's Plan for Lifetime Success through Education." 2008. http://www.barackobama.com/pdf/issues/PreK-12EducationFactSheet.pdf (accessed November 1, 2008).

7 "Remarks of Senator Barack Obama: Renewing American Competitiveness." 2008. http:// www.barackobama.com/2008/06/16/remarks_of_senator_barack_obam_79.php (accessed November 1, 2008).

8 Zeleny, Jeff. 2008. "Obama Borrows Page from Clinton," *New York Times.* http://www .nytimes.com/2008/07/14/us/politics/14obama.html?_r=2&oref=slogin&oref=slogin (accessed November 1, 2008).

9 "Economy." 2008. http://www.barackobama.com/issues/economy/ (accessed November 1, 2008).

10 "Remarks of Senator Barack Obama: A Serious Energy Policy for Our Future." 2008. http://www.barackobama.com/2008/06/24/remarks_of_senator_barack_obam_81.php (accessed November 1, 2008).

11 "Economy." 2008. http://www.barackobama.com/issues/economy/ (accessed November 1, 2008).

12 "Barack Obama on Tax Reform." 2008. http://ontheissues.org/Tax_Reform .htm#Barack_Obama (accessed November 1, 2008).

13 "Remarks of Senator Barack Obama (Abington, PA)." 2008. http://www.barackobama .com/2008/10/03/remarks_of_senator_barack_obam_131.php (accessed November 1, 2008).

14 Ibid.

15 "Remarks of Senator Barack Obama: Health Care." 2008. http://www.barackobama
.com/2008/10/04/remarks_of_senator_barrack_obam_129.php (accessed November 1,
2008).

16 "Democratic Debate Transcript, Philadelphia." 2008. Council on Foreign Relations.
http://www.cfr.org/publication/16044/ (accessed November 1, 2008).

17 "Democratic Primary Debate." 2007. *Special Edition: This Week, Hosted by George
Stephanopoulos*, ABC. http://www.ontheissues.org/2007_Stephanopoulos_Dems.htm
(accessed November 1, 2008).

18 "Jan. 15 Democratic Debate Transcript." 2008. MSNBC. http://www.msnbc.msn.com/
id/22682821/print/l/displaymode/1098/ (accessed November 1, 2008).

19 "The Presidential Field: Barack Obama on the Issues." 2008. *The Washington Post.* http://
projects.washingtonpost.com/2008-presidential-candidates/issues/candidates/barack-
obama/ (accessed November 2, 2008).

20 "Obama to NAACP: 'Our Work Is Not Over.'" 2008. Salon.com. http://www.salon.com/
news/primary_sources/2008/07/15/obama/index1.html (accessed November 1, 2008).

21 "Remarks of Senator Barack Obama: A Serious Energy Policy for Our Future." 2008.
http://www.barackobama.com/2008/06/24/remarks_of_senator_barack_obam_81.php
(accessed November 1, 2008).

22 "Economy." 2008. http://www.barackobama.com/issues/economy/ (accessed November
1, 2008).

23 "Barack Obama on Tax Reform," 2008. http://www.ontheissues.org/2008/Barack_
Obama_Tax_Reform.htm (accessed November 1, 2008).

24 "Remarks of Senator Barack Obama: Renewing American Competitiveness." 2008.
http://www.barackobama.com/2008/06/16/remarks_of_senator_barack_obam_79.php
(accessed November 1, 2008).

25 "Interviews of Presidential Candidates Throughout 2008." 2008. *Late Edition with Wolf
Blitzer.* CNN. http://www.ontheissues.org/2008_Late_Edition.htm (accessed November 1,
2008).

26 Arrington, Michael. 2007. "Q&A with Senator Barack Obama on Key Technology Issues."
TechCrunch. http://www.techcrunch.com/2007/11/26/qa-with-senator-barack-obama-on-
key-technology-issues/ (accessed November 1, 2008).

27 "The Democratic Debate in South Carolina." 2008. *New York Times.* http://www.nytimes
.com/2008/01/21/us/politics/21demdebate-transcript.html?pagewanted=4&_r=1&fta=y
(accessed November 1, 2008).

28 "Economy." 2008. http://www.barackobama.com/issues/economy/ (accessed November
1, 2008).

29 "The Democratic Debate [in Iowa]." 2007. *New York Times.* http://www.nytimes
.com/2007/12/13/us/politics/13text-debate.html?pagewanted=all (accessed November 1,
2008).

30 "The Presidential Field: Barack Obama on the Issues." 2008. *Washington Post.* http://
projects.washingtonpost.com/2008-presidential-candidates/issues/candidates/barack-
obama/ (accessed November 2, 2008).

31 "Economy." 2008. http://www.barackobama.com/issues/economy/ (accessed November
1, 2008).

32 "Remarks of Senator Barack Obama: Reclaiming the American Dream." 2007. http://
www.barackobama.com/2007/11/07/remarks_of_senator_barack_obam_31.php (accessed
November 1, 2008).

33 "Economy." 2008. http://www.barackobama.com/issues/economy/ (accessed November
1, 2008).

34 "Transcript of questions and answers with Sen. Barack Obama." 2008. http://www
.therepublic.com/main.asp?SectionID=1&SubSectionID=111&ArticleID=119206 (accessed
November 1, 2008).

35 "Remarks of Senator Barack Obama: Reclaiming the American Dream." 2007. http://
www.barackobama.com/2007/11/07/remarks_of_senator_barack_obam_31.php (accessed
November 1, 2008).

36 "The Presidential Field: Barack Obama on the Issues." 2008. *Washington Post.* http://
projects.washingtonpost.com/2008-presidential-candidates/issues/candidates/barack-
obama/ (accessed November 2, 2008).

37 "Economy." 2008. http://www.barackobama.com/issues/economy/ (accessed November
1, 2008).

38 Ibid.

39 "Remarks of Senator Barack Obama: Renewing American Competitiveness." 2008.
http://www.barackobama.com/2008/06/16/remarks_of_senator_barack_obam_79.php
(accessed November 1, 2008).

40 "Remarks of Senator Barack Obama (Grand Rapids, MI)." 2008. http://www
.barackobama.com/2008/10/02/remarks_of_senator_barack_obam_130.php (accessed
November 1, 2008).

41 "Economy." 2008. http://www.barackobama.com/issues/economy/ (accessed November
1, 2008).

42 Ibid.

43 Ibid.

44 Ibid.

45 Ibid.

46 Ibid.

47 Ibid.

48 Ibid.

49 Ward, Lee. 2008. "McCain Rips Off Obama Mortgage Purchase Idea." http://
wizbangblue.com/2008/10/08/mccain-rips-off-obama-mortgage-purchase-idea.php
(accessed November 1, 2008).

50 "Economy." 2008. http://www.barackobama.com/issues/economy/ (accessed November
1, 2008).

51 Ibid.

52 Ibid.

53 "Remarks of Senator Barack Obama: Reclaiming the American Dream." 2007. http://
www.barackobama.com/2007/11/07/remarks_of_senator_barack_obam_31.php (accessed
November 2, 2008).

54 Ibid.

Affordable Housing

1 Pierce, Neil. 2008. "McCain vs. Obama: Who's Best for Cities?" http://citiwire.net/
post/211/ (accessed November 2, 2008).

2 Dade, Corey. 2008. "Obama Promotes Plan for Urban Development." *Wall Street Journal.*
http://online.wsj.com/article/SB121962139246367581.html?mod=googlenews_wsj
(accessed November 2, 2008).

3 "Barack Obama and Joe Biden: New Energy for America." 2008. http://www
.barackobama.com/pdf/factsheet_energy_speech_080308.pdf (accessed November 2, 2008).

4 "Poverty." 2008. http://www.barackobama.com/issues/poverty/ (accessed November 2,
2008).

5 "Urban Policy." 2008. http://origin.barackobama.com/issues/urban_policy/#crime-and-
law-enforcement (accessed November 2, 2008).

6 "The Presidential Field: Barack Obama on the Issues." 2008. *Washington Post.* http://
projects.washingtonpost.com/2008-presidential-candidates/issues/candidates/barack-
obama/ (accessed November 2, 2008).

7 "Urban Policy." 2008. http://origin.barackobama.com/issues/urban_policy/ (accessed
November 2, 2008).

8 "Remarks of Senator Barack Obama: Changing the Odds for Urban America." 2007.
http://www.barackobama.com/2007/07/18/remarks_of_senator_barack_obam_19.php
(accessed November 2, 2008).

Rural Areas

1 "Transcript: Barack Obama's Speech on Race." 2008. National Public Radio. http://www.npr.org/templates/story/story.php?storyId=88478467 (accessed November 2, 2008).

2 Sweet, Lynn. 2008. "Obama Education Speech in Ohio. Transcript." *Chicago Sun-Times.* http://blogs.suntimes.com/sweet/2008/09/obama_education_speech_in_ohio.html (accessed November 1, 2008).

3 "Barack Obama and Joe Biden's Plan for Lifetime Success through Education." 2008. http://www.barackobama.com/pdf/issues/PreK-12EducationFactSheet.pdf (accessed November 1, 2008).

4 Arrington, Michael. 2007. "Q&A with Senator Barack Obama on Key Technology Issues." *TechCrunch.* http://www.techcrunch.com/2007/11/26/qa-with-senator-barack-obama-on-key-technology-issues/ (accessed November 1, 2008).

5 "Rural." 2008. http://www.barackobama.com/issues/rural/ (accessed November 2, 2008).

6 Ibid.

7 "Democratic Primary Debate." 2007. *Special Edition: This Week, Hosted by George Stephanopoulos.* ABC. http://www.ontheissues.org/2007_Stephanopoulos_Dems.htm (accessed November 1, 2008).

8 "Rural." 2008. http://www.barackobama.com/issues/rural/ (accessed November 2, 2008).

9 Ibid.

10 Ibid.

11 Ibid.

12 Ibid.

13 Ibid.

14 Ibid.

15 Ibid.

Criminal Justice

1 "Remarks of Senator Barack Obama: The Great Need of the Hour." 2008. http://www.barackobama.com/2008/01/20/remarks_of_senator_barack_obam_40.php (accessed November 1, 2008).

2 "Civil Rights." 2008. http://origin.barackobama.com/issues/civil_rights/ (accessed November 1, 2008).

3 "Barack Obama and Joe Biden: Creating Equal Justice and Opportunity for All." 2008. http://www.barackobama.com/pdf/issues/Fact_Sheet_Civil_Rights_and_Criminal_Justice_FINAL.pdf (accessed November 1, 2008).

4 Ibid.

5 Ibid.

6 "Remarks of Senator Barack Obama: Howard University Convocation." 2007. http:// www.barackobama.com/2007/09/28/remarks_of_senator_barack_obam_26.php (accessed November 1, 2008).

7 "Barack Obama and Joe Biden: Creating Equal Justice and Opportunity for All." 2008. http://www.barackobama.com/pdf/issues/Fact_Sheet_Civl_Rights_and_Criminal_Justice_ FINAL.pdf (accessed November 1, 2008).

8 "2008 U.S. Presidential Candidates Respond to the IACP's Questions on Crime, Terrorism, and Homeland Security." 2008. International Association of Chiefs of Police. http:// www.theiacp.org/documents/pdfs/PressRelease/Candidates_Q&A_10-08.pdf (accessed November 1, 2008).

9 Ibid.

10 Ibid.

11 Ibid.

12 Ibid.

13 Ibid.

14 Ibid.

15 "2008 Presidential Candidates on Marijuana Raids." 2007. http://medicalmarijuana .procon.org/viewresource.asp?resourceID=885#obama (accessed November 1, 2008).

16 "Remarks of Senator Barack Obama: Howard University Convocation." 2007. http:// www.barackobama.com/2007/09/28/remarks_of_senator_barack_obam_26.php (accessed November 1, 2008).

17 "Barack Obama and Joe Biden: Creating Equal Justice and Opportunity for All." 2008. http://www.barackobama.com/pdf/issues/Fact_Sheet_Civil_Rights_and_Criminal_Justice_ FINAL.pdf (accessed November 1, 2008).

18 Ibid.

19 "The Criminal Justice Moment of the South Carolina Debate." 2008. http://www.talkleft .com/story/2008/1/22/14739/7882 (accessed November 1, 2008).

20 "Civil Rights." 2008. http://origin.barackobama.com/issues/civil_rights/ (accessed November 1, 2008).

21 "Barack Obama and Joe Biden: Creating Equal Justice and Opportunity for All." 2008. http://www.barackobama.com/pdf/issues/Fact_Sheet_Civil_Rights_and_Criminal_Justice_ FINAL.pdf (accessed November 1, 2008).

22 "Obama to NAACP: 'Our Work Is Not Over.'" 2008. Salon.com. http://www.salon.com/ news/primary_sources/2008/07/15/obama/index1.html (accessed November 1, 2008).

23 "Barack Obama and Joe Biden: Creating Equal Justice and Opportunity for All." 2008. http://www.barackobama.com/pdf/issues/Fact_Sheet_Civil_Rights_and_Criminal_Justice_FINAL.pdf (accessed November 1, 2008).

24 Ibid.

25 "The Presidential Field: Barack Obama on the Issues." 2008. *Washington Post.* http://projects.washingtonpost.com/2008-presidential-candidates/issues/candidates/barack-obama/ (accessed November 2, 2008).

26 "Civil Rights." 2008. http://origin.barackobama.com/issues/civil_rights/ (accessed November 1, 2008).

27 "Urban Policy." 2008. http://origin.barackobama.com/issues/urban_policy#crime-and-law-enforcement (accessed November 1, 2008).

28 Ibid.

29 "If Obama Wins You Better Hide Your Guns." 2008. The Daily Conservative. http://64.233.169.104/search?q=cache:5mFXEKpjensJ:www.thedailyconservative.net/2008/10/13/if-obama-wins-you-better-hide-your-guns/+down+on+the+various+loopholes+that+exist+in+terms+of+background+checks+for+children,+the+mentally+ill&hl=en&ct=clnk&cd=5&gl=us (accessed November 1, 2008).

30 "Urban Policy." 2008. http://origin.barackobama.com/issues/urban_policy#crime-and-law-enforcement (accessed November 1, 2008).

31 Ibid.

32 "2007 NAACP Presidential Primary Forum: On Gun Control." 2007. http://www.ontheissues.org/Archive/2007_NAACP_Primary_Gun_Control.htm (accessed November 1, 2008).

33 "2008 U.S. Presidential Candidates Respond to the IACP's Questions on Crime, Terrorism, and Homeland Security." 2008. International Association of Chiefs of Police. http://www.theiacp.org/documents/pdfs/PressRelease/Candidates_Q&A_10-08.pdf (accessed November 1, 2008).

34 "Urban Policy." 2008. http://origin.barackobama.com/issues/urban_policy#crime-and-law-enforcement (accessed November 1, 2008).

Community Policing

1 "2008 U.S. Presidential Candidates Respond to the IACP's Questions on Crime, Terrorism, and Homeland Security." 2008. International Association of Chiefs of Police. http://www.theiacp.org/documents/pdfs/PressRelease/Candidates_Q&A_10-08.pdf (accessed November 1, 2008).

2 "Urban Policy." 2008. http://origin.barackobama.com/issues/urban_policy/#crime-and-law-enforcement (accessed November 1, 2008).

3 "Barack Obama and Joe Biden: Supporting Urban Prosperity." 2008. http://www
.barackobama.com/pdf/issues/UrbanFactSheet.pdf (accessed November 1, 2008).

4 Sweet, Lynn. 2008. "Obama Latin America Speech in Miami." *Chicago Sun-Times*. http://
blogs.suntimes.com/sweet/2008/05/obama_latin_america_speech_in.html (accessed
November 1, 2008).

5 "Read Barack Obama's Speech." 2008. *The Times-Picayune* (New Orleans). http://www.nola
.com/news/index.ssf/2008/02/barack_obamas_speech.html (accessed November 1, 2008).

Energy

1 "Transcript: Obama's 'New Energy for America' Speech." 2008. PBS. http://www.pbs.org/
newshour/bb/politics/july-dec08/obamaenergy_08-04.html (accessed November 1, 2008).

2 Little, Amanda Griscom. 2007. "Obama on the Record." *Grist*. http://www.grist.org/
feature/2007/07/30/obama/index.html (accessed November 1, 2008).

3 Ibid.

4 "Barack Obama and Joe Biden: New Energy for America." 2008. http://www
.barackobama.com/pdf/factsheet_energy_speech_080308.pdf (accessed November 1, 2008).

5 "Remarks of Senator Barack Obama: The Clinton Global Initiative." 2008. http://www
.barackobama.com/2008/09/25/remarks_of_senator_barack_obam_122.php (accessed
November 1, 2008).

6 "Barack Obama and Joe Biden: New Energy for America." 2008. http://www
.barackobama.com/pdf/factsheet_energy_speech_080308.pdf (accessed November 1, 2008).

7 "Remarks of Senator Barack Obama: The Clinton Global Initiative." 2008. http://www
.barackobama.com/2008/09/25/remarks_of_senator_barack_obam_122.php (accessed
November 1, 2008).

8 Witze, Alexandra. 2008. "U.S. election: Questioning the candidates." *Nature*. http://www
.nature.com/news/2008/080903/full/455446a.html (accessed November 1, 2008).

9 "Remarks of Senator Barack Obama: Real Leadership for a Clean Energy Future." 2007.
http://www.barackobama.com/2007/10/08/remarks_of_senator_barack_obam_28.php
(accessed November 1, 2008).

10 "The Democratic Debate in New Hampshire." 2008. *New York Times*. http://www.nytimes
.com/2008/01/05/us/politics/05text-ddebate.html?pagewanted=all ("[W]hat you have to
do is you have to combine it with a hundred percent auction.") (accessed November 1, 2008).

11 "Special Report: The Presidential Election." 2008. *National Wildlife Federation*. http://
www.nwf.org/NationalWildlife/article.cfm?issueID=124&articleID=1650.

12 Witze, Alexandra. 2008. "U.S. election: Questioning the candidates." *Nature*. http://www
.nature.com/news/2008/080903/full/455446a.html (accessed November 1, 2008).

13 "Barack Obama and Joe Biden: New Energy for America." 2008. http://www
.barackobama.com/pdf/factsheet_energy_speech_080308.pdf (accessed November 1, 2008).

14 "New Energy for America." 2008. http://my.barackobama.com/page/content/ newenergy_more#emissions (accessed November 1, 2008).

15 "Barack Obama and Joe Biden: New Energy for America." 2008. http://www .barackobama.com/pdf/factsheet_energy_speech_080308.pdf (accessed November 1, 2008).

16 Witze, Alexandra. 2008. "U.S. election: Questioning the Candidates." *Nature.* http://www .nature.com/news/2008/080903/full/455446a.html (accessed November 1, 2008).

17 "Remarks of Senator Barack Obama: Real Leadership for a Clean Energy Future." 2007. http://www.barackobama.com/2007/10/08/remarks_of_senator_barack_obam_28.php (accessed November 1, 2008).

18 Ibid.

19 "Democratic Debate Transcript, Philadelphia." 2008. Council on Foreign Relations. http://www.cfr.org/publication/16044/ (accessed November 1, 2008).

20 "Remarks of Senator Barack Obama (Abington, PA)." 2008. http://www.barackobama .com/2008/10/03/remarks_of_senator_barack_obam_131.php (accessed November 1, 2008).

21 Obama, Barack. 2008. "Barack Obama (Presidential Candidate): Candidate Questionnaire." http://sharp.sefora.org/people/presidential-candidates/barack-obama-presidential-candidate/ (accessed November 1, 2008).

22 "Remarks of Senator Barack Obama: Real Leadership for a Clean Energy Future." 2007. http://www.barackobama.com/2007/10/08/remarks_of_senator_barack_obam_28.php (accessed November 1, 2008).

23 "Transcript: Obama's 'New Energy for America' Speech." 2008. PBS. http://www.pbs .org/newshour/bb/politics/july-dec08/obamaenergy_08-04.html (accessed November 1, 2008).

24 "New Energy for America." 2008. http://my.barackobama.com/page/content/ newenergy_more#emissions (accessed November 1, 2008).

25 Ibid.

26 "Remarks of Senator Barack Obama: A Serious Energy Policy for Our Future." 2008. http://www.barackobama.com/2008/06/24/remarks_of_senator_barack_obam_81.php (accessed November 1, 2008).

27 "Transcript: Obama's 'New Energy for America' Speech." 2008. PBS. http://www.pbs .org/newshour/bb/politics/july-dec08/obamaenergy_08-04.html (accessed November 1, 2008).

28 Ibid.

29 Ibid.

30 Ibid.

31 "The Presidential Field: Barack Obama on the Issues." 2008. *Washington Post.* http://projects.washingtonpost.com/2008-presidential-candidates/issues/candidates/barack-obama/ (accessed November 1, 2008).

32 "Barack Obama and Joe Biden: New Energy for America." http://www.barackobama.com/pdf/factsheet_energy_speech_080308.pdf (accessed November 1, 2008).

33 "Transcript: Obama's 'New Energy for America' Speech." 2008. PBS. http://www.pbs.org/newshour/bb/politics/july–dec08/obamaenergy_08-04.html (accessed November 1, 2008).

34 "Transcript of Second McCain, Obama Debate." 2008. CNN. http://www.cnn.com/2008/POLITICS/10/07/presidential.debate.transcript/index.html (accessed November 1, 2008).

35 "New Energy for America." 2008. http://my.barackobama.com/page/content/newenergy_more#emissions (accessed November 1, 2008).

36 Ibid.

37 "Barack Obama and Joe Biden: New Energy for America." 2008. http://www.barackobama.com/pdf/factsheet_energy_speech_080308.pdf (accessed November 1, 2008).

38 "Remarks of Senator Barack Obama: Real Leadership for a Clean Energy Future." 2007. http://www.barackobama.com/2007/10/08/remarks_of_senator_barack_obam_28.php (accessed November 1, 2008).

39 "Barack Obama and Joe Biden: New Energy for America." 2008. http://www.barackobama.com/pdf/factsheet_energy_speech_080308.pdf (accessed November 1, 2008).

40 Ibid.

41 "New Energy for America." 2008. http://my.barackobama.com/page/content/newenergy_more#emissions (accessed November 1, 2008).

42 "Transcript: Obama's 'New Energy for America' Speech." 2008. PBS. http://www.pbs.org/newshour/bb/politics/july–dec08/obamaenergy_08-04.html (accessed November 1, 2008).

43 "Transcript of Second McCain, Obama Debate." 2008. CNN. http://www.cnn.com/2008/POLITICS/10/07/presidential.debate.transcript/index.html (accessed November 1, 2008.)

44 "Special Report: The Presidential Election." 2008. *National Wildlife Federation.* http://www.nwf.org/NationalWildlife/article.cfm?issueID=124&articleID=1650 (accessed November 1, 2008).

45 "Transcript: Obama's 'New Energy for America' Speech." 2008. PBS. http://www.pbs.org/newshour/bb/politics/july-dec08/obamaenergy_08-04.html (accessed November 1, 2008).

46 "New Energy for America." 2008. http://my.barackobama.com/page/content/newenergy_more#emissions (accessed November 1, 2008).

47 "Barack Obama and Joe Biden: New Energy for America." 2008. http://www.barackobama.com/pdf/factsheet_energy_speech_080308.pdf (accessed November 1, 2008).

48 "Transcript: Obama's 'New Energy for America' Speech." 2008. PBS. http://www.pbs.org/newshour/bb/politics/july-dec08/obamaenergy_08-04.html (accessed November 1, 2008).

49 Ibid.

50 "New Energy for America." 2008. http://my.barackobama.com/page/content/newenergy_more#emissions (accessed November 1, 2008).

51 "Transcript: Obama's 'New Energy for America' Speech." 2008. PBS. http://www.pbs.org/newshour/bb/politics/july-dec08/obamaenergy_08-04.html (accessed November 1, 2008).

52 Witze, Alexandra. 2008. "U.S. election: Questioning the candidates," *Nature.* http://www.nature.com/news/2008/080903/full/455446a.html (accessed November 1, 2008).

53 Obama, Barack. 2008. "Barack Obama (Presidential Candidate): Candidate Questionnaire." http://sharp.sefora.org/people/presidential-candidates/barack-obama-presidential-candidate/ (accessed November 1, 2008).

54 Witze, Alexandra. 2008. "U.S. election: Questioning the Candidates." *Nature.* http://www.nature.com/news/2008/080903/full/455446a.html (accessed November 1, 2008).

55 Little, Amanda Griscom. 2007. "Obama on the Record." *Grist.* http://www.grist.org/feature/2007/07/30/obama/index.html (accessed November 1, 2008).

56 Obama, Barack. 2008. "Barack Obama (Presidential Candidate): Candidate Questionnaire." http://sharp.sefora.org/people/presidential-candidates/barack-obama-presidential-candidate/ (accessed November 1, 2008).

57 "The Presidential Field: Barack Obama on the Issues." 2008. *Washington Post.* http://projects.washingtonpost.com/2008-presidential-candidates/issues/candidates/barack-obama/ (accessed November 1, 2008).

58 "Barack Obama and Joe Biden: New Energy for America." 2008. http://www.barackobama.com/pdf/factsheet_energy_speech_080308.pdf (accessed November 1, 2008).

59 "Transcript: The Democratic Debate in New Hampshire." 2008. *New York Times.* http://www.nytimes.com/2008/01/05/us/politics/05text-ddebate.html?pagewanted=all (accessed November 1, 2008).

60 "Barack Obama and Joe Biden: New Energy for America." 2008. http://www.barackobama.com/pdf/factsheet_energy_speech_080308.pdf (accessed November 1, 2008).

61 Ibid.

62 Ibid.

63 "Transcript: Sen. Obama, Part 2." 2008. *Sixty Minutes* Interview, CBS News, http://www.cbsnews.com/stories/2008/09/24/60minutes/main4476126.shtml (accessed November 1, 2008).

64 Lam, Tina. 2008. "Obama Proposes $5 Billion Fund to Restore Great Lakes." http://www.freep.com/apps/pbcs.dll/article?AID=/20080917/NEWS15/809170386 (accessed November 1, 2008).

65 "Special Report: The Presidential Election." 2008. *National Wildlife Federation.* http://www.nwf.org/NationalWildlife/article.cfm?issueID=124&articleID=1650 (accessed November 1, 2008).

Democracy

1 "Jan. 15 Democratic Debate Transcript." 2008. MSNBC. http://www.msnbc.msn.com/id/22682821/print/1/displaymode/1098/ (accessed November 1, 2008).

2 "Remarks of Senator Barack Obama: Renewing American Competitiveness." 2008. http://www.barackobama.com/2008/06/16/remarks_of_senator_barack_obam_79.php (accessed November 1, 2008).

3 Mark, David. 2008. "Full Text: Obama Interview." Politico.com. http://www.politico.com/news/stories/0208/8457_Page2.html (accessed November 2, 2008).

4 "Selma Voting Rights March Commemoration." 2007. http://www.barackobama.com/2007/03/04/selma_voting_rights_march_comm.php (accessed November 2, 2008).

5 "Remarks of Senator Barack Obama (La Crosse, WI)." 2008. http://www.barackobama.com/2008/10/01/remarks_of_senator_barack_obam_127.php (accessed November 2, 2008).

6 "Remarks of Senator Barack Obama (Greensboro, NC)." 2008. http://www.barackobama.com/2008/09/27/remarks_of_senator_barack_obam_124.php (accessed November 2, 2008).

7 "Barack Obama and Joe Biden: Creating Equal Justice and Opportunity for All." 2008. http://www.barackobama.com/pdf/issues/Fact_Sheet_Civil_Rights_and_Criminal_Justice_FINAL.pdf (accessed November 1, 2008).

8 "Civil Rights." 2008. http://origin.barackobama.com/issues/civil_rights/#voting (accessed November 2, 2008).

9 "Service." 2008. http://www.barackobama.com/issues/service/ (accessed November 2, 2008).

10 Ibid.

11 Ibid.

12 Ibid.

13 Ibid.

14 Ibid.

15 Ibid.

INDEX

CARTOON PERMISSIONS

CHAPTER 1. HEALTH CARE AND WELL-BEING: WHO HOLDS THE CURE?

R. J. Matson, "Miracle of Modern Medicine," originally printed in *The St. Louis Post-Dispatch*, June 23, 2008. Available at: http://www.politicalcartoons.com.

Larry Wright, "Health Care Woes," originally printed in *The Detroit News*, September 14, 2004. Available at: http://www.politicalcartoons.com.

CHAPTER 2. EDUCATION: SUCCESS IN OUR SCHOOLS

John Cole, "No Child Left Behind," originally printed in *The Scranton Times-Tribune*, April 22, 2002. Available at: http://www.politicalcartoons.com.

Jeff Parker, "Teacher Shortage," originally printed in *Florida Today*, October 30, 2002. Available at: http://www.politicalcartoons.com.

CHAPTER 3. UNEQUAL JUSTICE: BALANCING THE SCALES

Mike Keefe, "Prison Population," originally printed in *The Denver Post*, February 28, 2008. Available at: http://www.politicalcartoons.com.

Pavel Constantin, "Blind Justice," September 24, 2007. Available at: http://www.politicalcartoons.com.

CHAPTER 4. THE ECONOMY: SECURING THE MEANS NECESSARY FOR PURSUING HAPPINESS

Larry Wright, "Minimum Wage," originally printed in *The Detroit News*, July 24, 2008. Available at: http://www.politicalcartoons.com.

Ares, "Mortgage Heavy Load," August 4, 2008. Available at: http://www.politicalcartoons.com.

CHAPTER 5. THE ENVIRONMENT, ENERGY, AND OUR AGING INFRASTRUCTURE: PROTECTING OURSELVES AND OUR PLANET

Adam Zyglis, "Commuting Without SUVs," originally printed in *The Buffalo News*, June 19, 2008. Available at: http://www.politicalcartoons.com.

John Trever, "Oil Supply," originally printed in *The Albuquerque Journal*, June 17, 2008. Available at: http://www.politicalcartoons.com.

**CHAPTER 6. DEMOCRACY: WE THE PEOPLE IN ORDER
TO FORM A MORE PERFECT UNION**

Pavel Constantin, "Democracy," January 7, 2008. Available at: http://www.politicalcartoons
.com.

Jeff Parker, "Right to Gripe," originally printed in *Florida Today*, January 28, 2008. Available
at: http://www.politicalcartoons.com.

ABOUT THE AUTHORS

Tavis Smiley is a nationally known public intellectual, political commentator, philanthropist, and radio and television personality. His bestselling books include the *Covenant with Black America,* THE COVENANT *In Action,* and his memoir, *What I Know for Sure.* He lives in Los Angeles. Visit his website at http://www.tavistalks.com.

Stephanie Robinson is a nationally recognized social commentator and political analyst. She is the president & CEO of the Jamestown Project, a lecturer at Harvard Law School, and former chief counsel to Senator Edward M. Kennedy. She lives with her family in Massachusetts. Visit her website at http://www.stephanierobinsonspeaks.com.